# THE LETTERING JOURNEY BEGINS ...

THIS BOOK BELONGS TO:

DEDICATED TO
THOSE WHO USE MARKERS
TO INCREASE GROUP UNDERSTANDING
AND ENCOURAGE BREAKTHROUGH CONVERSATIONS
BY HOLDING A SPACE
FOR OTHERS TO BE SUCCESSFUL.


YOU KNOW WHO YOU ARE.

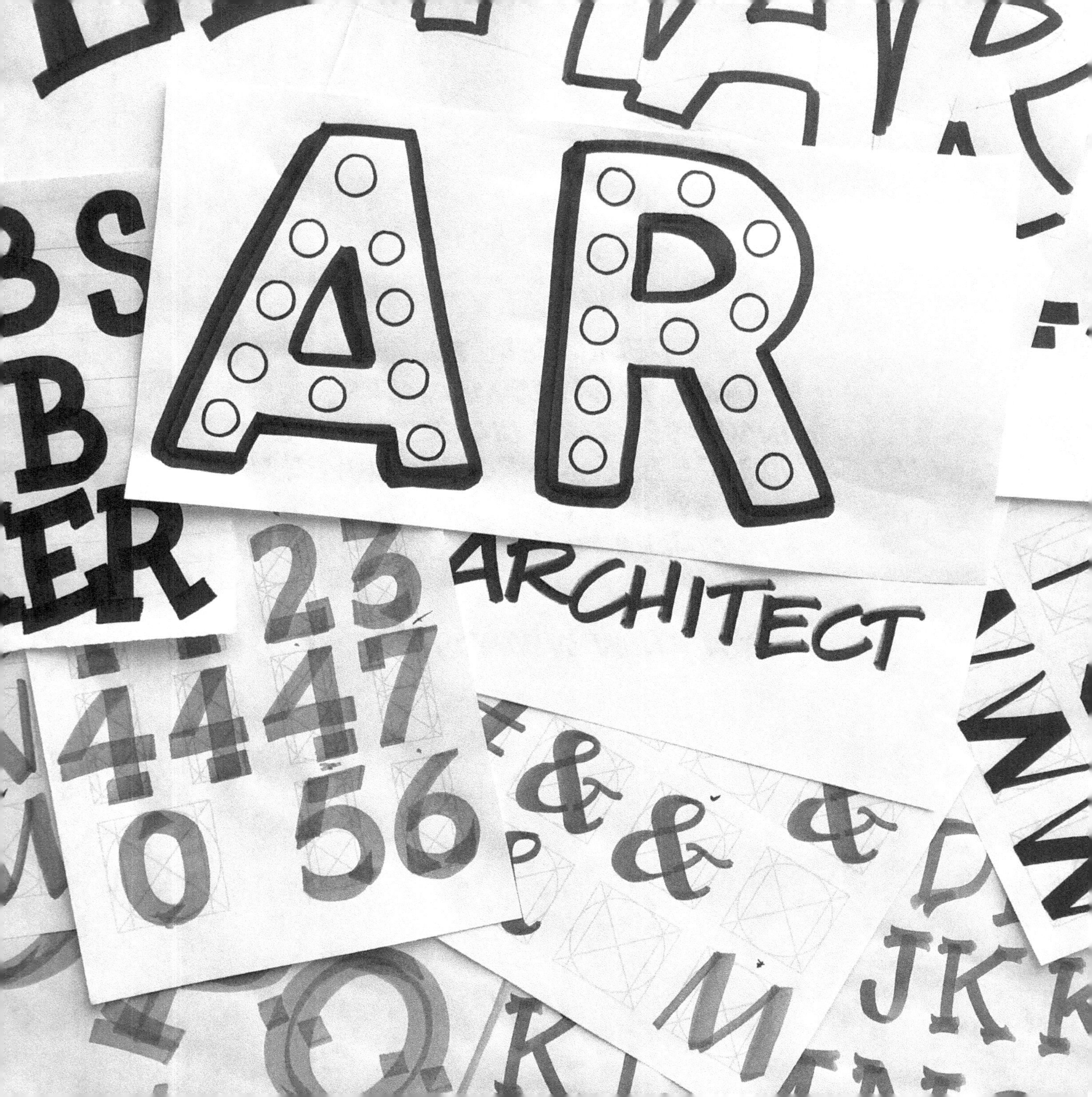

A R
ARCHITECT
23
447
0 56
&

# TABLE OF CONTENTS



## GRAB YOUR MARKERS!



## LETTERING STYLES



## USE IT!



**Let's letter together!**
Download free templates at www.LetsLetterTogether.com/resources

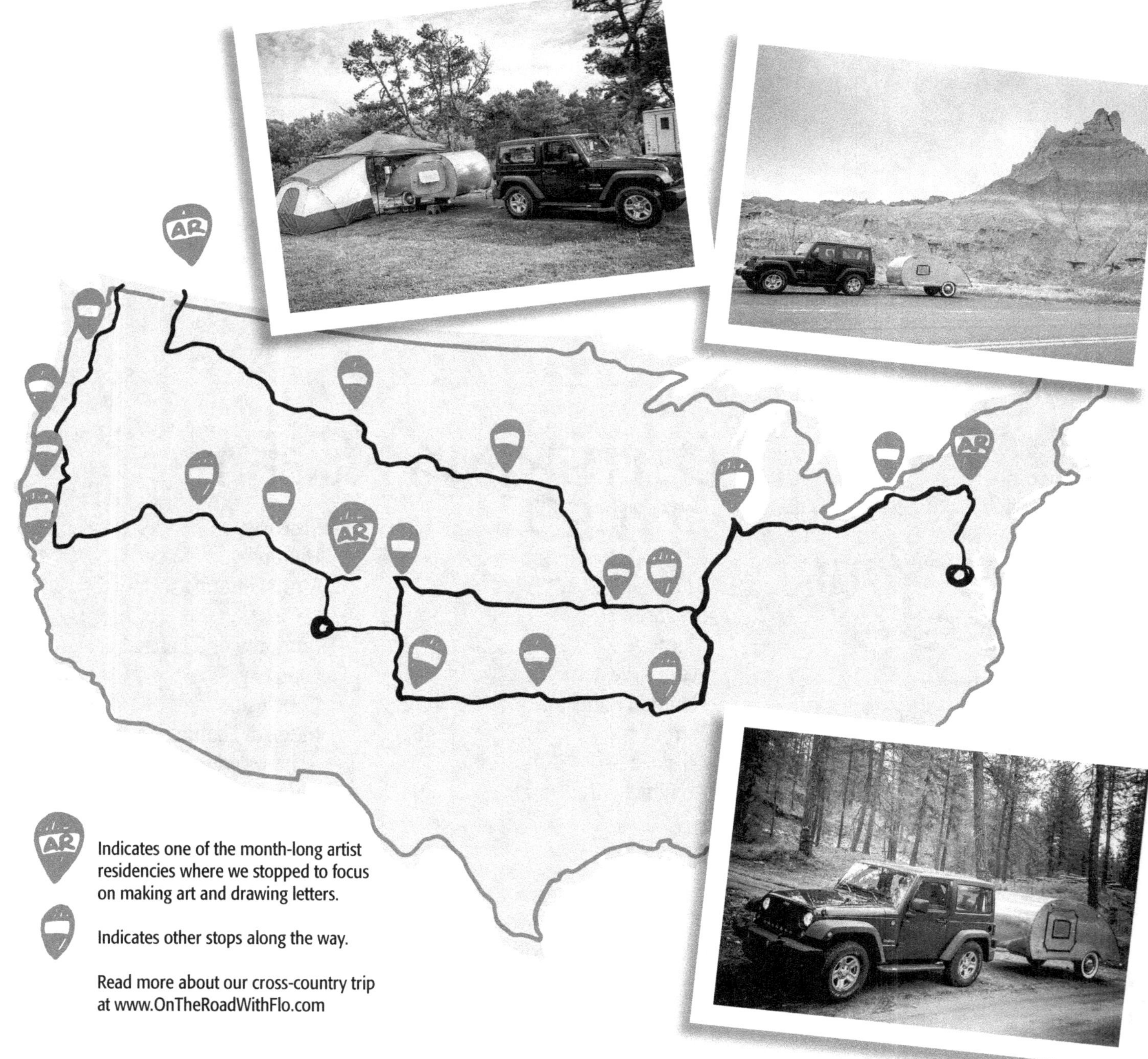


Flo as she makes her way across North America, including stops at the South Dakota Badlands, crossing the border into Canada and on the coast of Oregon.

# PREFACE

This book is about how I found inspiration while traveling and the letters that grew from that inspiration.

Shortly after the 2016 United States election, I left Washington, DC, and the strong community of visual practitioners, including my beloved colleagues on the Visioneering team at OGSystems. This values-based decision led me to follow my dream to return to my life as an artist, independent visual practitioner and coach.

My husband, Ray, and I set out on a cross-country journey, visiting month-long artist residencies and camping in a 1947 teardrop trailer named Flo.

As we traveled across the country, I drew inspiration from every stop, and on many occasions I pulled out the Hands-On poster by Neuland and asked Ray to take a picture so that I could capture the essence of the scene for future reference. Research from our stops led to the discovery of letterforms in books, online and on signage and creation of new letterforms along the way. I quickly found that just about any lettering style I saw could be broken down into repeatable strokes with the tools we use as visual practitioners.

While our trip was an adventure of a lifetime, the lettering journey continues. I got here by standing on the shoulders of giants, and I suspect as a visual practitioner, you did too. The work of a scribe starts as an apprentice, and in our field, we have a wealth of seasoned professionals who share their expertise, allowing us the opportunity to increase our understanding, develop skills that bring value to the client and ultimately be in service to those in leadership positions to make great change. My contribution of lettering tips is just one small facet of the skills you need to do your job well. As life-long learners, I look forward to seeing you in workshops—mine and those of others—along the way.

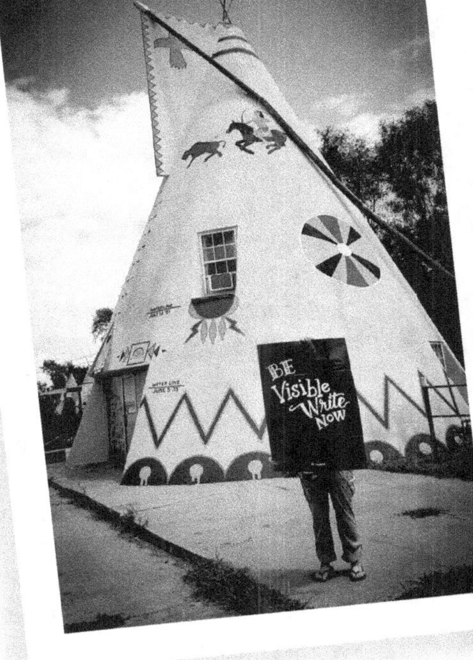



Throughout this book, you will find photos taken during our journey across the country, the tools recommended to create the letters, quick-reference scales to help you determine when and where to use the styles and exemplars with my studio notes on how to create the letters. I invited Avril to write the Foreword because she is known in our field, as the queen of lettering. I had the great fortune of sharing these lettering styles with some of our peers in the field and they were gracious enough to share back how they used them. I'm proud to feature their work throughout the book, and I hope that the next book I write includes your work, too!

As the lettering journey continues for all of us, I hope our paths cross so we may letter together. Remember to keep your markers full of ink and plenty of practice paper on hand and to visualize the letters as you go. We have important work to do as visual practitioners. Let's make our letters look good as we do it!

Your Friend in Lettering,
Heather

*pictured above*
**Tee Pee Junction**
**US Highway 24, Lawrence, Kansas**
*This landmark has been a meaningful icon located near where I grew up and went to college.*

# FOREWORD by Avril Orloff

I've been a lettering geek ever since I learned how to write. My favourite library book as a kid was *The Art of Freehand Lettering*. I took it out so often they should have just given it to me, and I spent many hours happily copying serif, sans serif, script and Old English letterforms into my sketchbooks. In high school, I was the go-to person for making posters, signs, theatre programs—pretty much anything that contained letters. I invented fanciful typefaces, doodled alphabets on my exams, turned letters into pictures and photographed hand-lettered signs all over the world. Since 2006, I've been a graphic recorder, with a reputation for having particularly good lettering skills. Heather calls me The Lettering Queen (though we argue about that every time we get together).

But if I'm a lettering queen, Heather Leavitt Martinez is The Lettering Goddess. (Yes, you are, Heather—don't argue!) Because Heather not only has outstanding lettering skills but also has an insatiable drive to perfect those skills and to keep learning more, and her generosity in sharing her knowledge is legendary. Look at her online offerings: you could become a master just by watching her videos and practicing what she shows you. On top of which, she teaches in-person workshops filled with tips, tricks and detailed instructions for creating different letterforms and provides exemplars and handouts galore to aid you in your practice. I know. I've taken her workshops, both online and in-person, and I learn tons more about lettering every time. I was also honoured to be a guest "master" in her *Lettering with the Masters*

series, in which she brought together some of the best people in the biz to share their skills. Just another example of Heather's generosity. (And a shameless plug for the series, which you should really take!)

This is why I say Heather is The Lettering Goddess. Because while we both adore letters and are serious about our craft, my approach tends toward "Oh, let's see what it looks like this time," while Heather is systematic and consistent and very clear about connecting the dots between what she does and how she does it. That's why her letters always look like they're supposed to and why her techniques are so readily transferable.

So, I'm thrilled that Heather has written this book for visual practitioners. Lettering is such a critical part of our craft, and in these pages, you'll find not only a wealth of letterforms to add to your palette but also all the information you'll need to create them—from what markers to use, to attributes and mechanics of the lettering, to how to work quickly (very important for visual practitioners!), all liberally interspersed with examples of different practitioners' work and delightful stories of her typographic travels.

I feel sure this book will be as important to me now as *Freehand Lettering* was to me as a kid—and I know it will quickly join the growing list of books visual practitioners must have.

And now…let's grab our markers and dive in!

# INTRODUCTION

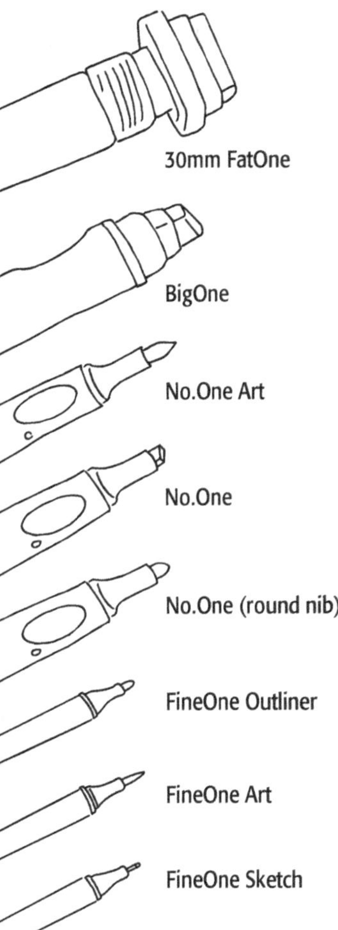

**Markers to use:**

30mm FatOne

BigOne

No.One Art

No.One

No.One (round nib)

FineOne Outliner

FineOne Art

FineOne Sketch

## Who is this book for?

This book was designed with you, the visual practitioner, in mind:

- graphic recorders
- graphic facilitators
- sketchnoters
- anyone using flip charts or whiteboards in their facilitation work or for training
- lettering artists
- glyphophiles who use markers
- anyone who wants to join the fun!

**You are welcome to use these lettering styles in your work. Allow this book to serve as a reference guide. Here's how...**

In each chapter of this book, I suggest markers to use (pictured left) and attributes of each lettering style along three spectra (pictured below). Consider this a quick guide to determining the right lettering style for the job. Some letters are fast and easy to write, while others will take some time to get right. How long it takes to master each style depends on how intentional you make your practice.

## Remember...

Lettering with markers, especially when writing fast, means you need to take it easy on yourself regarding imperfections. These are hand-drawn letters, so they aren't perfect. Add speed and the fact that the felt/nylon nibs wear with age and you have a mark-making tool that has a personality of its own. I suggest you learn to dance with it and enjoy the marks that you make.

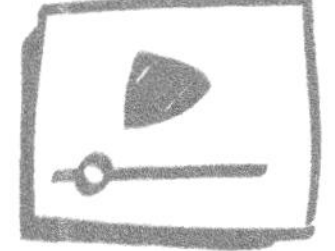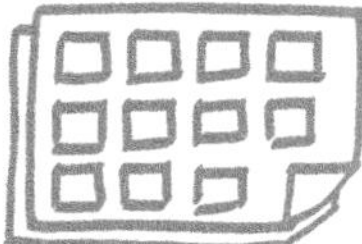

When you see either of these icons, check out the *Lettering Journey* resources page at www.LetsLetterTogether.com/resources for downloadable PDF handouts videos and other lettering tips.

Throughout the book, you will see that I reference *lettering styles* and *courses* that I teach; these are typeset in *italic.*

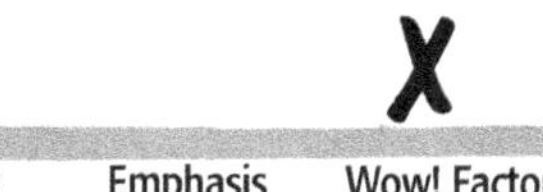

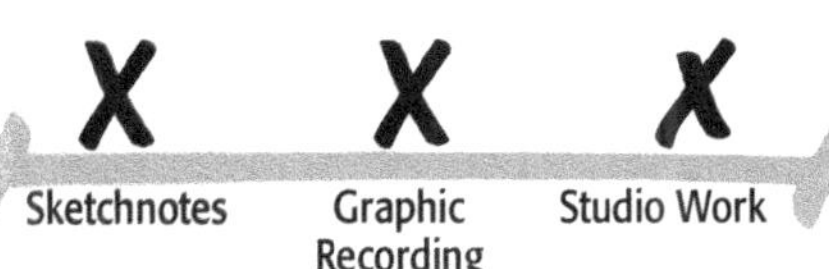

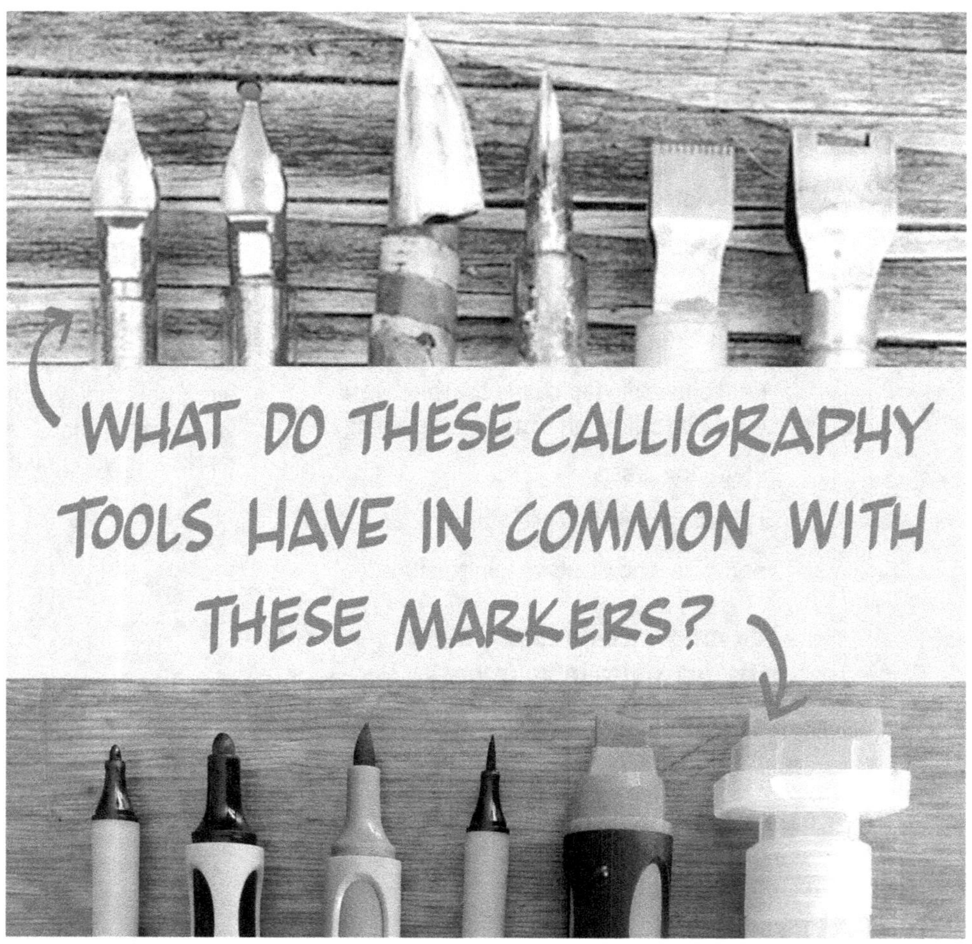



After learning Bone script, folded pen and monoline Italic from master calligrapher Carol DuBosch, I realized that nearly every lettering style can be translated from calligraphy tools into Neuland's wedge, brush and round nib markers.

Carol shares what our tools have in common in the May 2018 session of *Lettering with the Masters*. She offers monoline and broad-edge Uncial, how to write with bleach and a demo using the folded pen.

# TOOLS OF THE TRADE designed by Neuland®

The **FatOne** empty marker offers a wider broad edge (30 mm and 50 mm) and can be filled with your favorite Neuland ink color or you can mix your own. After writing the letterforms in ink, you can outline the letters with a darker color or add a drop shadow.

The broad side of the **Neuland BigOne®** allows for bold lines, perfect for chart titles and filling in large areas.

The brush nib of the **Neuland No.One® Art** gives you a gestural line that can be used to liven up your existing handwriting or create letters much like those written by calligraphers and sign painters.

The **Neuland No.One®** is the workhorse of the bunch. The grooves (also found in the No.One Art and BigOne) provide a comfortable grip when capturing large amounts of content. The wedge nib provides a variety of line widths and can be held at different angles to achieve a variety of styles, while the round nib is monoline.

The **Neuland FineOne® Sketch** with the fineliner nib is available in 4 sizes: 0.1, 0.3, 0.5, 0.7 mm, which captures detail and is proportionate for sketchnoting. The **Neuland FineOne® Art** comes in a brush nib and the FineOne Outliner comes in a 1mm round nib.

**AcrylicOne** markers are in a league of their own. They work great on many types of surfaces and come in a variety of nib widths.

**Choosing the right tool for the job will give you the marks you are looking for and save you time.**

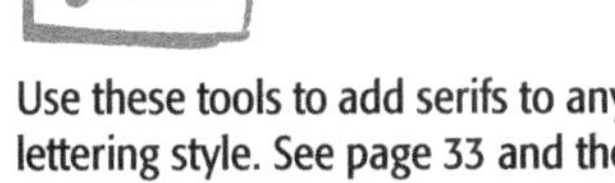

Use these tools to add serifs to any lettering style. See page 33 and the online video mentioned there.

These and more tools designed for visual practitioners are available at www.Neuland.com.

# ANATOMY OF MARKER NIBS

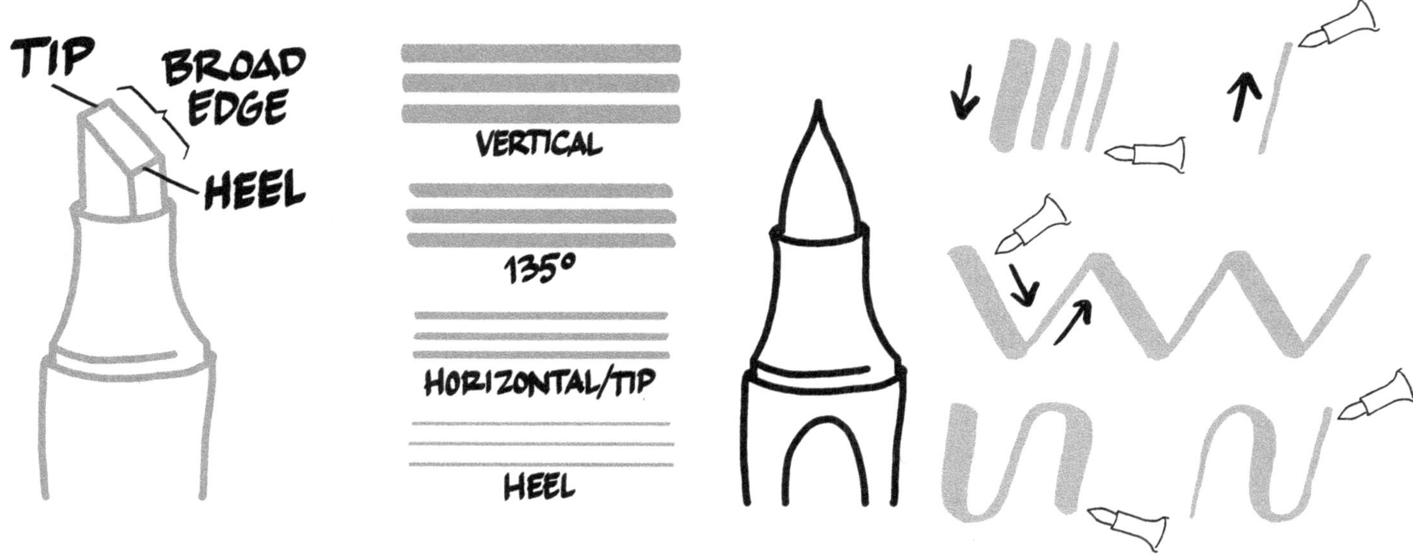



**No.One** (wedge nib)

Holding the wedge (or chisel) nib of a marker vertically and moving horizontally will give you the widest line.

Holding the nib at a common 135° angle (with the tip of the nib pointed up and to the left) makes the vertical and horizontal lines closer in nib width, making them look more natural.

Writing with the nib pointed horizontally and moving horizontally is very similar to just writing with the tip.

The most underused part of the nib is the heel. It makes the thinnest line and is useful when underlining or when drawing lines between lines of bulleted items.

**No.One Art** (brush nib)

While the wedge nib has defined angles that make a variety of marks, a brush nib's marks are varied by using pressure and angle.

Holding the nib of the No.One Art horizontal and moving down vertically will make the widest mark. Using less pressure and moving the marker more vertically with each stroke will show you the range of stroke widths you can make. Above are some practice strokes to help you warm up.

A video is available about the anatomy of a marker nib and how to hold the marker to get a variety of marks.

# MARKER GRIP

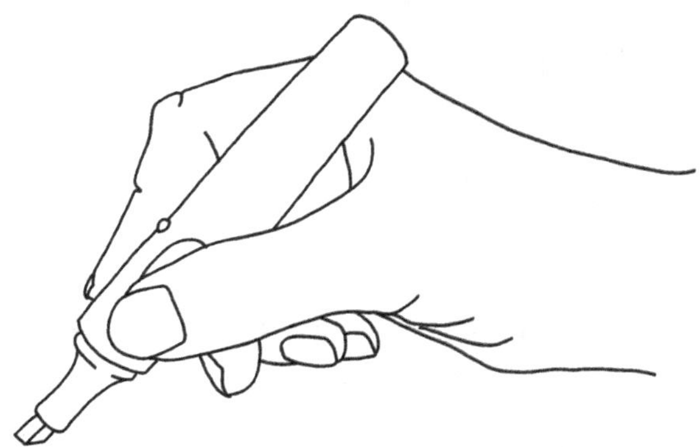

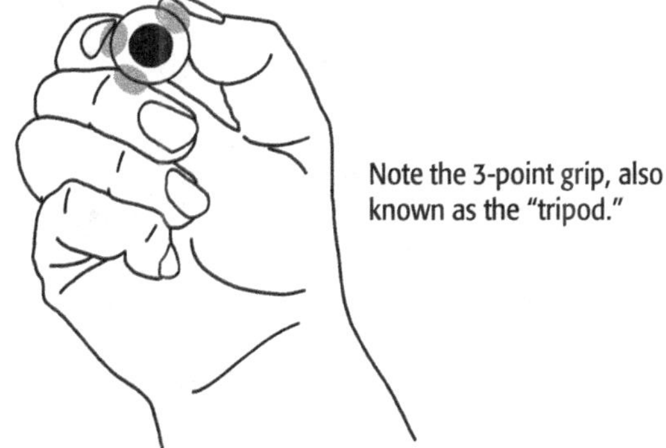

Note the 3-point grip, also known as the "tripod."

One of the questions I am asked most frequently is how to hold a marker. Luckily, Neuland has made it easy by offering ergonomic indentations you can use to place your thumb and forefinger. However, sometimes these don't line up for some grips.

I'm not here to tell others they are holding their markers wrong, but I do want to offer up these illustrations of how I was taught to hold a pencil/pen. It reflects how every traditionally trained calligrapher and handwriting expert with whom I have studied holds their mark-making tool. It allows you to have the maximum range of motion when writing with your fingers and stability when using your wrist, elbow and shoulders for larger letters.

I see a lot of contemporary pointed pen and marker calligraphers emulate grips that are trending on social media. I wouldn't recommend changing your grip unless it improves your handwriting and lettering abilities, just as I wouldn't recommend a left-hander switching to be a "righty."

Left-handers can also mirror this grip. And while there is not a right or wrong way for lefties to angle their marker—some write below the line, some hook and some wear gloves to prevent smearing—I would like to take this opportunity to mention my left-handed policy. If you take one of my in-person classes or have signed up for one of my paid online courses, I will offer you a free 1:1 session. Most lettering styles are not "lefty friendly," but I want you to know that I am. I want you to feel confident about your lettering, so I'm happy to make the extra time to work with you. Plus, I always learn something about writing as a lefty that I can share with other lefties!

Another note about grip...if you are finding that you are clenching your jaw or feeling tension in your shoulders, chances are you are holding the marker too tight. To loosen up, try holding the marker very tight, then loosen your grip to the point where it's about to fall out of your hand. Then, slowly increase your grip until it feels comfortable to hold and you are able to write. You may need to take a moment to stretch or breathe deeply.

Relax! And get a grip!

# BRICK

## A slab-serif lettering style suitable for chart titles and emphasizing words.

This lettering style, inspired by bricks, works well for chart titles or topics using the broad edge of large markers like the 30mm FatOne and the BigOne. This style is not recommended for use with smaller markers because the lettering style takes time to write—it is too slow to rapidly capture real-time content.

*Brick* can be embellished and can easily be modified, but watch out! It's important to create the serifs as you are writing out the letterforms. Adding them later can create spacing issues. And while you can certainly take liberty on where to place the serifs, I have outlined here where it makes sense to add serifs and where to omit or only add a serif to one side of a terminal.

*Brick* was inspired by a day trip to Albany and Troy, New York, during my art residency at Arts Letters and Numbers in Averill Park. This was the first photograph Ray took of me holding the poster that I co-designed with Neuland for their *Hands On* poster series. I had just received it in the mail, and I wanted to take photos of me holding the poster in the same environments that inspired me to design lettering styles for graphic recording. Bricks can be interpreted as strong foundations, building blocks and structure—all metaphors commonly found in the work of a visual practitioner.

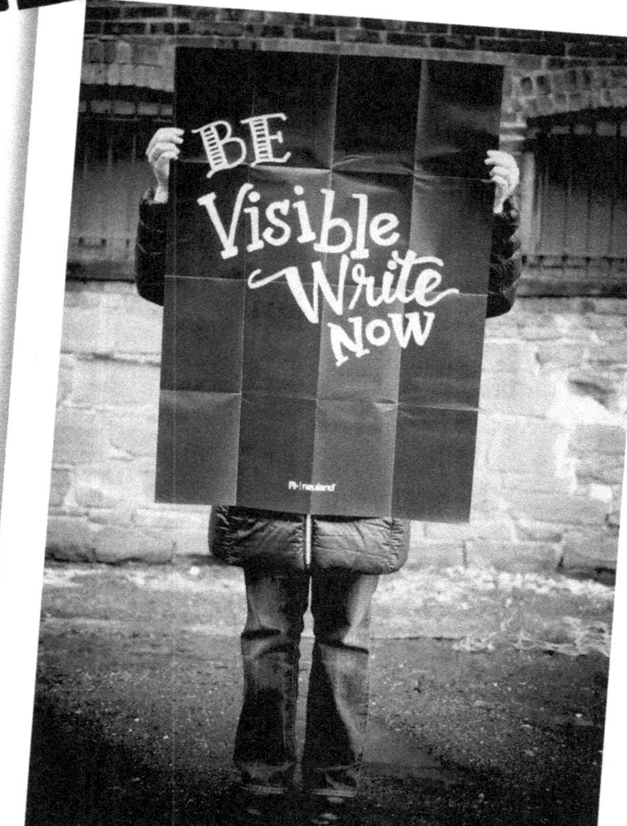


Brick building
Troy, New York

# ATTRIBUTES

## Markers to use:

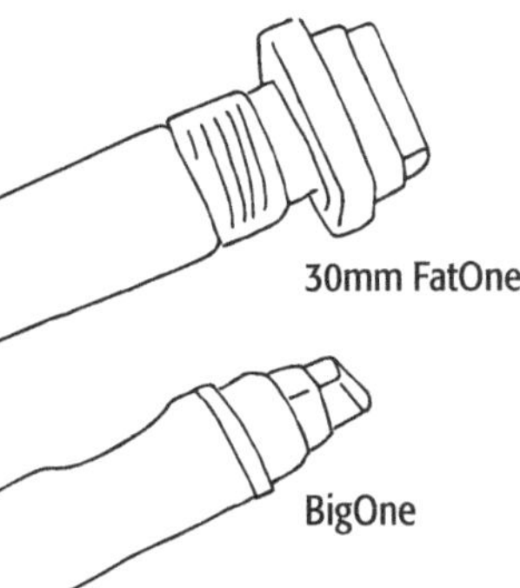

30mm FatOne

BigOne

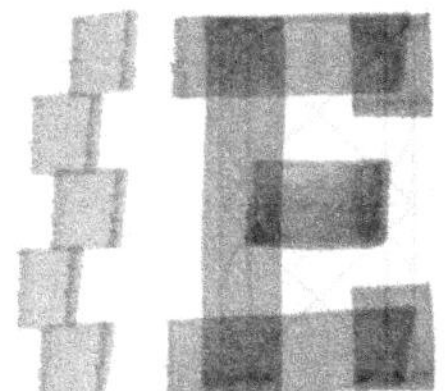

Notice how the letter lives in relationship to the grid.

### Lettering style attributes:
- Five nib widths tall or taller
- Uses entire broad edge of marker, requiring nib position changes
- Letterforms based on Roman majuscules/uppercase letters
- Serif placement based on the font Rockwell
- Great to use in conjunction with brick frames, containers and motifs
- To help liven it up or make it look less mechanical, try rotating, bouncing letters or using a varied baseline
- May be varied to include bold, light and italic styles

**Pro Tip:** While condensed and compressed styles can be adapted, they are far less readable, especially if you are varying the style in a single chart or project.

## What is a pen scale and why is it important?

Have you ever started writing a title only to get to a capital "E" and realize that you didn't make your letters big enough for there to be counter space between the horizontal strokes? Make a quick pen scale by stacking marks made with the broad edge of the marker nib. This scale will help you determine the minimum height of your letters before you begin writing. Want to go smaller? Use a smaller marker. Want to go bigger? Use a bigger marker or double up your lines.

Whatever you do, don't let this happen to you. Be sure to write your letters tall enough to ensure they each have adequate counter space. And avoid placing round or slab serifs at the end of terminals, like the image below. It looks juvenile and amateurish.

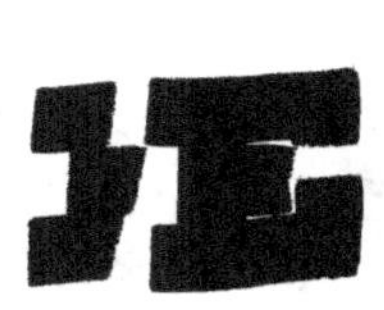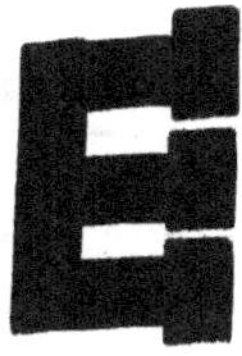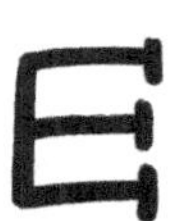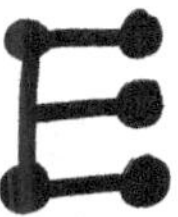

### Notes on the placement of serifs
First, determine how your serifs will lie perpendicular to stems at the terminal. Tips: Centering them allows you cover up any mistakes. Determine whether you want very straight letters (draw angles with your marker nib at 0 degrees) or whether you want to make your letters bounce and dance (keep your broad edge flat and marker tip pointing perpendicular to the line you want to draw).

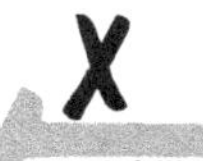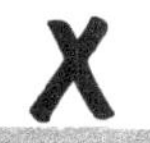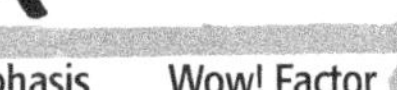

Readability   Emphasis   Wow! Factor

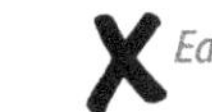 *Easy but slow* 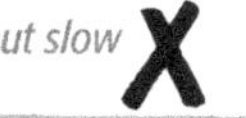

Fast/Easy   Slow/Involved

*Can be adapted*

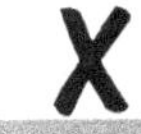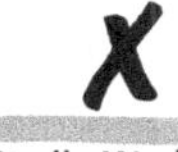

Sketchnotes   Graphic Recording   Studio Work

# LETTER WIDTHS

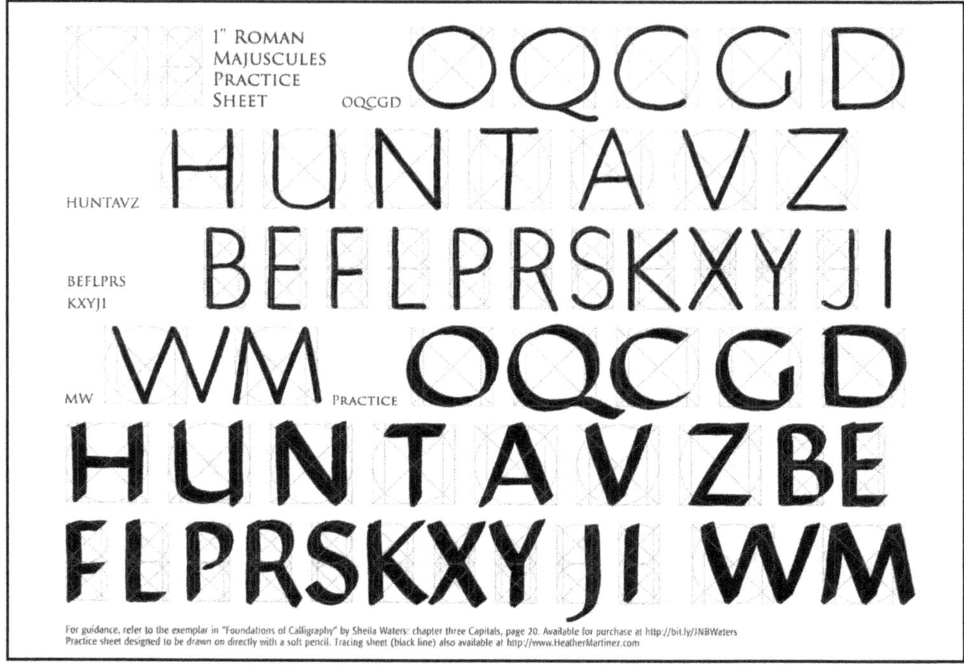



The letterforms found in *Brick* is based on *Roman Hand* with the addition of serifs. Based on the templates used to learn and practice *Roman Hand*, there are four different letter widths. Here, they are separated into groups showing the letters that go in each group. This is important to note so that you can consider the space your words will take up during layout or when writing.

Full width: Round group
**OQCGD**
3/4 width: Rectangular group
**HUNTAVZ**
1/2 width: Narrow group
**BEFLPRSKXYJI**
Full+ width: Wide group
**MW**

There are two different ways you can learn this lettering style: either by width or by likeness of other letters so that you can learn the easiest letters as a foundation and build from there. Below, they are organized by families of likeness, starting with vertical and horizontal strokes, moving to diagonal strokes and then considering curved strokes.

**I, H, L, E, F, T**
**A, V, W, M, N, X, Y, Z**
**O, Q, C, G**
**D, B, P, R, K**
**U, J, S**

The letters on the following pages are in alphabetical order for easy reference.

# PRACTICE STROKES

Start by creating a 5-nib-width pen scale.

Note: These marks were made with a BigOne but have been scaled down to fit on the page. All other letters in this chapter are shown at 100% so you can see how they are created. Follow the broad edge "ticks" to determine nib angle.

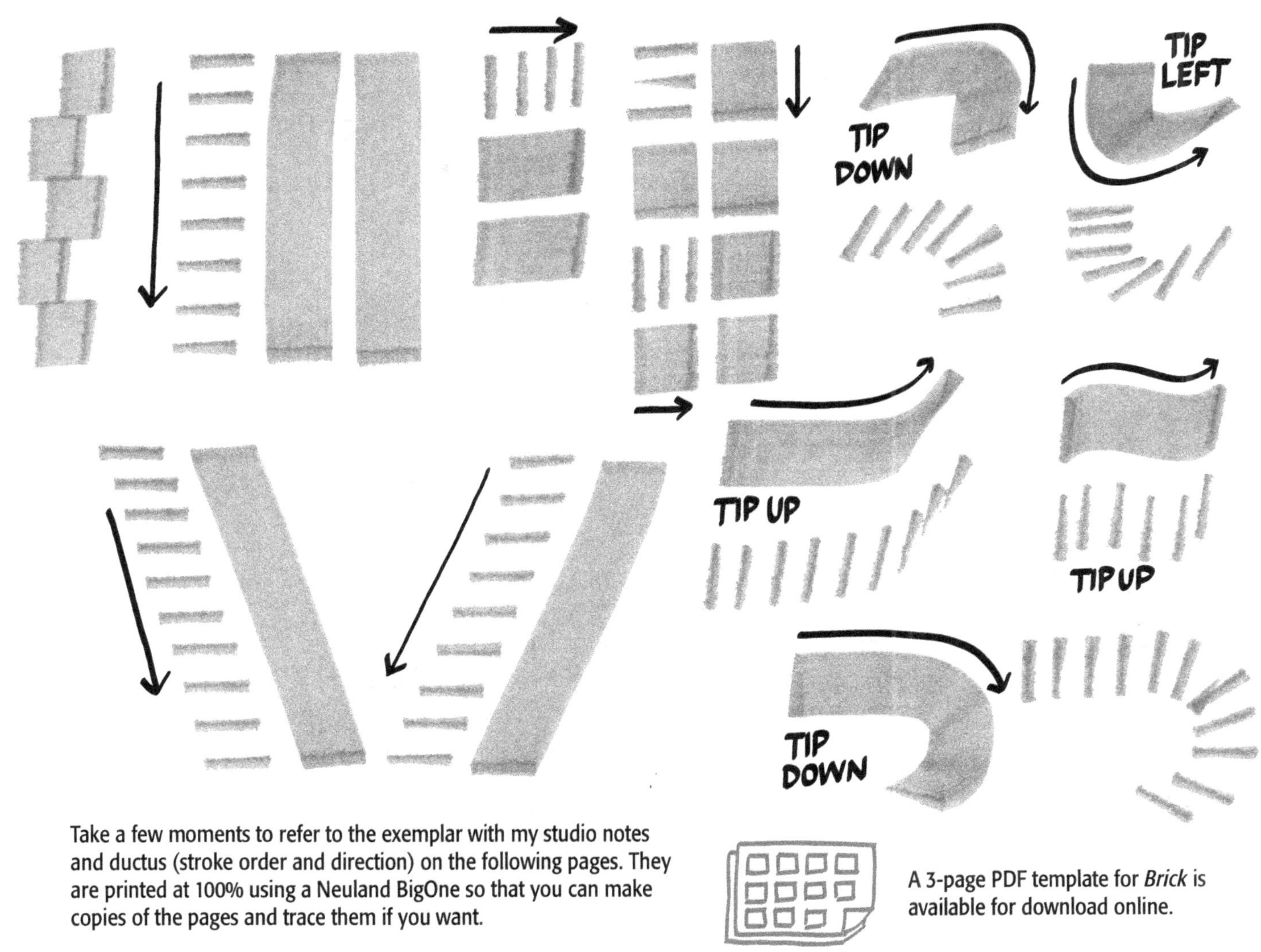


Take a few moments to refer to the exemplar with my studio notes and ductus (stroke order and direction) on the following pages. They are printed at 100% using a Neuland BigOne so that you can make copies of the pages and trace them if you want.

A 3-page PDF template for *Brick* is available for download online.

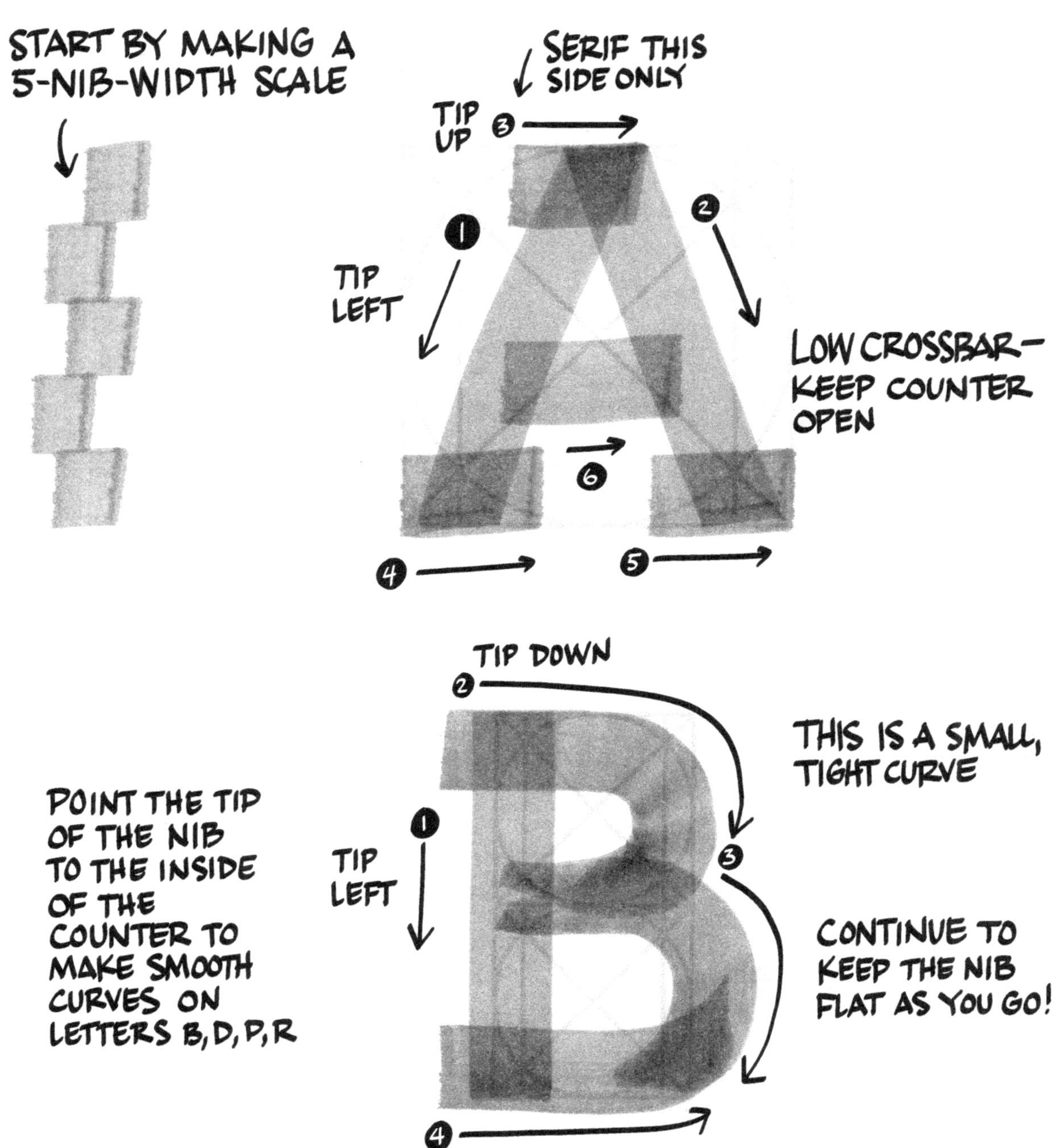

START BY MAKING A 5-NIB-WIDTH SCALE
SERIF THIS SIDE ONLY
TIP UP
3
1
2
TIP LEFT
LOW CROSSBAR— KEEP COUNTER OPEN
6
4
5
TIP DOWN
2
THIS IS A SMALL, TIGHT CURVE
POINT THE TIP OF THE NIB TO THE INSIDE OF THE COUNTER TO MAKE SMOOTH CURVES ON LETTERS B, D, P, R
1
TIP LEFT
3
CONTINUE TO KEEP THE NIB FLAT AS YOU GO!
4
TIP UP

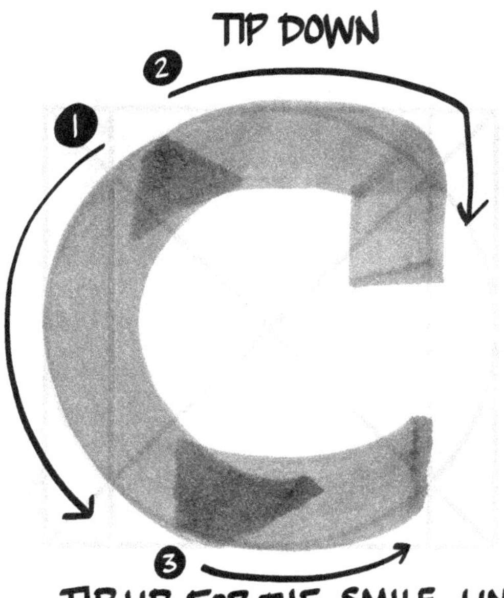




**An important note on stroke order and direction:**
While I offer up how I create these letters based on my training, I understand that you may use a different stroke order to create your letters. If you find that your forms meet or exceed these using your approach, by all means, you don't have to adopt mine.

**A note to lefties:**
In most cases, you will want to pull your strokes instead of pushing them. Try going in the opposite direction than indicated here and see what feels right. This will be the case for most crossbars and horizontal, diagonal and curved strokes. Also, note the position of the nib and what feels most comfortable to you.

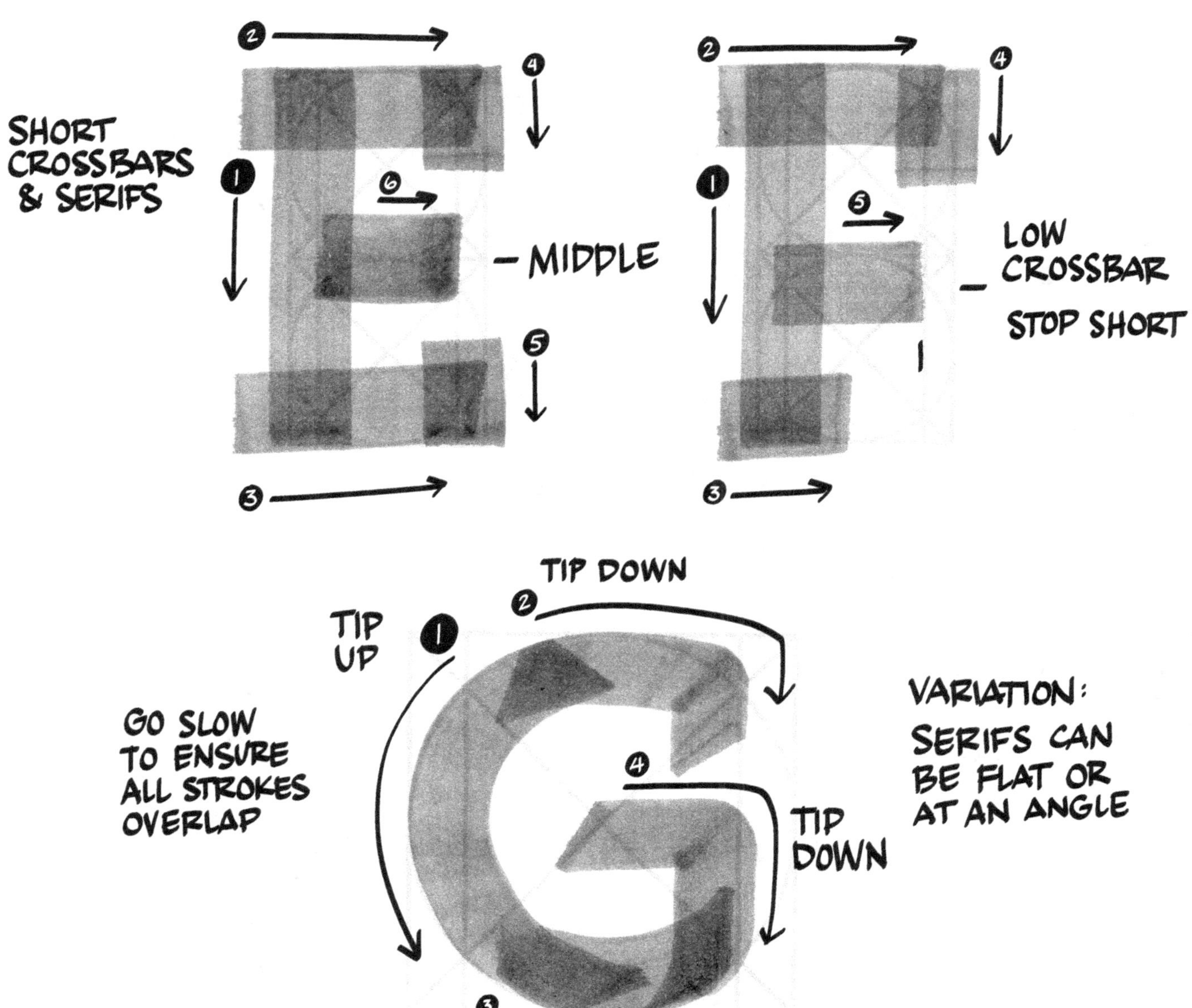

SHORT CROSSBARS & SERIFS
2
4
1
6
MIDDLE
5
3
2
4
1
5
LOW CROSSBAR
STOP SHORT
3
TIP DOWN
TIP UP
1
2
GO SLOW TO ENSURE ALL STROKES OVERLAP
4
TIP DOWN
VARIATION: SERIFS CAN BE FLAT OR AT AN ANGLE
3
TIP UP

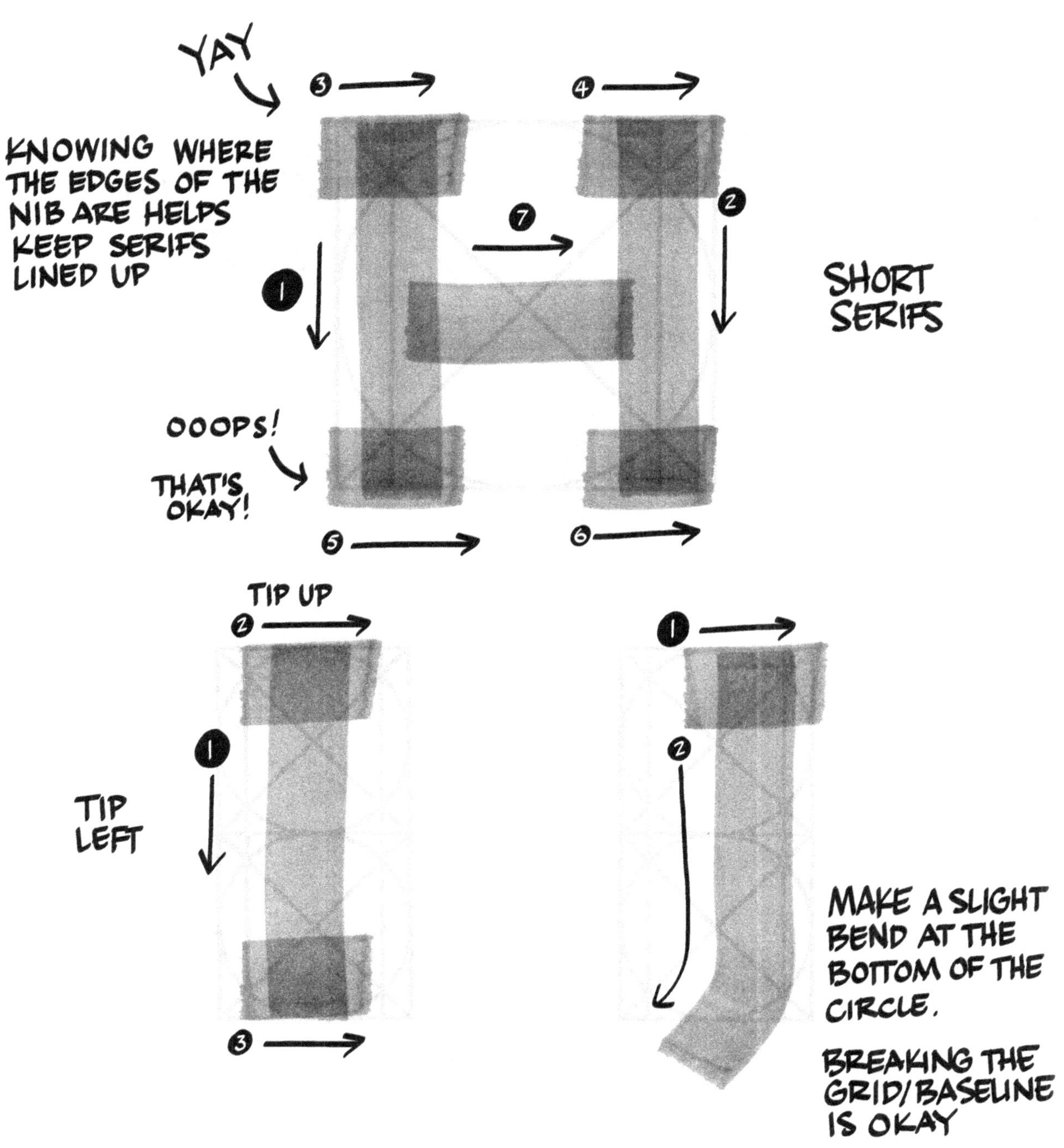

YAY
KNOWING WHERE THE EDGES OF THE NIB ARE HELPS KEEP SERIFS LINED UP
3
4
7
2
1
SHORT SERIFS
OOOPS!
THAT'S OKAY!
5
6
TIP UP
2
1
TIP LEFT
3
1
2
MAKE A SLIGHT BEND AT THE BOTTOM OF THE CIRCLE.
BREAKING THE GRID/BASELINE IS OKAY

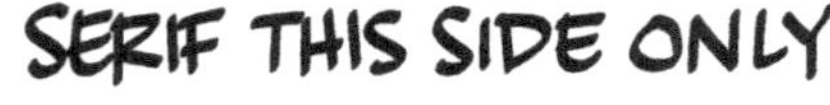


REMEMBER TO PAY ATTENTION TO HOW THE LETTERS LIVE IN RELATIONSHIP TO THE GRID

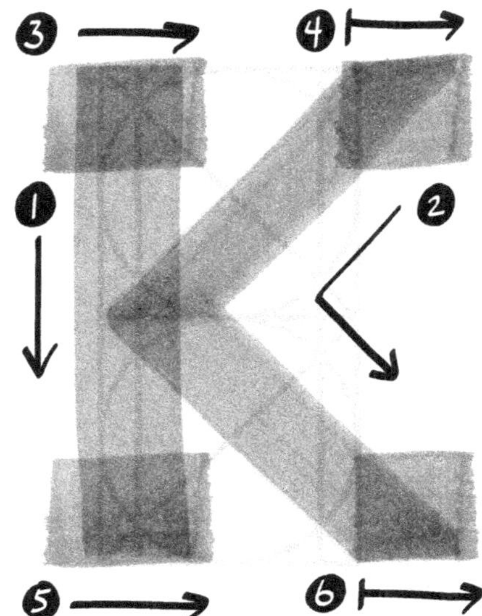


KEEP ANGLE OF NIB FLAT ON THE DIAGONALS AND NOTE THE JUNCTURE

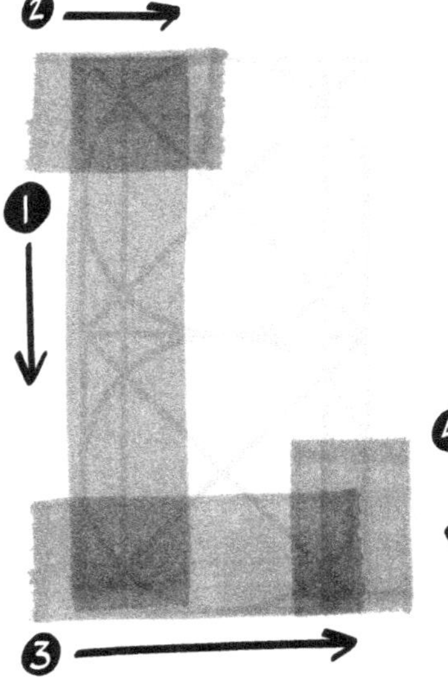


SIMPLE AND SIMILAR TO "I" & "F"

BE SURE TO KEEP SERIFS SHORT & CONSISTENT

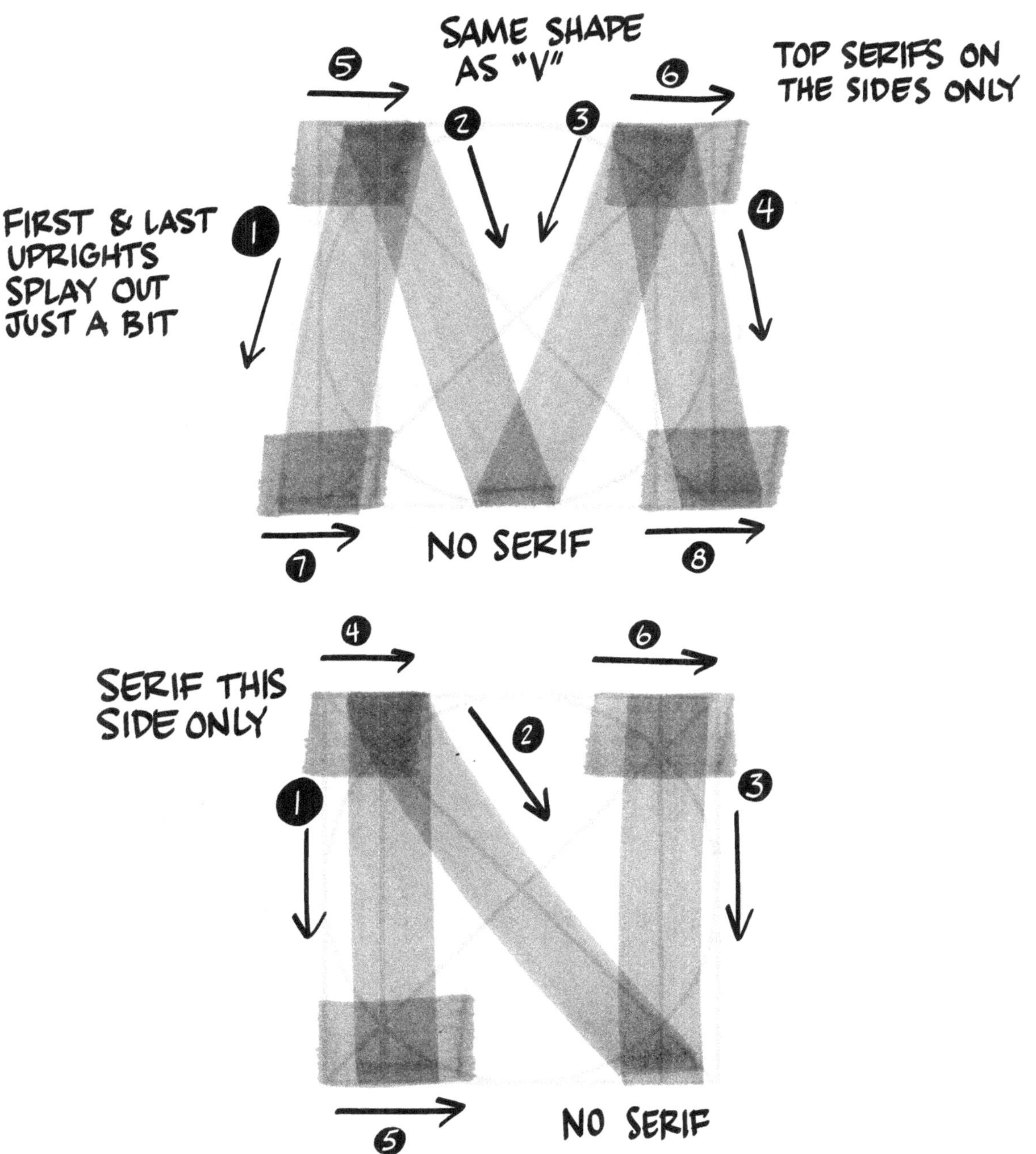

SAME SHAPE AS "V"
TOP SERIFS ON THE SIDES ONLY
FIRST & LAST UPRIGHTS SPLAY OUT JUST A BIT
NO SERIF
SERIF THIS SIDE ONLY
NO SERIF

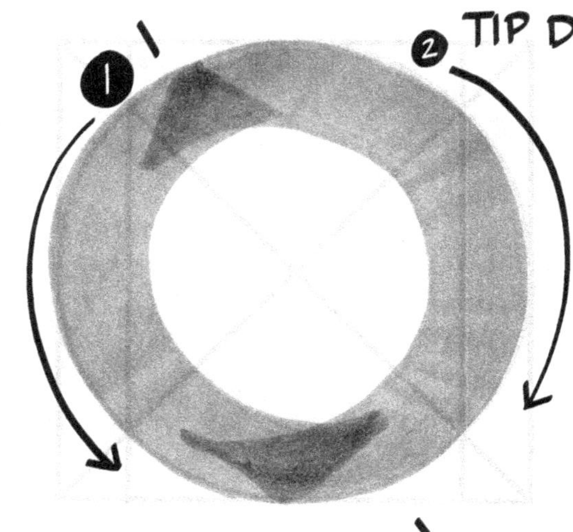


START AND
END AT
~11 & 5 —
LIKE ON
A CLOCK

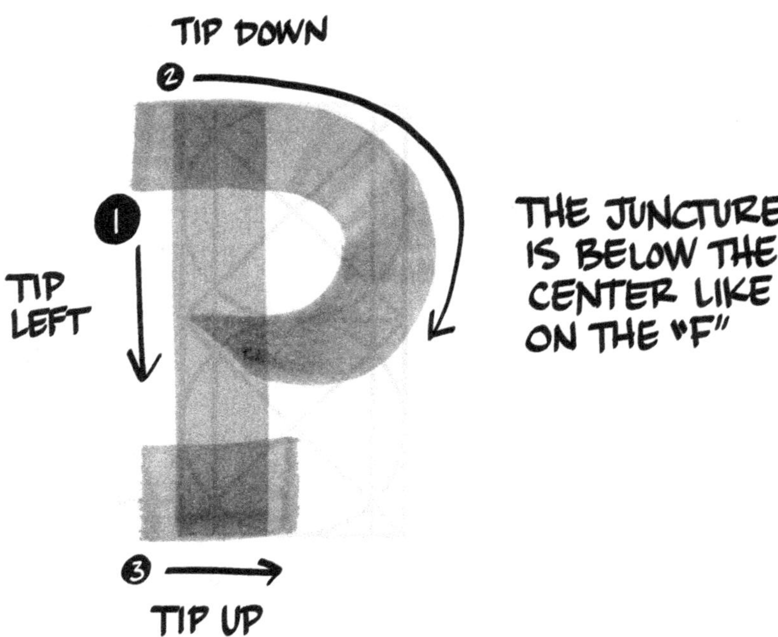

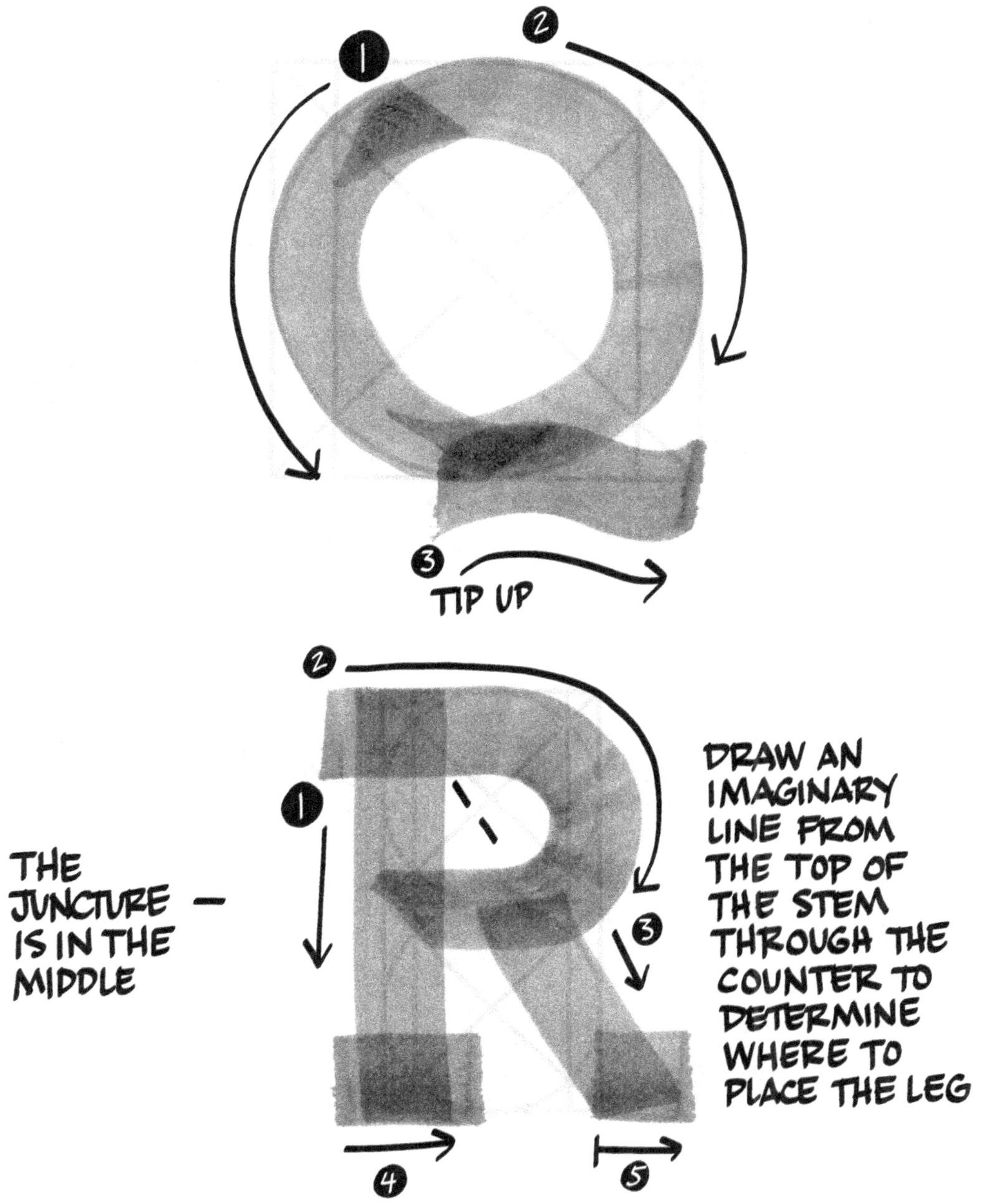
1
2
3
TIP UP
2
1
3
4
5
THE JUNCTURE — IS IN THE MIDDLE
DRAW AN IMAGINARY LINE FROM THE TOP OF THE STEM THROUGH THE COUNTER TO DETERMINE WHERE TO PLACE THE LEG

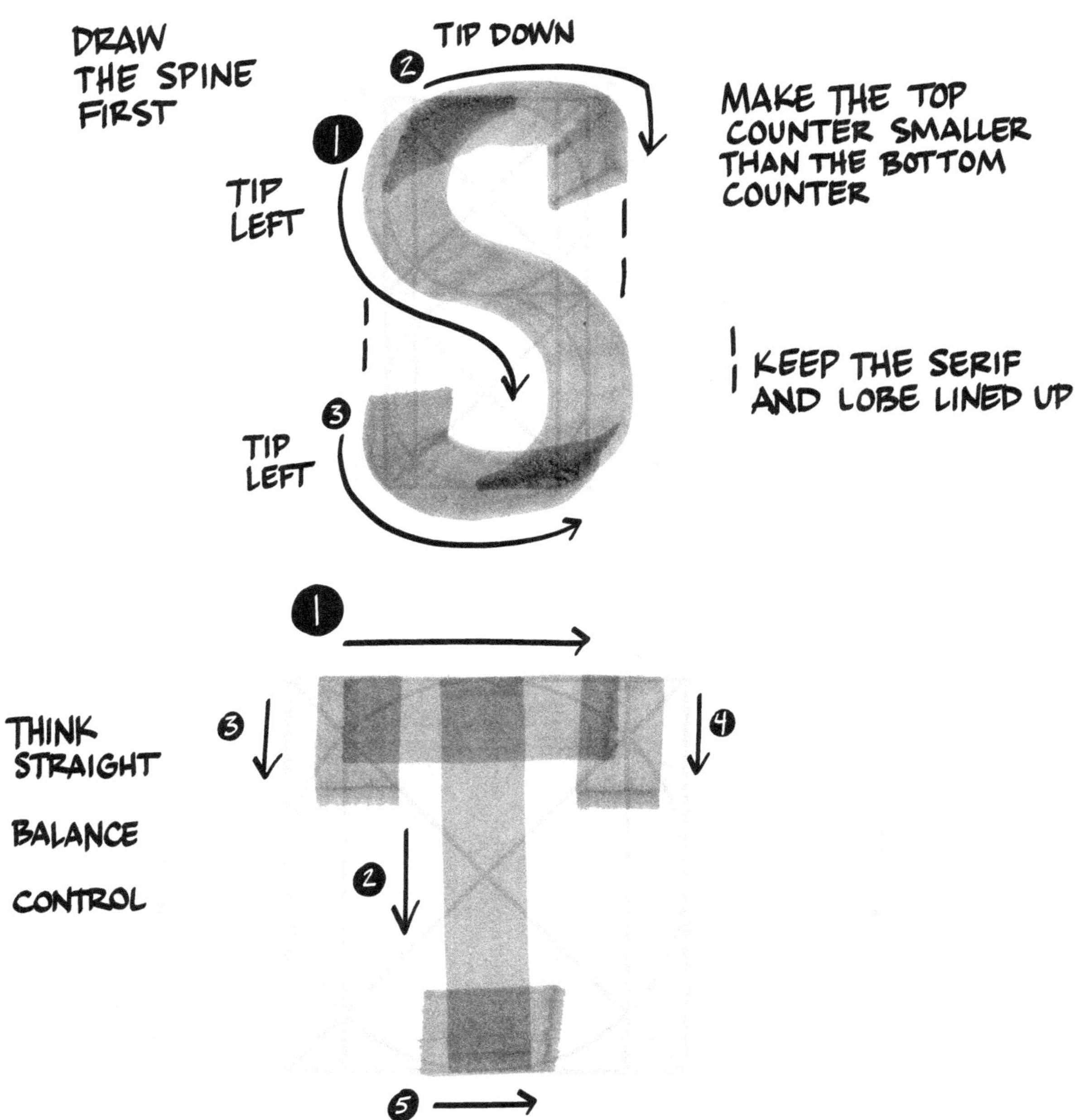
DRAW
THE SPINE
FIRST

TIP DOWN

MAKE THE TOP
COUNTER SMALLER
THAN THE BOTTOM
COUNTER

TIP
LEFT

KEEP THE SERIF
AND LOBE LINED UP

TIP
LEFT

THINK
STRAIGHT

BALANCE

CONTROL

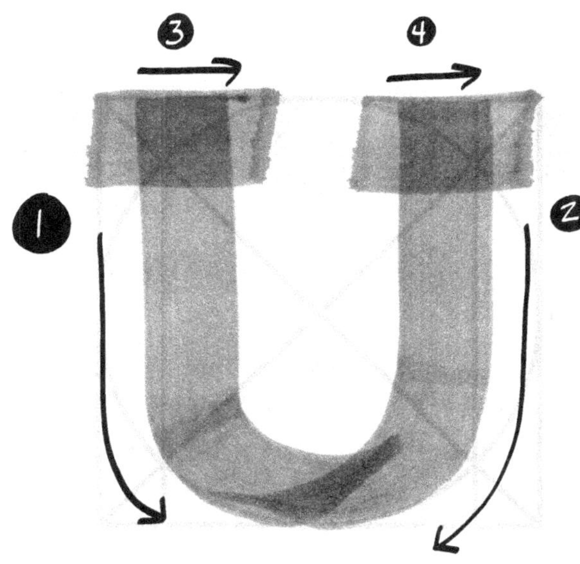


FOLLOW THE INSIDE
UPRIGHTS AND
CIRCLE OF THE GRID

TIP LEFT BOTH SIDES

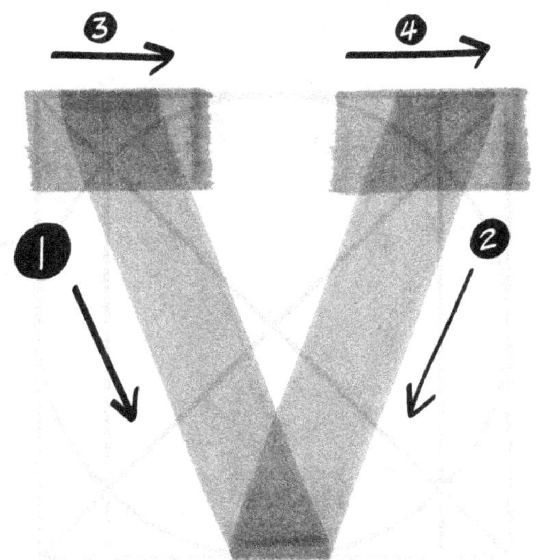


KEEP THE NIB
AT 0° FOR THE
DOWNSTROKES

# WRITE AS A DOUBLE "V" - SERIFS ON THE TOP ONLY

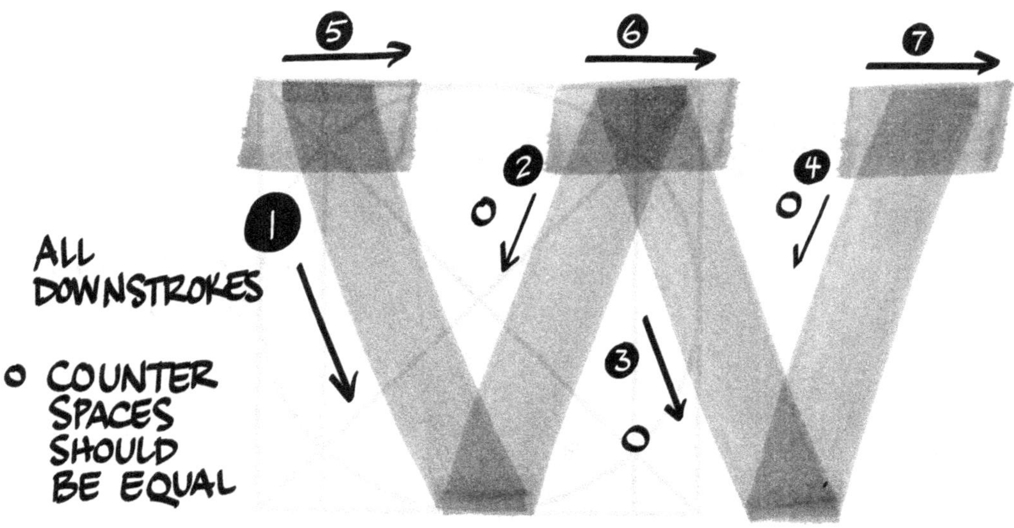


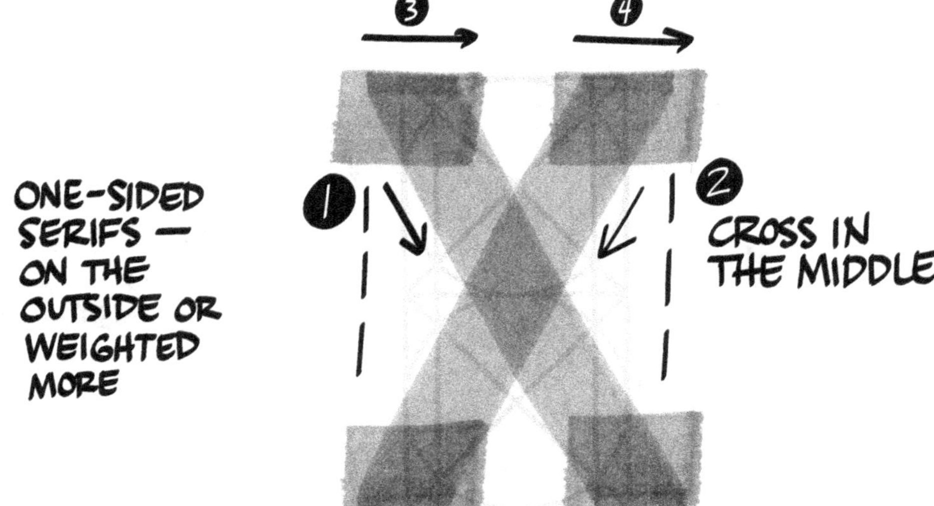

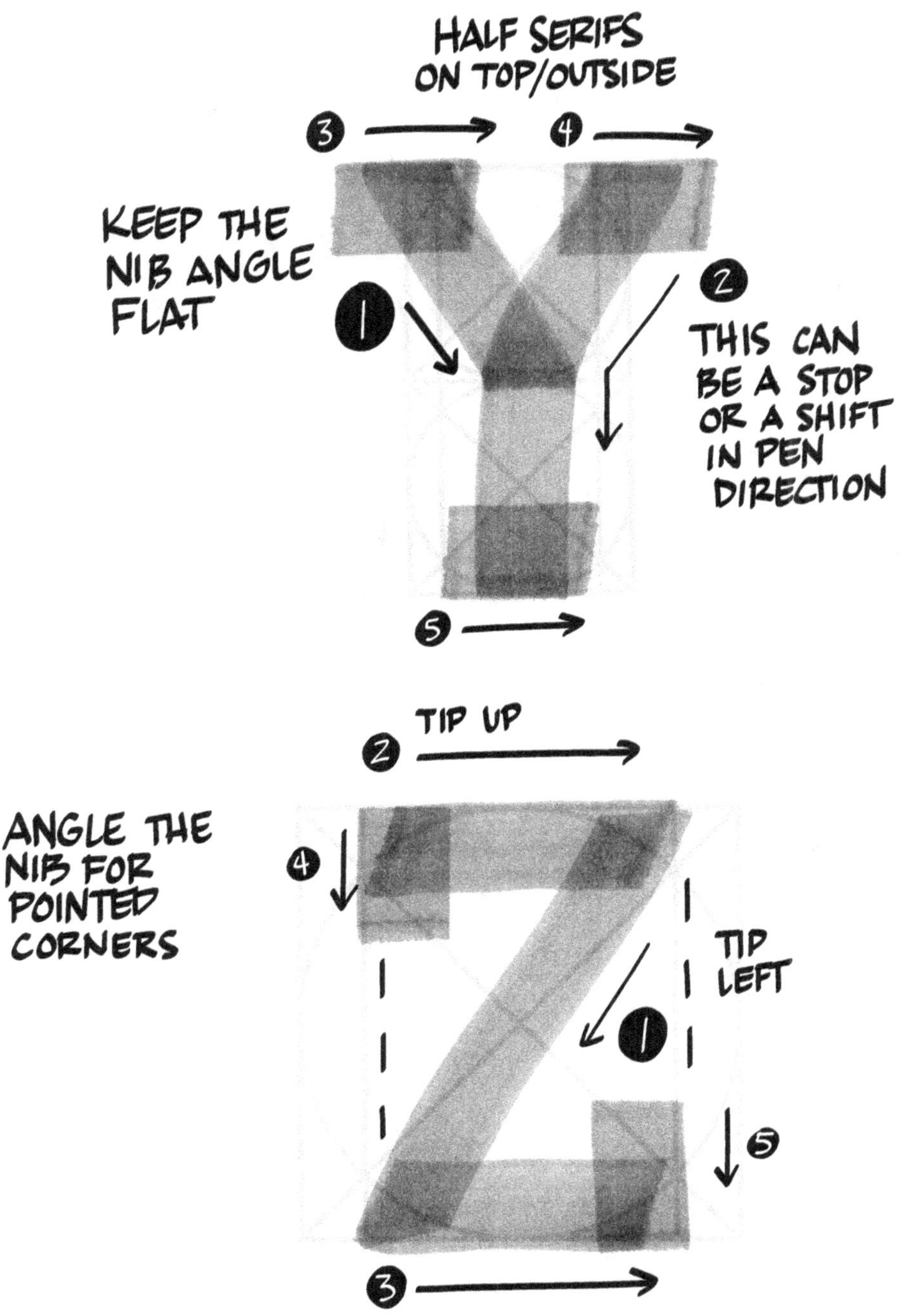

HALF SERIFS ON TOP/OUTSIDE
KEEP THE NIB ANGLE FLAT
THIS CAN BE A STOP OR A SHIFT IN PEN DIRECTION
TIP UP
ANGLE THE NIB FOR POINTED CORNERS
TIP LEFT

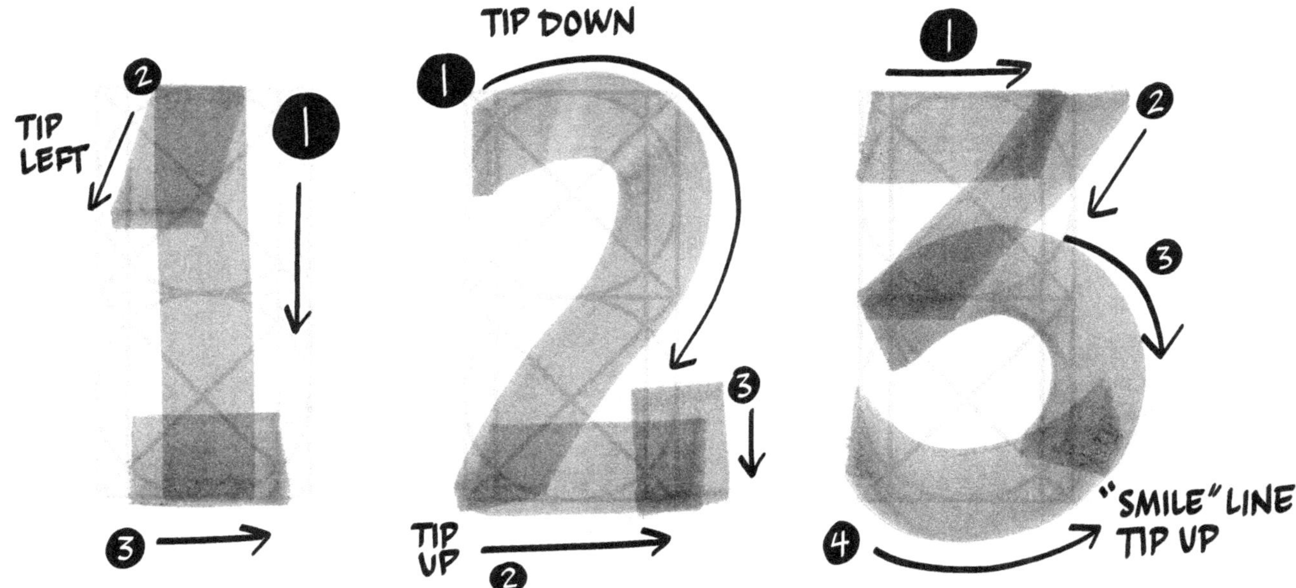


PAY ATTENTION TO JUNCTURES AND WHERE STROKES COME TOGETHER

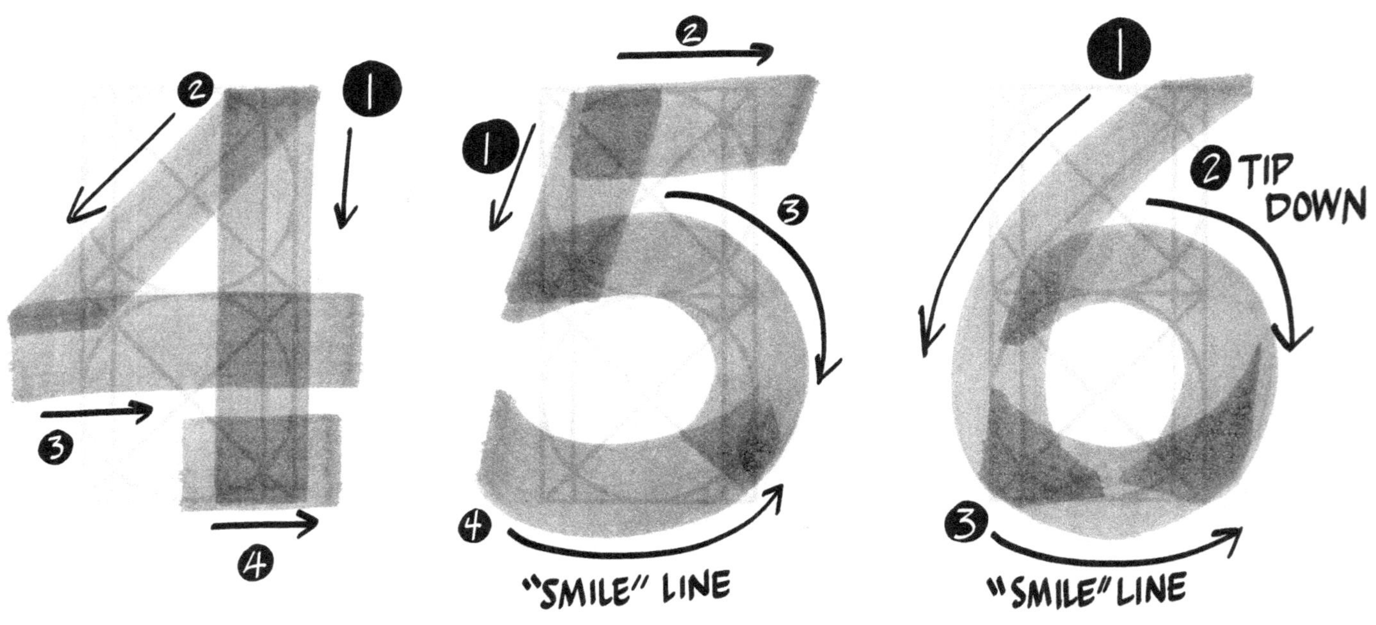

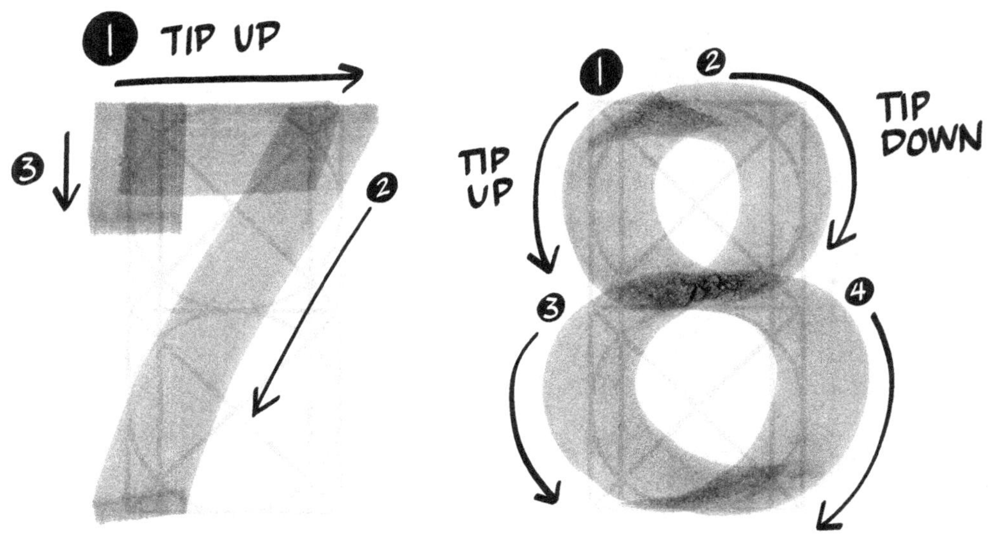


NOTE THE ANGLES OF THE BROAD
EDGE AND HOW THEY OVERLAP

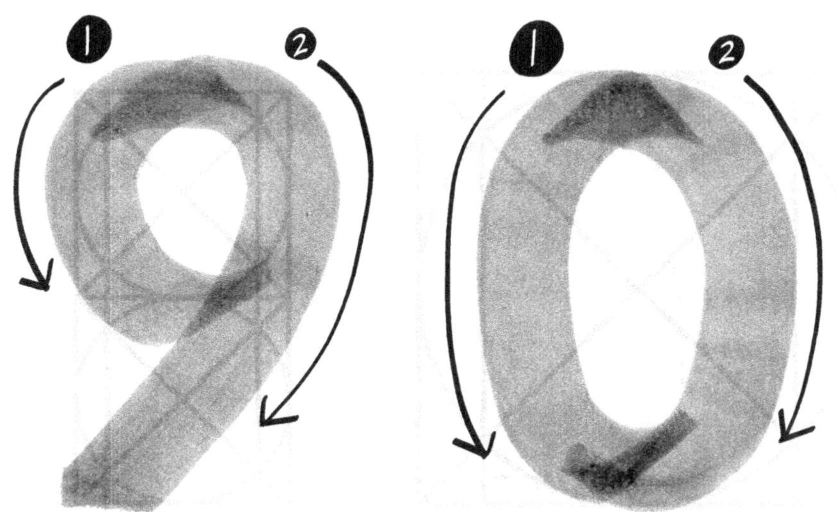

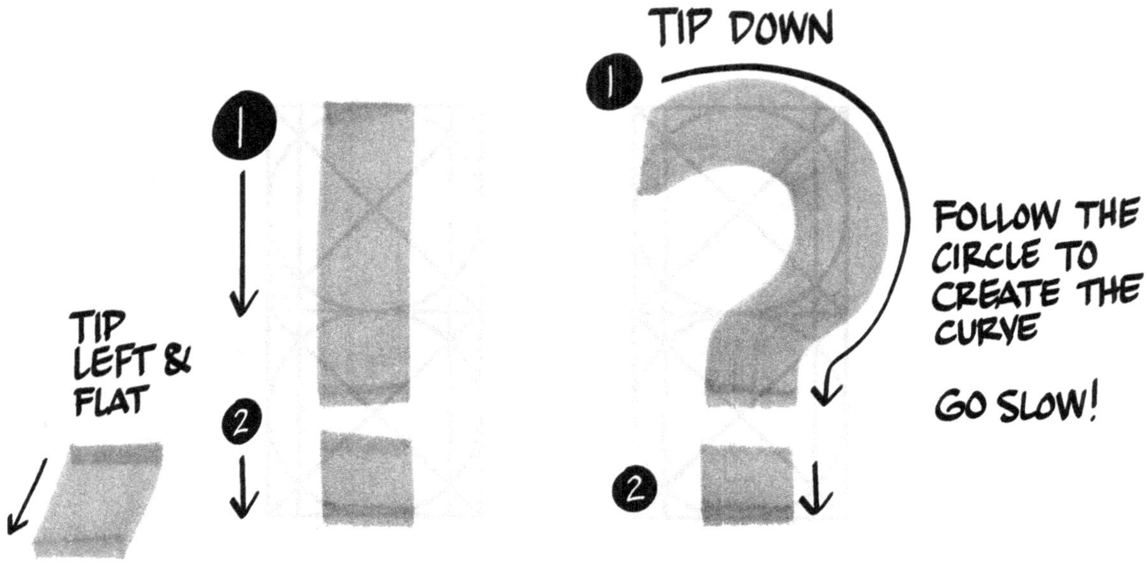

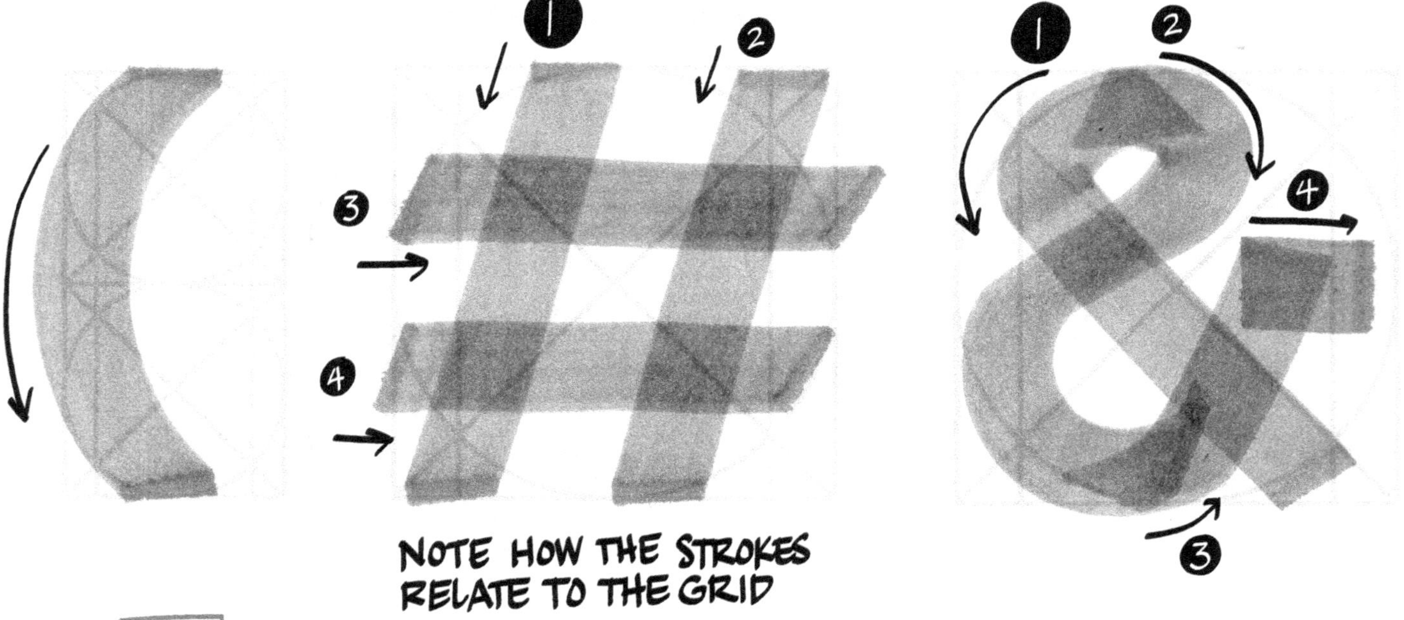

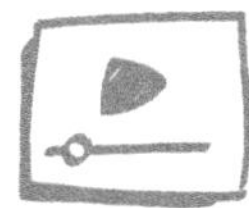

Interested in learning other punctuation marks, symbols or characters outside of the Latin alphabet? Please reach out to me directly, and I will cover them on the online resources page.

# VARIATIONS

## Add serifs to any lettering style using any Neuland marker nib!

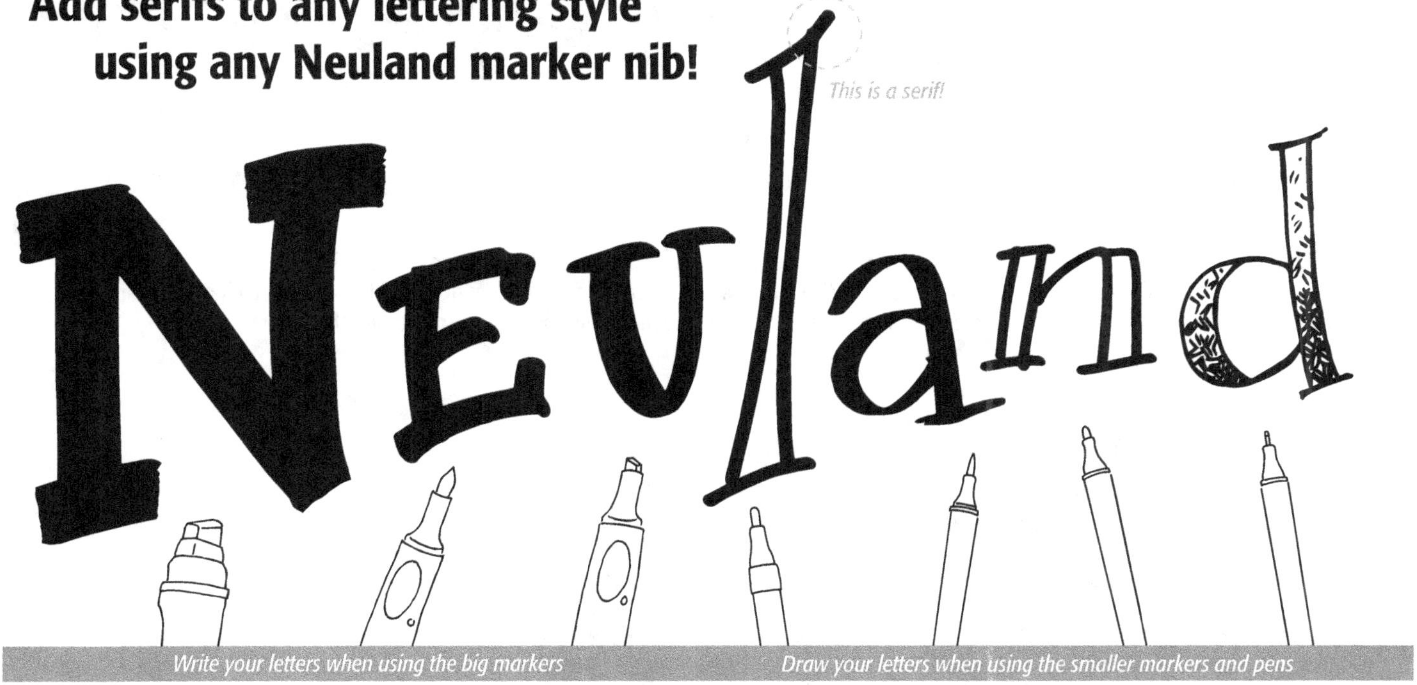

*This is a serif!*

Neuland



| **Neuland BigOne®** | **Neuland No.One® Art** | **Neuland No.One®** | **AcrylicOne** | **Neuland FineOne® Art** | **Neuland FineOne® Outliner** | **Neuland FineOne® Sketch** |
|---|---|---|---|---|---|---|
| Slab serif | Architect Variation | Double Stroke First Stroke | Versal Variation | Twinkle | Open Double Stroke First Stroke | |

As visual practitioners, we have to make letters fast. Sometimes we want to add variety to our work or need to show emphasis on a specific word or letter. Serifs can be added to nearly any lettering style quickly and give our letters a finished look. Here are some examples that you can try using different marker nibs and the lettering styles that go well with them.

### Writing vs. drawing letters

When we write, we allow the marker to define the letter width by using a series of single strokes. When we draw a letter, we define the outline of a letter and then choose whether to fill it in. Note that the uppercase "N" on the left took six written strokes. To draw the same letter with a smaller marker would require 20 strokes and then a fill to achieve the same result.

Writing big letters with big markers allows the markers to do the heavy lifting and gives you more time to letter and draw elsewhere in your chart.

Learn how to add a serif to any lettering style in: *Ambassador Talk: Are You a Lettering Addict?,* with Sandra Dirks. See resources on page 113.

# LETTERING EXAMPLES

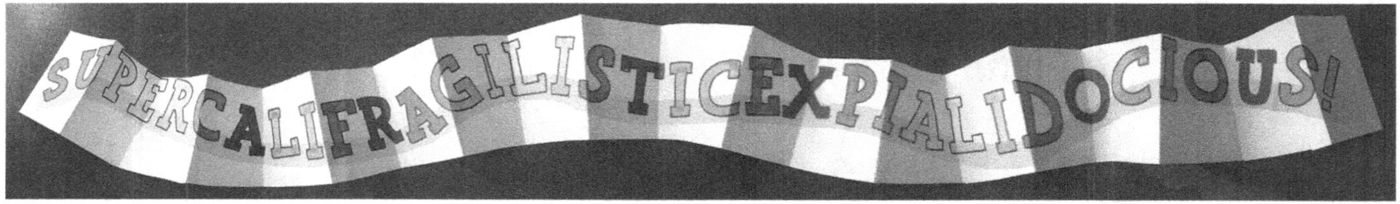

*pictured above*

**Tina Abert** of Madison, Wisconsin, is an early adopter of all things at www.LetsLetterTogether.com and utilizes her learnings in her work as a visual practitioner. Here, Tina used every BigOne she owns to create a very impressive card to wish me well on my trip to EuViz in Denmark. This is a stellar example of how to write on a wavy baseline by bouncing and rotating the letters.

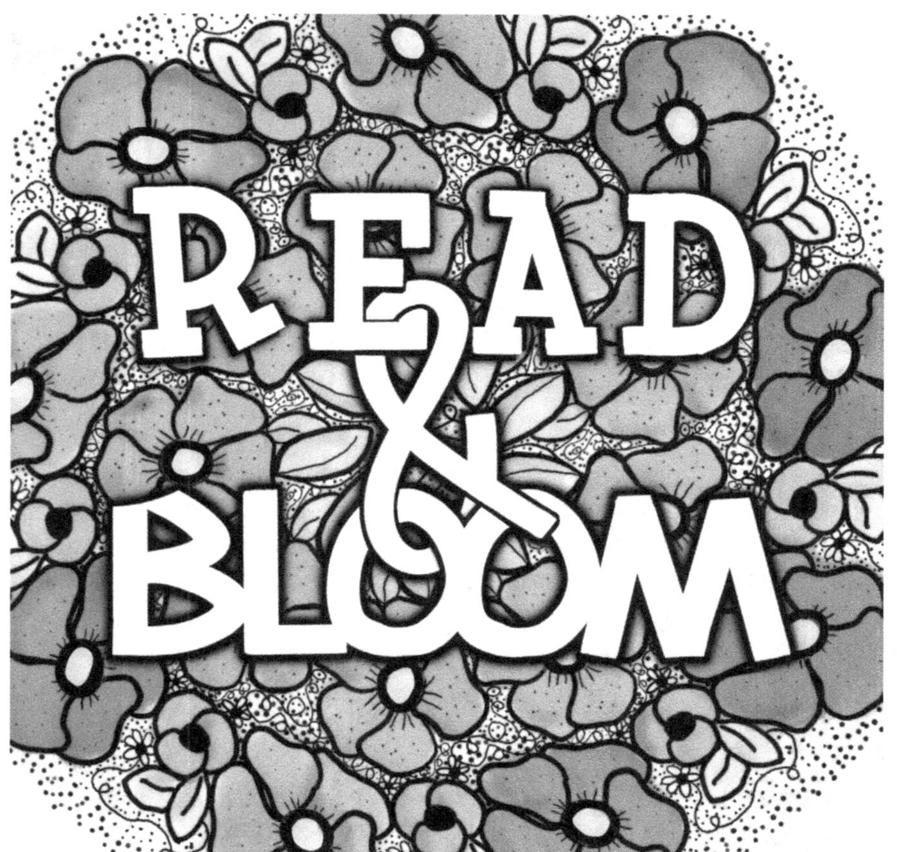

*pictured left*

**Karin Perry**, a.k.a. karinlibrarian, from Haworth, Oklahoma, is prolific on social media. Because she works in Procreate on her iPad Pro with Apple Pencil, she is able to create quickly. While she is working digitally, we can see that she is integrating the *Brick* letterform, the *Harbor* technique, and connecting it all together with that interlocking ampersand on a bed of flowers. The black glow really links the letters and flowers while making the letters pop out!

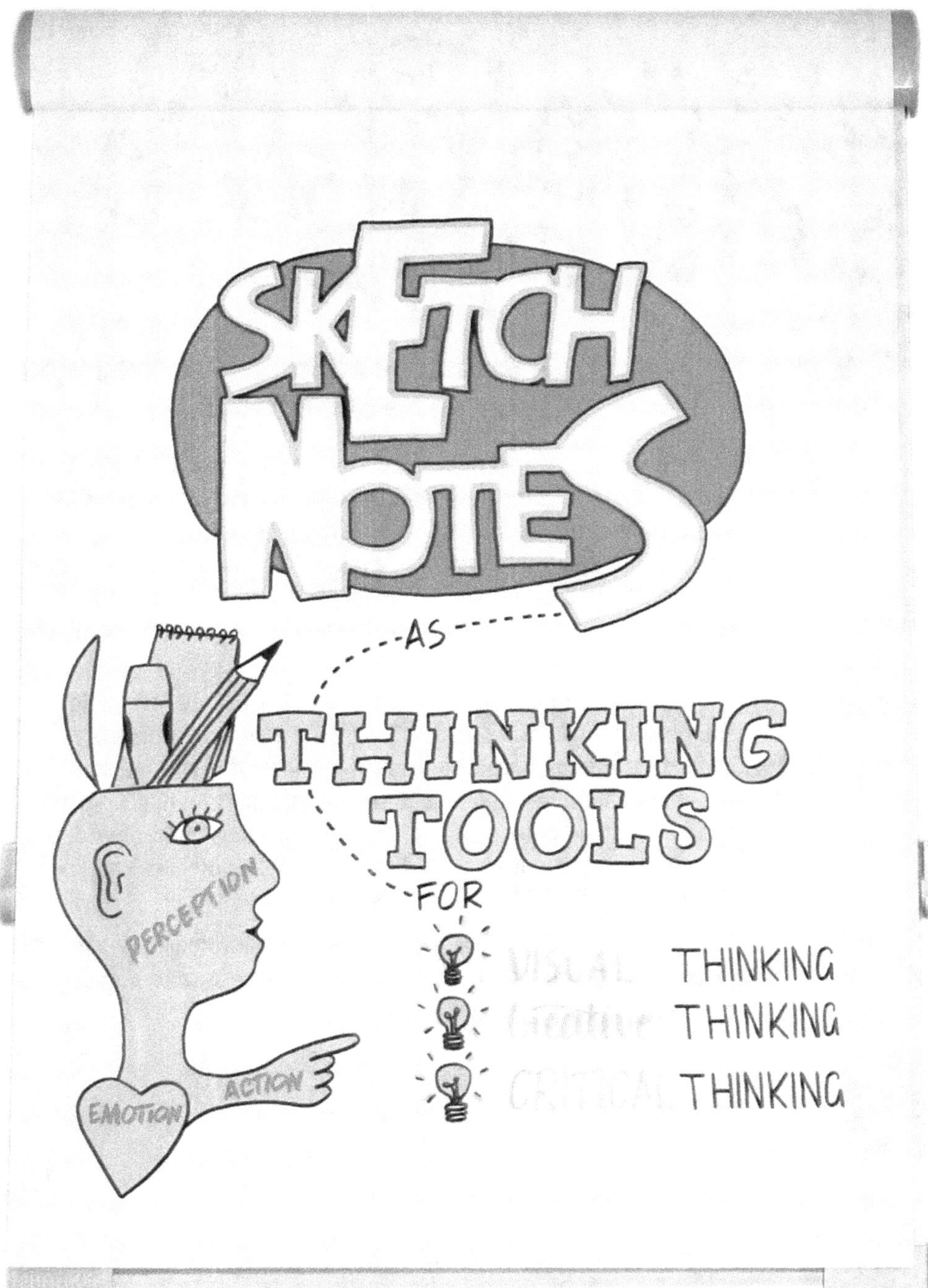




**Raffaelina Rossetti** of Frankfurt, Germany, is new to the field but has quickly picked up the skills needed to do the job well. In this flip chart, she utilizes both *Brick* and *Harbor*, found in this book, and several other lettering styles to show off an upcoming event where she will present how sketchnotes are an effective thinking tool.

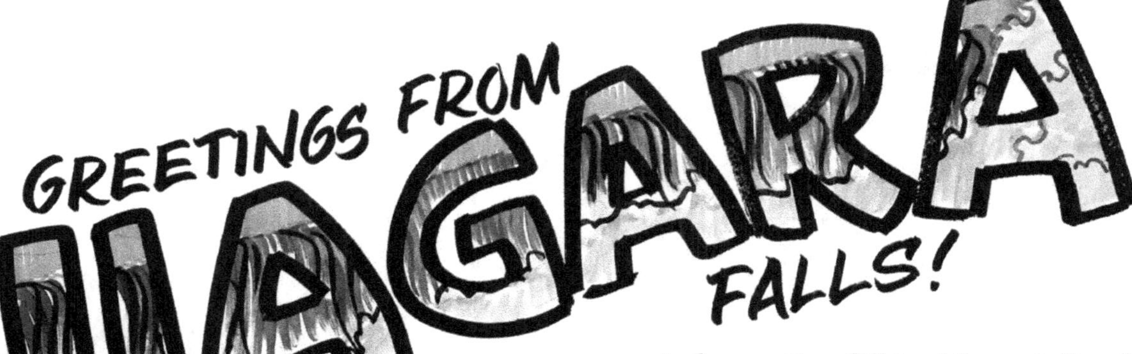


## A decorative fill inside a stylized block letter on a wavy baseline.

Remember those postcards from yesteryear that say "Greetings from..." in small letters and the destination's name in large block letters? They are making a comeback! While on the road, I saw many examples and thought they would make great chart titles for graphic recordings. Because Niagara Falls is such a touristy place with a long history, it conjured up the visual for me. And the letters were fun to fill with water.

The wow factor of this lettering can be immediate and incredible. You need to think through your design ahead of time—content, context, composition, color palette. You will need to commit some time beforehand to planning and sketching, but it can really pay off. In addition to graphic recording, other applications of this approach include customer journeys, roadmaps, historical timelines and finished studio pieces that will be reproduced.

In this chapter, I joined forces with letterer extraordinaire Ben Tinker to tackle the process for this lettering style. Ben shows us his design process and how he applies the concept.

Some ideas are simply bigger than me. That's why I like to collaborate with other creatives. Here are some quick sketches I made while on a call with Ben. As we discussed the concept, we also decided it would make for great content for his *Lettering with the Masters* session.

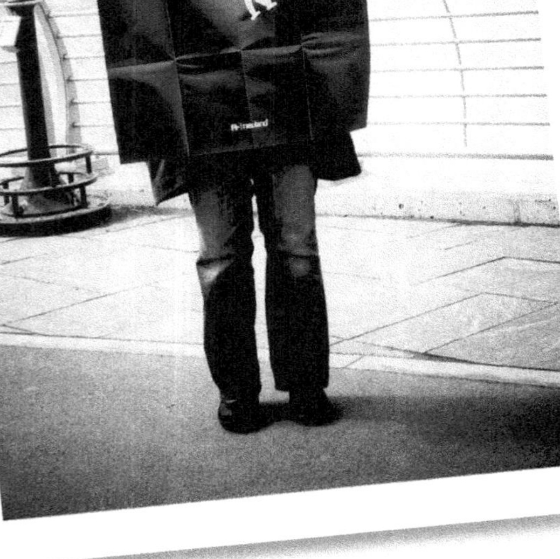


Niagara Falls
New York

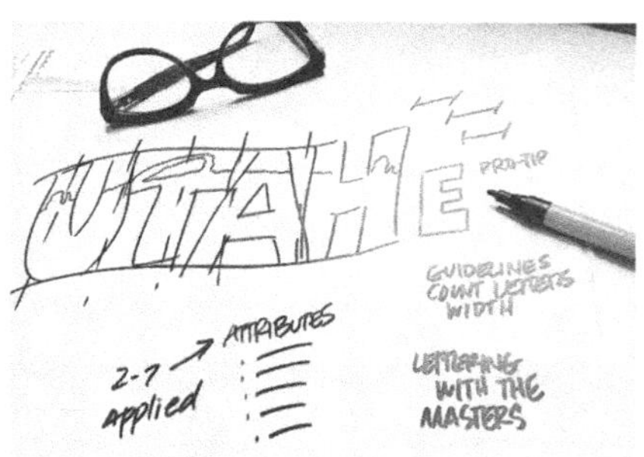

# ATTRIBUTES

**Markers to use:**

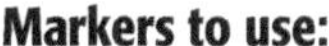
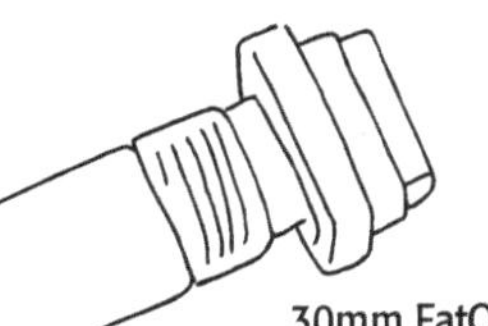
30mm FatOne

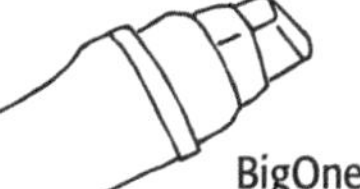
BigOne

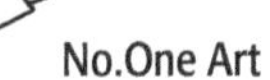
No.One Art

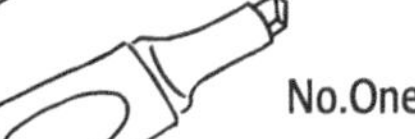
No.One

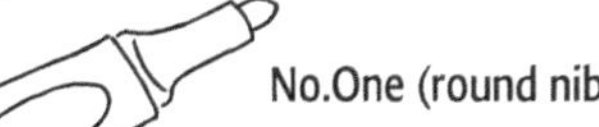
No.One (round nib)

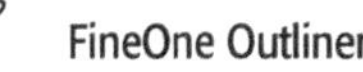
FineOne Outliner

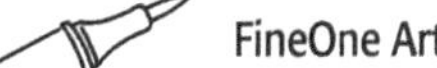
FineOne Art

FineOne Sketch

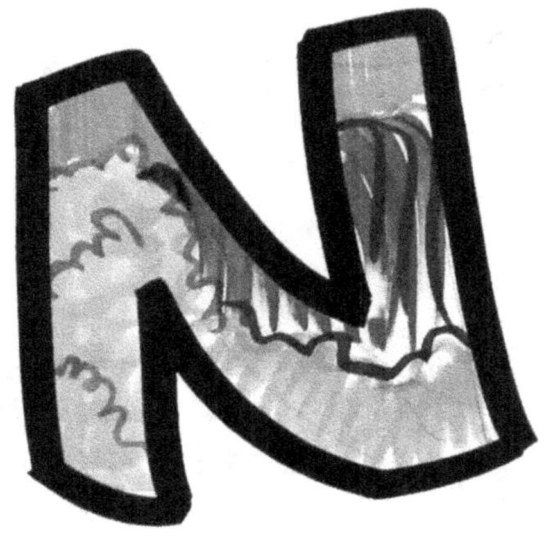

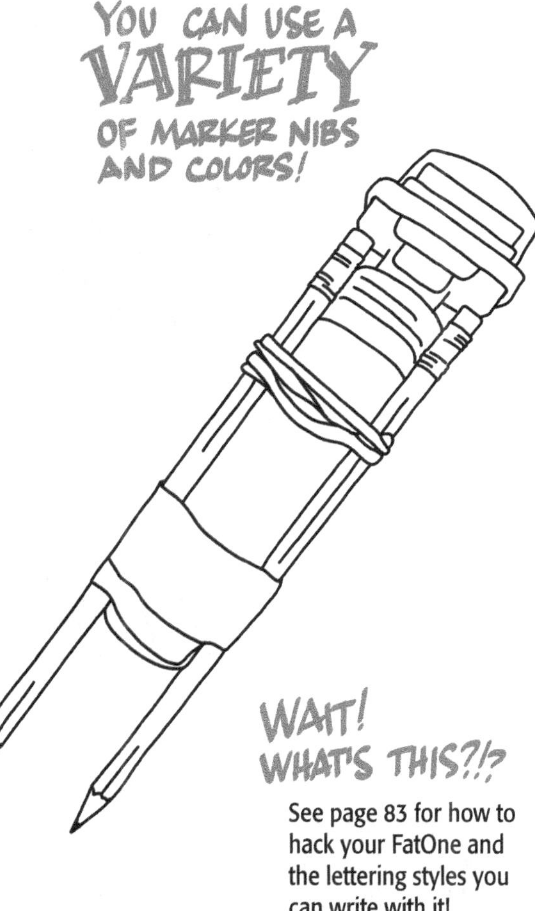


**Lettering style attributes:**
- Hand drawn
- Decorative
- Includes fills
- 3D/Perspective
- Arched or wavy baseline

**Important considerations:**
- Theme/motif
- Color palette
- Sketch it out! It's about composition
- Lots of steps
- Lots of iterations

See page 83 for how to hack your FatOne and the lettering styles you can write with it!

Drawings found on pages 38-41 are by Ben Tinker.

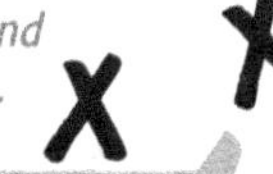
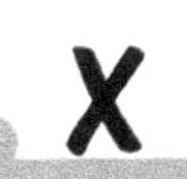
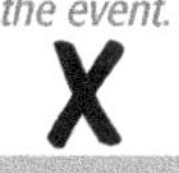
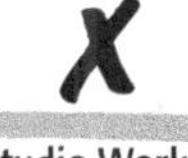

*Can easily be "off the chart" due to time involvement and commitment to final piece.*

*Create prior to the event.*

| Readability | Emphasis | Wow! Factor | | Fast/Easy | | Slow/Involved | | Sketchnotes | Graphic Recording | Studio Work |
|---|---|---|---|---|---|---|---|---|---|---|
| | | X | | | | X  X | | X | X | X |

# EXPLORE THE POSSIBILITIES

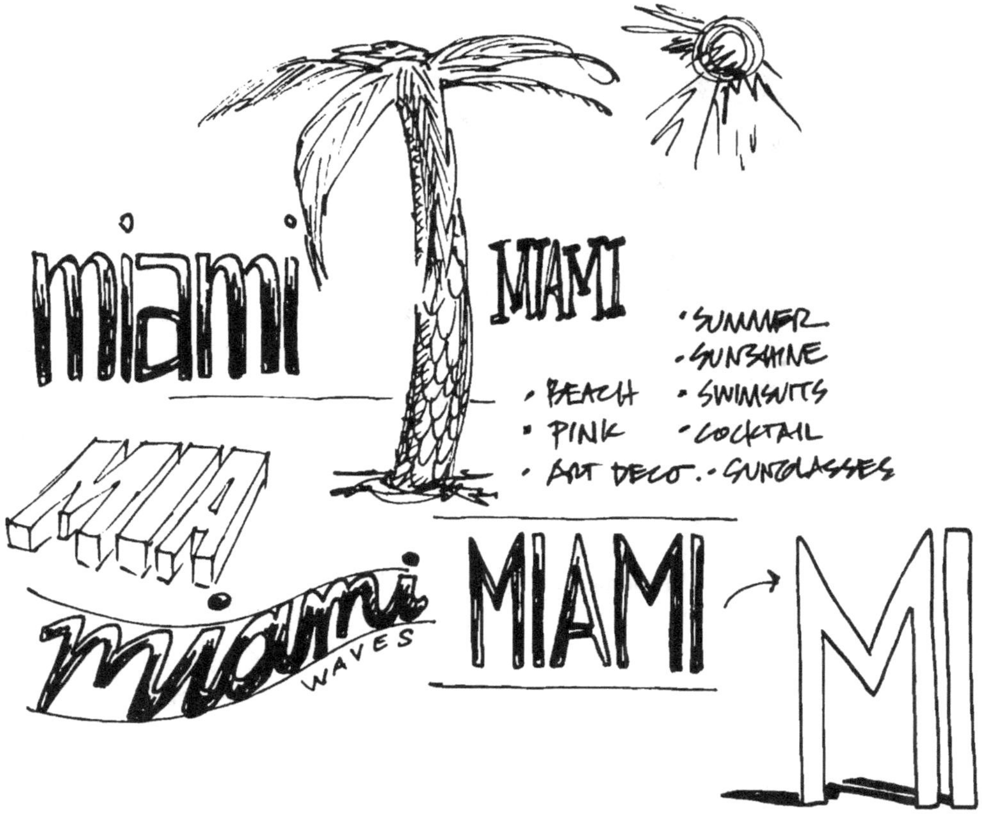


**Choose a lettering style that has a lot of open space.**
It can be block lettering, *Neuland Hand,* or something stylized. Just make sure there is enough space to draw an image inside of the letterforms.

In this example, Ben sketches preliminary ideas and themes during a discovery session. You can see that he starts with a variety of lettering styles.

**Consider the possibilities!**
What kind of letterform or picture will strengthen your message? What does the word inspire in you? Are you evoking a mood, setting a scene or conveying a concept?

**Once you've considered your inspiration and options, experiment and iterate!**
Consider whether the letterform you've chosen helps or hinders your product. Consider your color palette and its use. Fields of color and details will attract the viewer's eye—so make sure they are harmonious and complement the overall product.

Take a step back from your work and notice the balance, emphasis and composition. What is working? What is distracting? Take the time to sketch and refine. You've come this far—make it a show-stopper!

# SKETCH IT OUT

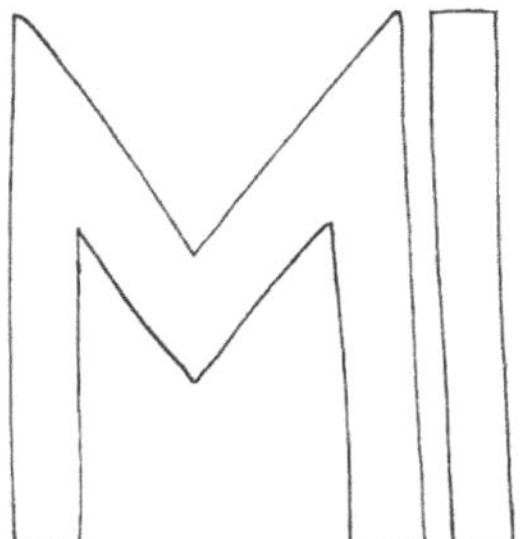

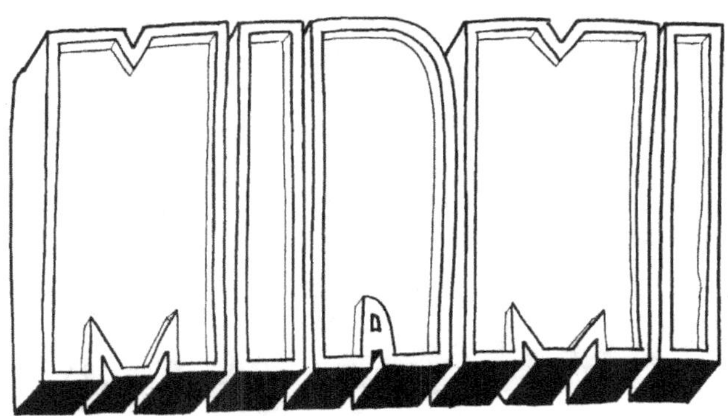

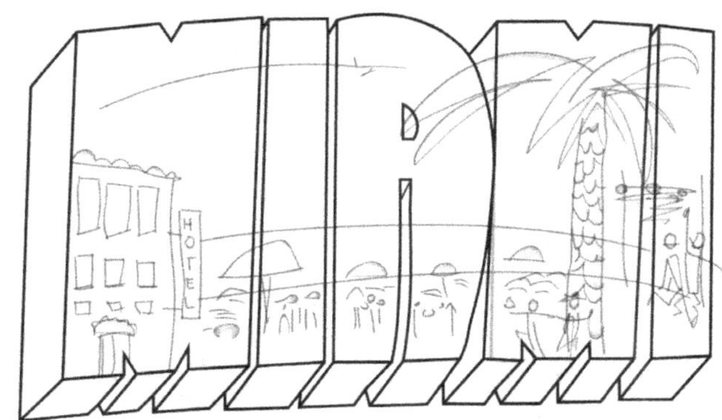

Here are a few of Ben's sketches where he is considering some lettering mechanics:
- The open space within and between the letters
- The structure (flat or 3D)
- baseline, height and size
- perspective, highlight and shadows

We can also see that his sketches include preliminary ideas for fills and landscapes, including depth, scale, iconography and color. All of these considerations can happen anywhere: sketchbooks, tablets, notebooks, scratch paper, found paper, back of the napkin, even the palm of your hand! Get it out of your head and in front of you visibly!

# MAKE NOTES

Sketch
Ben Tinker

ORIGINAL
LANDSCAPE
IDEAS:

BEACH
· simple, bold
· Palm tree
· low horizon, lots of sky
· colored umbrellas

ANGLES are too similar

Add a feature to the sky?

Use a DEEPER DIMENSION
to create a longer shadow

Keep the x-height low

Gradient treatment
@ the bend in
the A

PALETTE
— tans ~ sand, tree
— blue/green/red
— pink
— blues

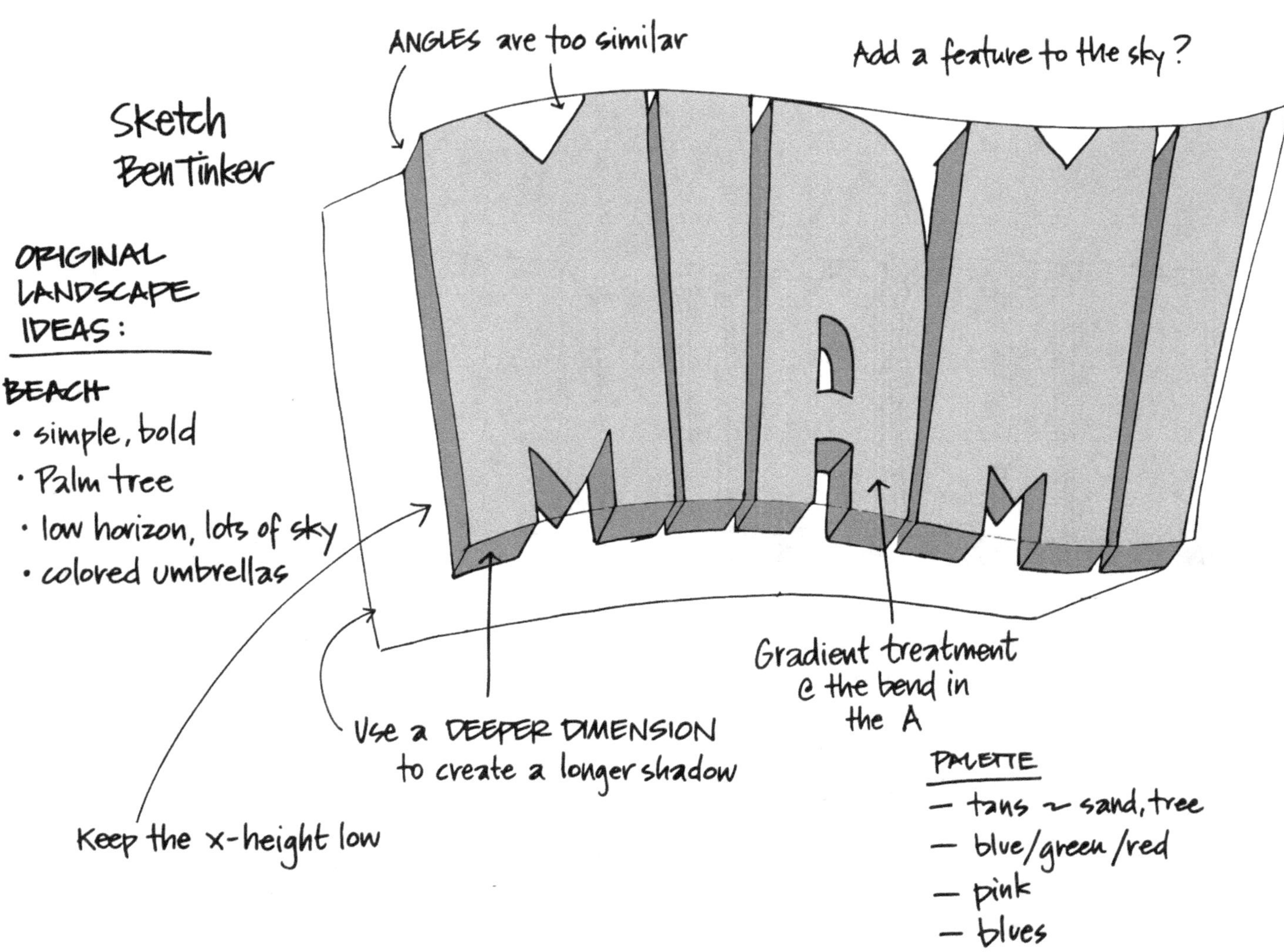

# FINAL DRAWING

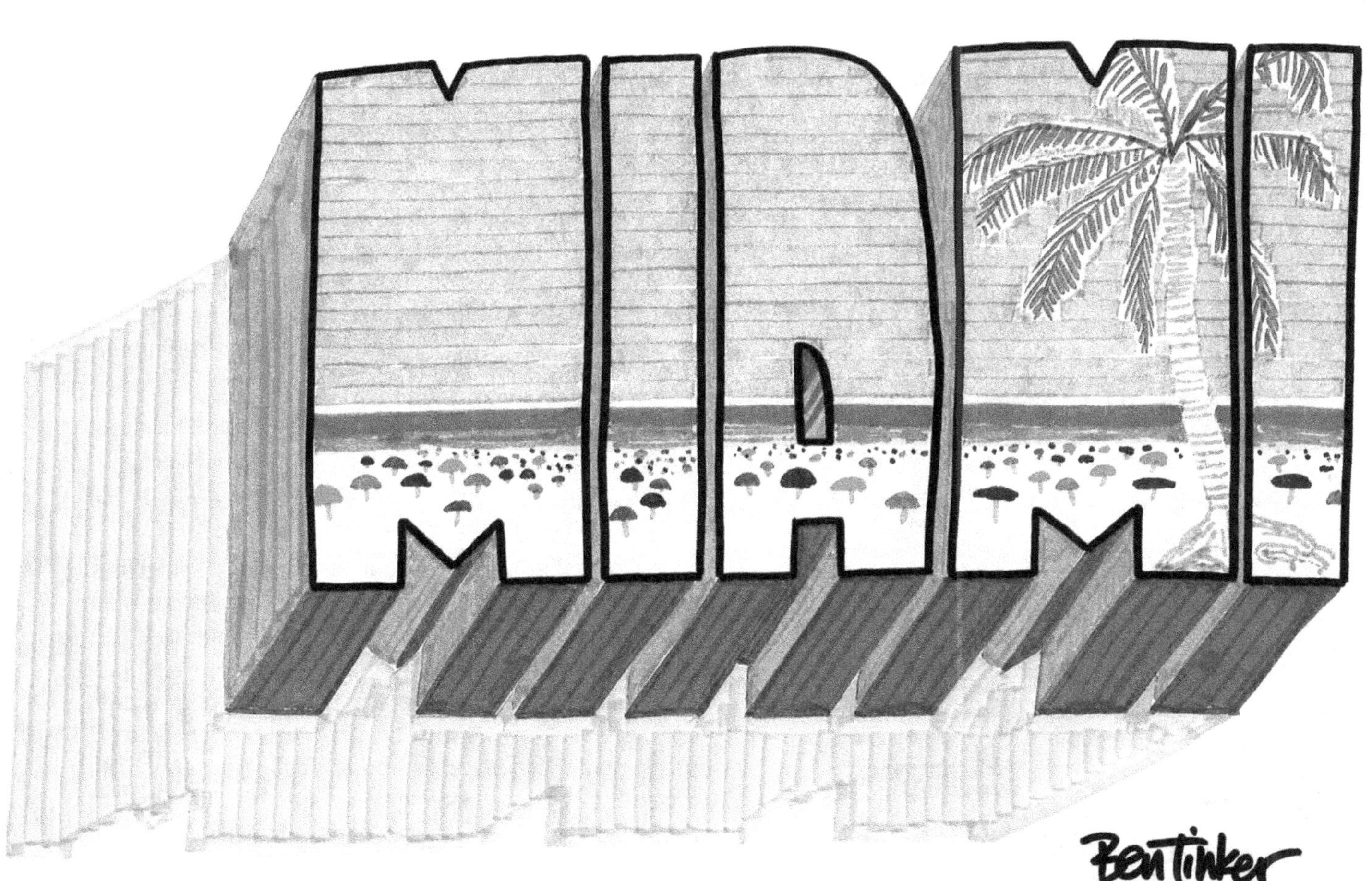

# MARQUEE

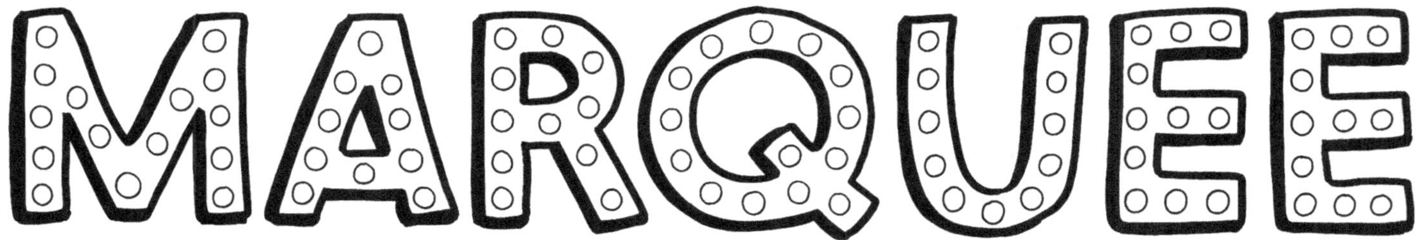

**An embellishment technique for block lettering—fit for a feature film.**

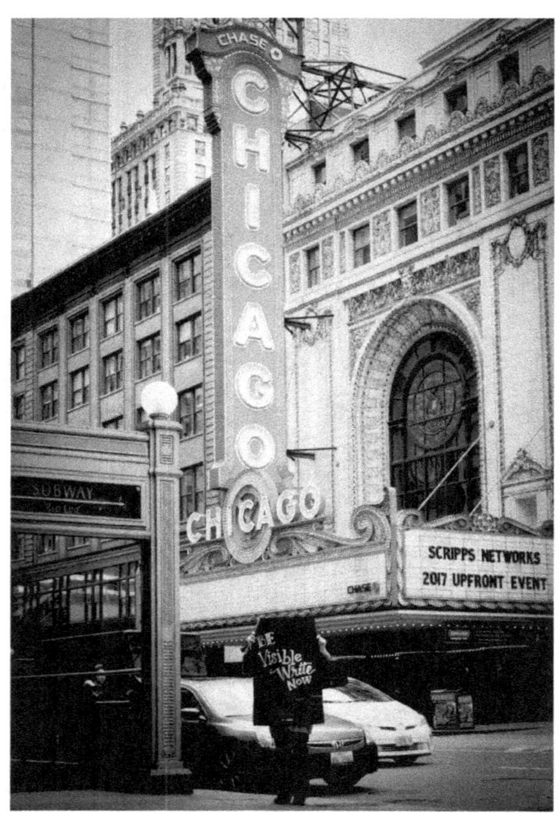


Chase Theatre
Chicago, Illinois

Marquees can be found in nearly every city, from the performance centers of major cities to small town theaters on Main Street. We saw many along the way, but it was the Chase Theatre in Chicago that popped out from its surroundings and inspired a very easy to re-create lettering style.

After a multi-day visit with Diane Bleck—where she featured me on a Facebook Live event for her Doodle Girls and Friends group—and lunch with Brandy Agerbeck in Chicago, Ray and I set out on foot to explore the city.

It's fun to find inspiration in your surroundings. Sometimes it's something you find foreign or out of place that pops out at you. Other times, it's the essence of an environment that you can see, feel, smell, hear or taste. We drove over 13,000 miles during our trip. Some places whizzed by and I could only see the obvious. Other times, we were fortunate to spend days in one place. This book is but a snippet of that trip and some of the lettering styles or embellishments that I feel might be useful to the visual practitioner.

When a sign this big and bright jumped out at me on an overcast day in the Windy City, I had to stop and consider the possibilities of how it could be incorporated into my next graphic recording or studio project.

# ATTRIBUTES

**Marquee is all about the grid!**
And where the lights sit within it. Let the width of your "hack" determine the size of your letters.

Pencil lines create both horizontal and vertical "nib width scales." Use 5 nib widths high and 3 nib widths wide for the letter 'E'. Not sure how wide to make other letters? The *Roman Hand* guide on page 16 is a great place to start.

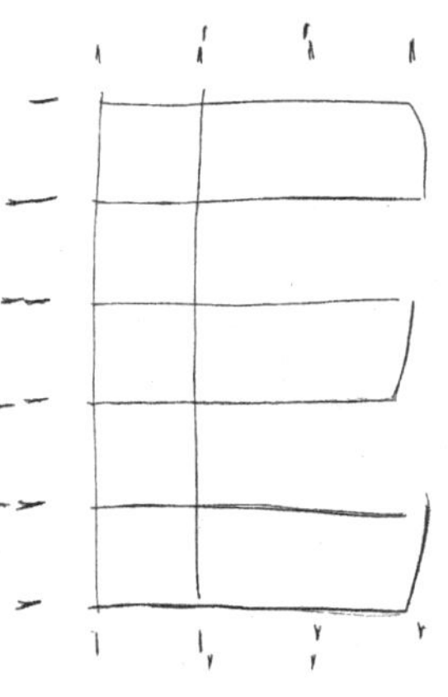

When drawing circles quickly, the tendency is to draw them small. Draw them slightly larger than usual and keep in mind when outlining whether you are going to fill them in or fill around them.

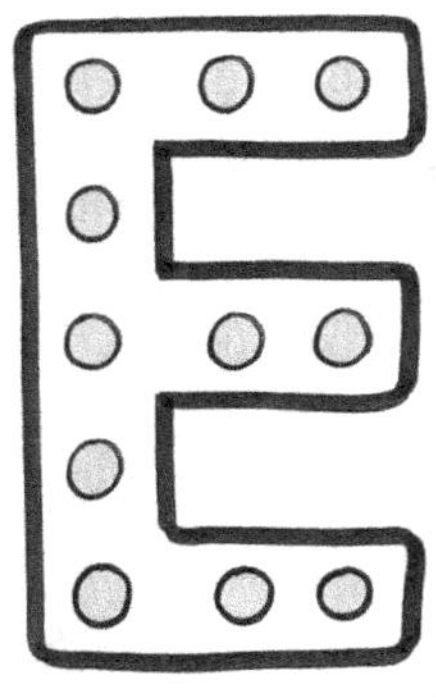

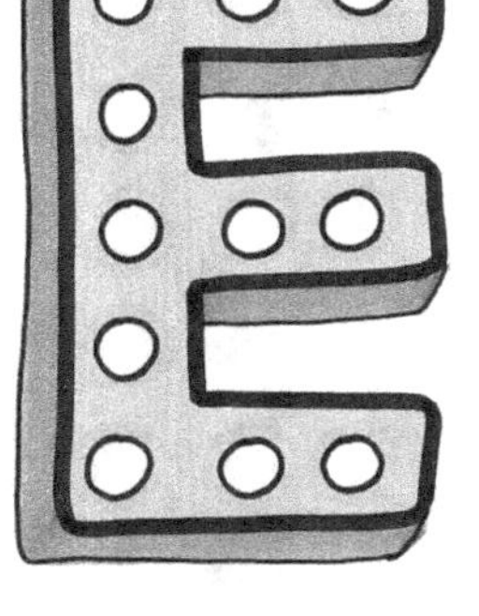

Use the pencil lines as a loose guide. Be as precise or expressive as you want when defining the shape by outlining your letter.

**Tips on drawing a circle:**
Don't look at where your nib is touching the paper. Look at where you want it to go!

Visualize a circle in quadrants. Keep your eye on the place where you want to go and draw an arc towards it!

**Less is more, here's why:**
Keep in mind the grid configuration. Draw the minimum number of circles necessary. It will save time and look better.

After defining the letterform with your outlines, erase all pencil marks, especially if you are planning to keep the white of the paper or are using a light colored marker. Otherwise the pencil marks will show through. Once you write with a marker over a pencil, you can't erase it. The ink locks it in!

Using the same hack that I feature in *Harbor* (page 83) be sure to use a 5-nib-width scale and use that scale like a grid to line up the lights. Once you know the formula, it's easy to show off your client's content by drawing their words big and "in lights!"

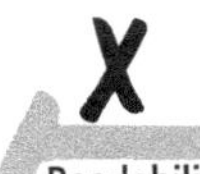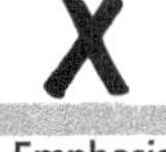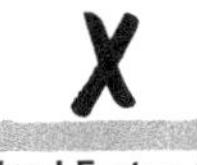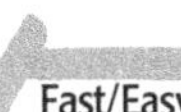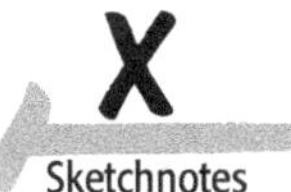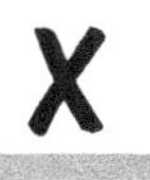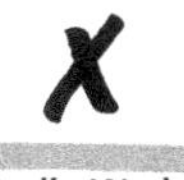

| Readability | Emphasis | Wow! Factor | Fast/Easy | Slow/Involved | Sketchnotes | Graphic Recording | Studio Work |

# LETTERING EXAMPLES

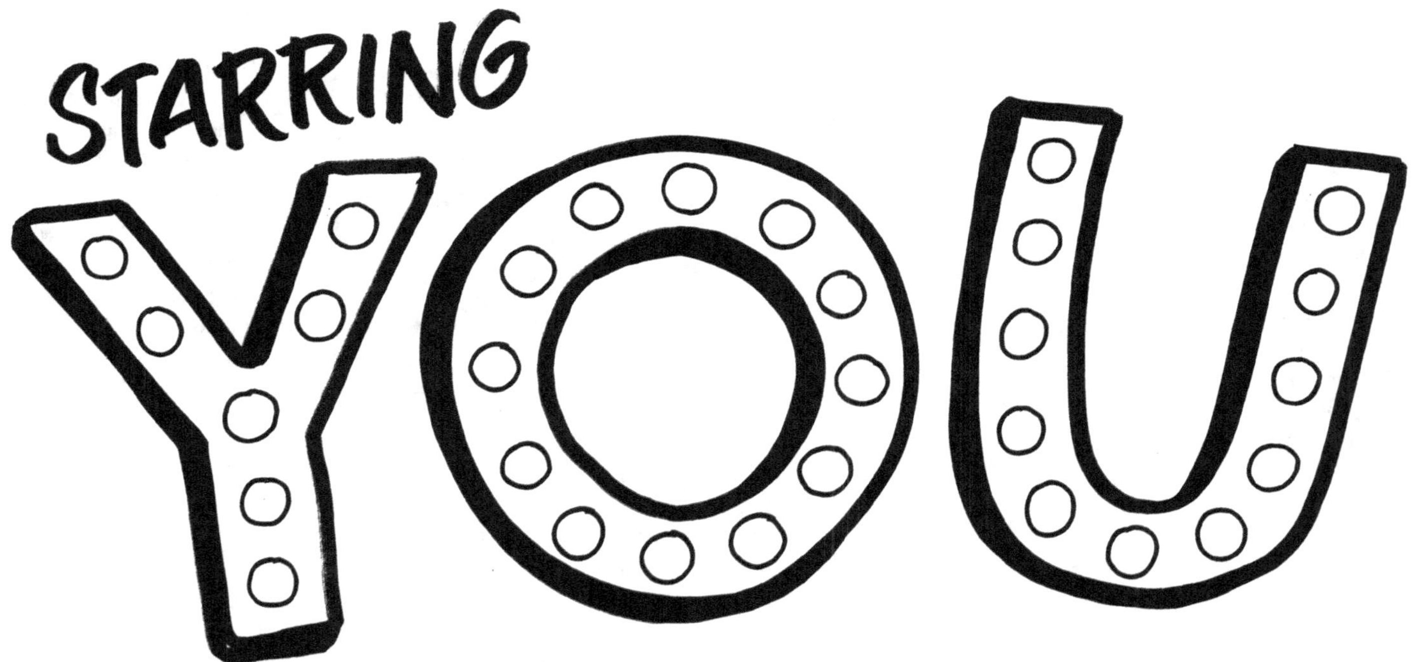



I hope you enjoy these lettering styles and techniques as much as I enjoyed dreaming about them and putting them to paper.

Please share your practice pages or how you incorporate these lettering styles into your work by #letslettertogether or #letteringjourney on social media. I will be seeking you out and giving away prizes to those with my favorite posts.

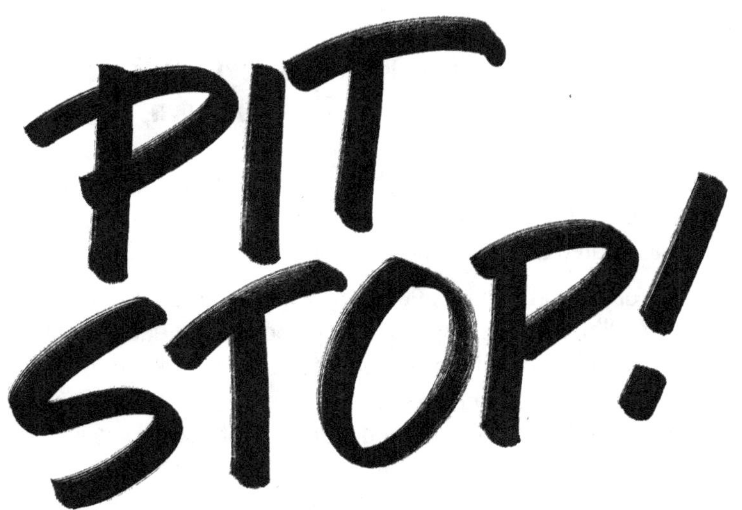


### It's time for a pit stop!

Race car drivers take them because they need new tires, a splash of fuel and maybe a clean wipe of the windshield. While on the road, travelers stop at rest stops to stretch their legs, use the restroom and get a breath of fresh air.

As visual practitioners, it's important that we take care of ourselves. Much like being in a race or on a road trip, as you work or practice be sure to

- wear comfortable shoes,
- stay hydrated and eat healthy foods, and
- stay centered so you can focus on the job at hand.

It's also important to take breaks and step away from your work so that you can come back to it with fresh eyes.

For those of you who plan to sit down and plow through this book in a day, good for you! But do us both a favor and practice your lettering like you are in it to win it! And that means that quality counts. If you haven't already skipped to the back of the book to read the practice tips (page 108), here's a reminder to work with intention.

Practice a few letters, but don't make a page full of them. Get your bearings straight and hop back on the road. You will do your best when you put these letters to use and make meaning by writing words and sentences. Sure, form is important, but it's important to have fun too!

So, take a pit stop and then get back on track. We have a long and wonderful lettering journey ahead of us. Let's enjoy it as we go.

# WACKY WESTERN

**A slab-serif lettering style that you can vary and make your own.**

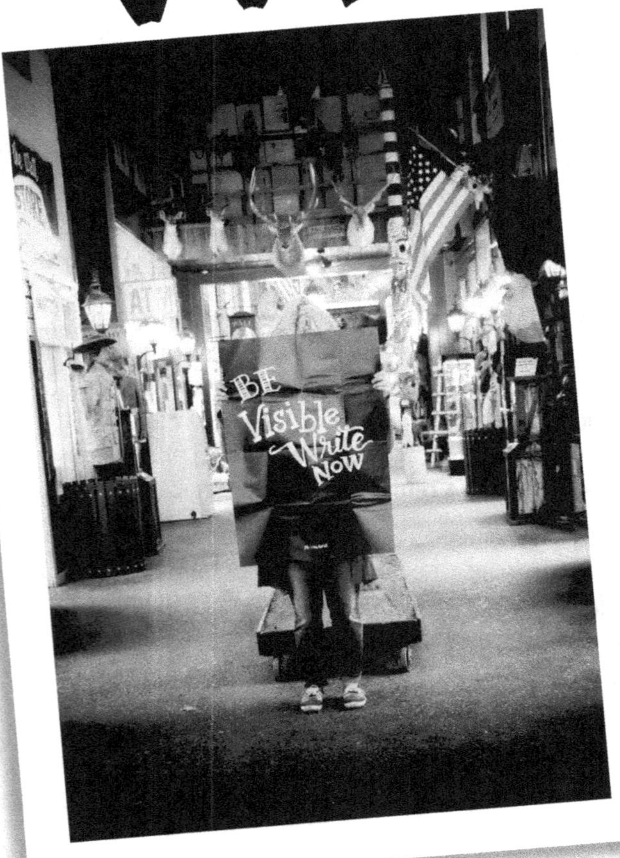



Wall Drug
Wall, South Dakota

There are many routes you can take when driving from coast to coast in the US, but in the plains, there isn't much to see unless you get as excited as I do about billboards.

If you are driving on Highway 90, for nearly 300 miles you will see Wall Drug billboards enticing you to stop and check it out. There is literally something for everyone: from food and toys to games and dinosaurs. Main Street and the shops therein offer complete visual overload. I loved all of the signs and made lots of notes. However, I'm only sharing one lettering style: *Wacky Western*. And it's not really a style as much as a slab-serif variation. It's fast, easy and fun. Just like the day we spent there.

Wall Drug, located in Wall, South Dakota, started out as a small drugstore that was purchased in 1931 by Ted and Dorothy Hustead when the town was poor and business was slow. Though the town was in the middle of nowhere, they figured out a way to use it to their advantage. People before us, long before us, traveled across the country in the heat and high winds and needed a place to stop, so Wall Drug advertised that they served "Free! Ice-cold Water!" And that was just the beginning of one of the most well-known tourist stops in America.

I think I could write an entire book of lettering inspired by Wall Drug. So if you are up for a roadtrip, let me know. I'm ready to go back for a few days and study.

# ATTRIBUTES



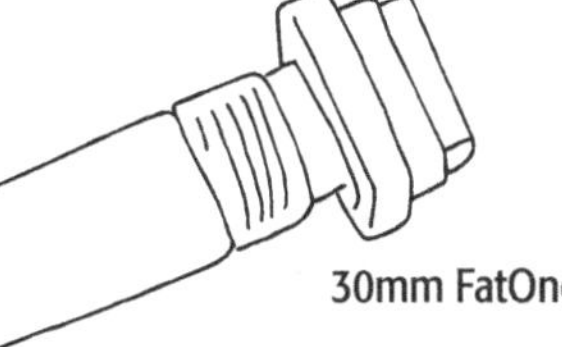



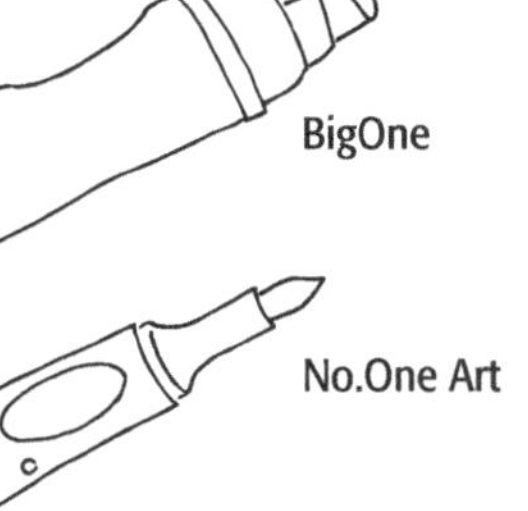



Note: Ductus and studio notes are offered on the following pages. They are printed at 100% using a BigOne so that you can make copies of the pages and trace them if you want.

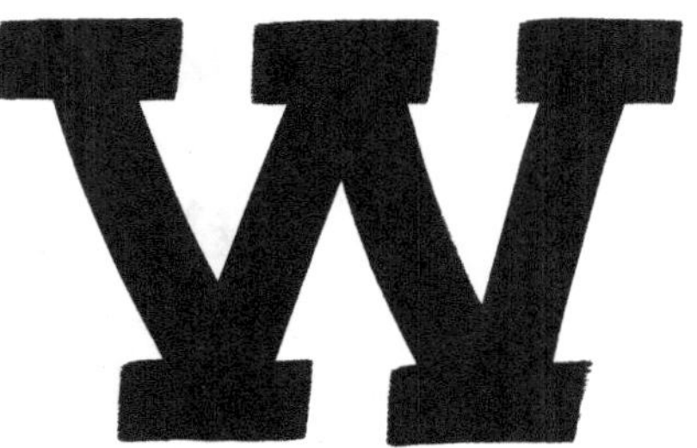

Formal slab-serif Western style written with a BigOne.

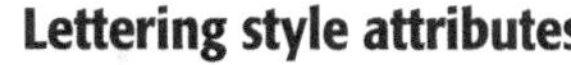

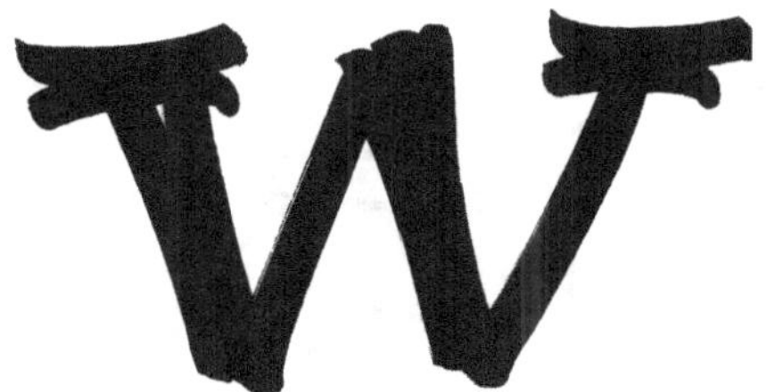

Casual double-slab-serif Western style written with a No.One Art.

## Lettering style attributes
- Influenced by the Western US cowboy culture
- Thick serifs
- Stylized serifs
- From simple and casual to fancy and ornate
- Easily scaled
- Variations are endless!

## When to use:
- Titles and bold topics
- Thematically or whimsically
- Fast for a "Cowboy Funky" look and feel
- Slow and deliberate for an "authoritative" tone
- "Wanted" posters

## Nib widths
The full-size examples of letterforms on the following pages were drawn at 8 nib widths high. When working with expressive and loose lettering styles like this one, 8 nibs of height is a good, loose guide to ensure you have enough height to accommodate counter spaces in your letters.

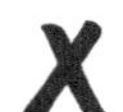

Readability   Emphasis   Wow! Factor

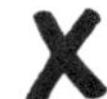

Fast/Easy   Slow/Involved

Sketchnotes   Graphic Recording   Studio Work

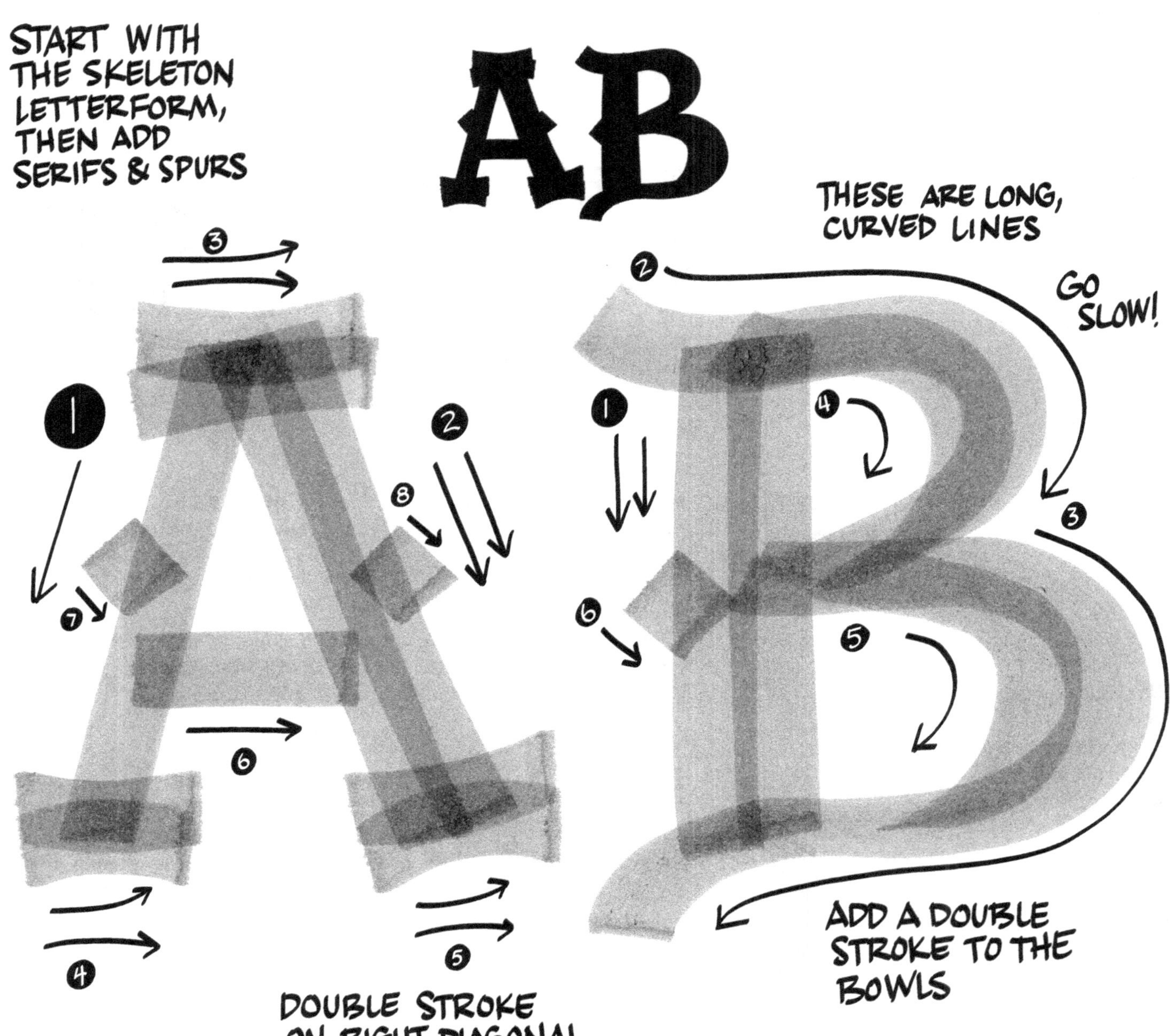


What gives this lettering style its Western flair? The diamond shapes that adorn each letter at its midpoint, which are called "spurs."

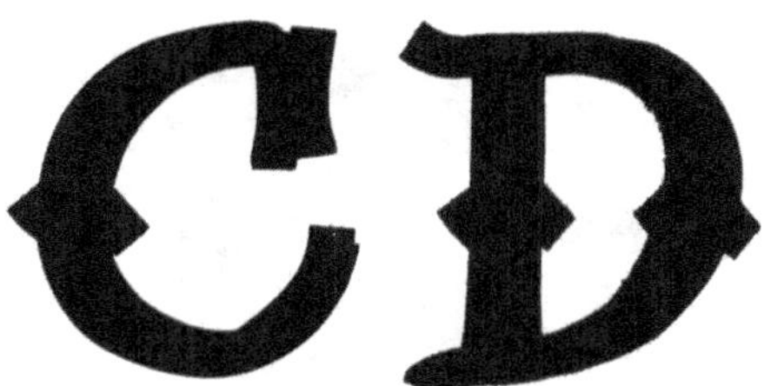

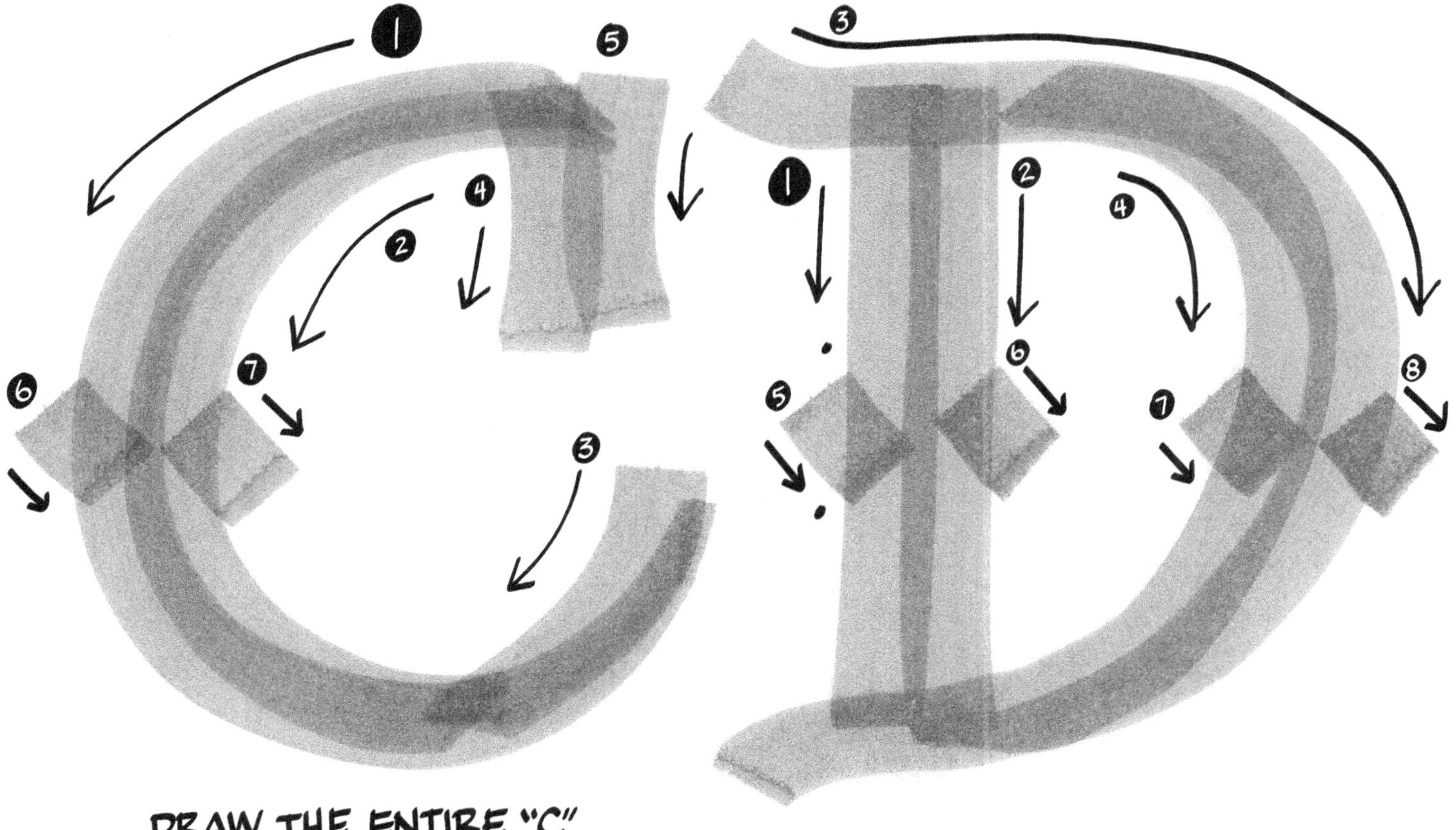

DRAW THE ENTIRE "C"
FIRST, THEN ADD A
DOUBLE STROKE FOR
THICKNESS

FINISH THE TERMINAL

LIKE THE "B"

- NOTE WHERE THE
SPURS START & STOP

# EF

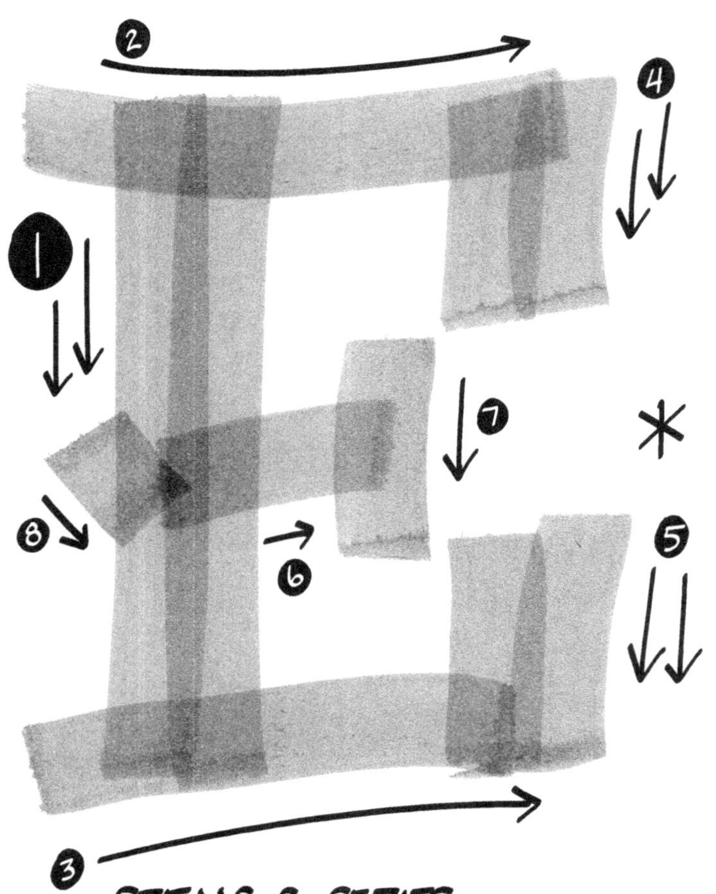

STEMS & SERIFS
ARE DOUBLE STROKES—
CROSSBARS ARE SINGLE

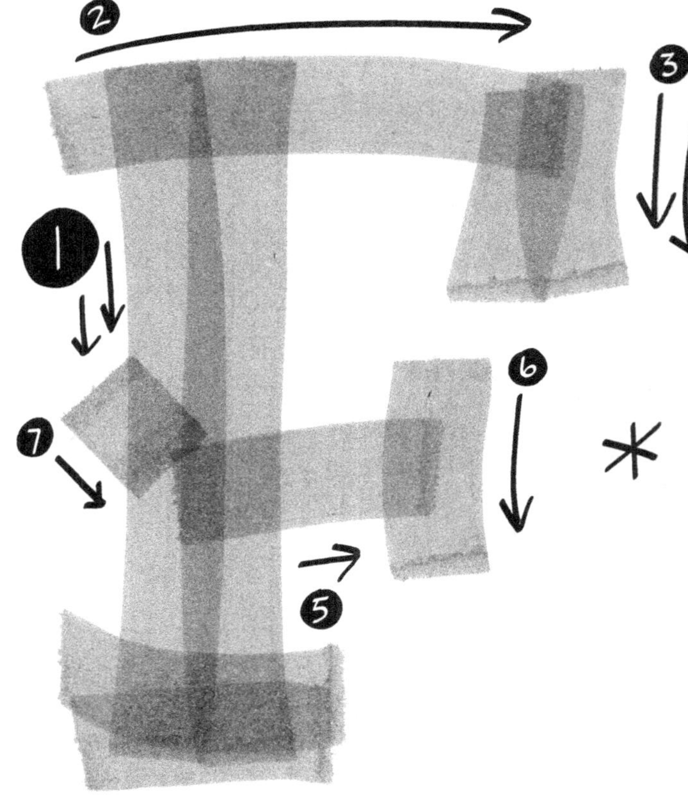

CROSSBARS & SERIFS
ARE SINGLE ON
"E" & "F"

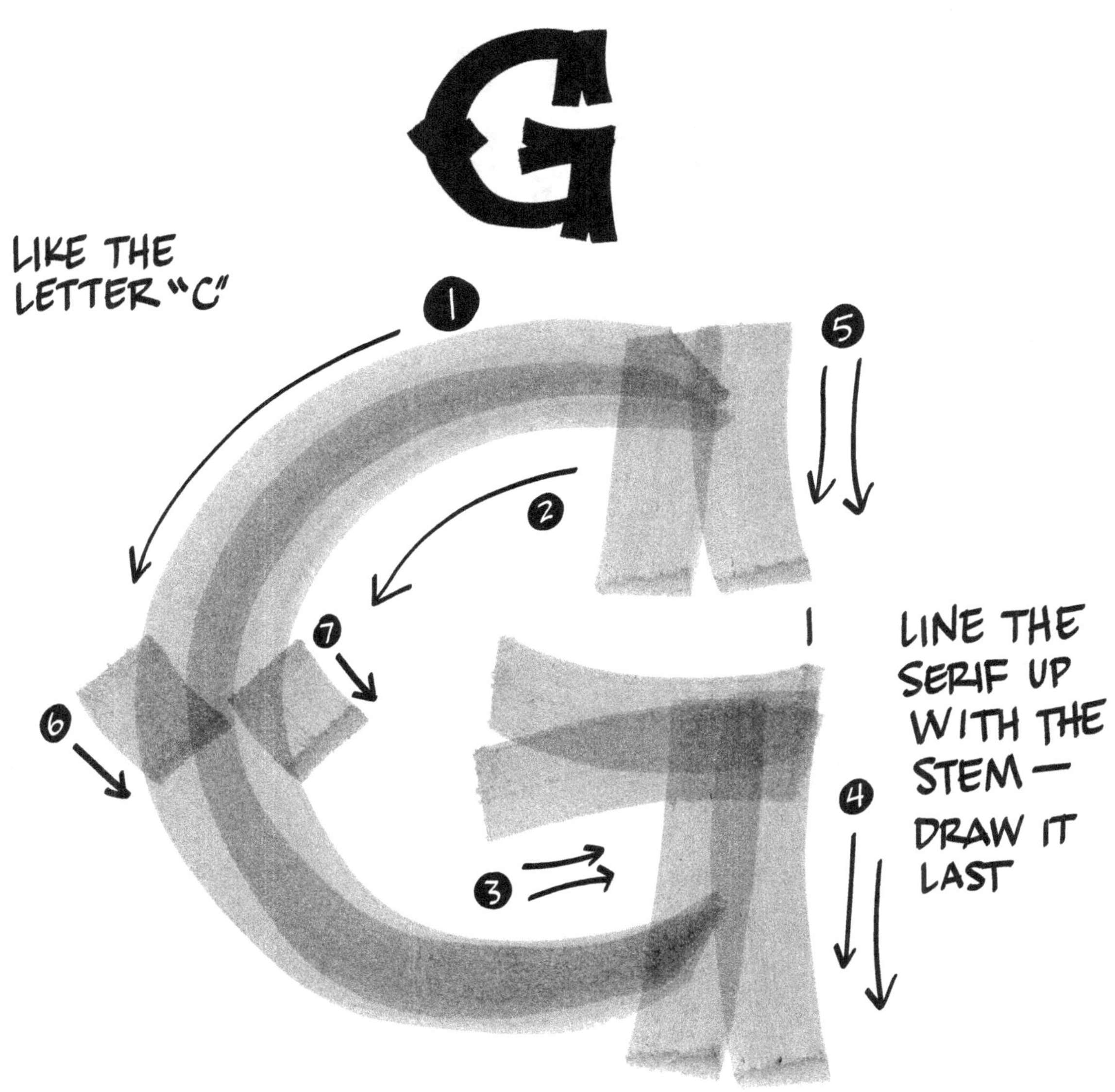

LIKE THE LETTER "C"
LINE THE SERIF UP WITH THE STEM — DRAW IT LAST
1
2
3
4
5
6
7

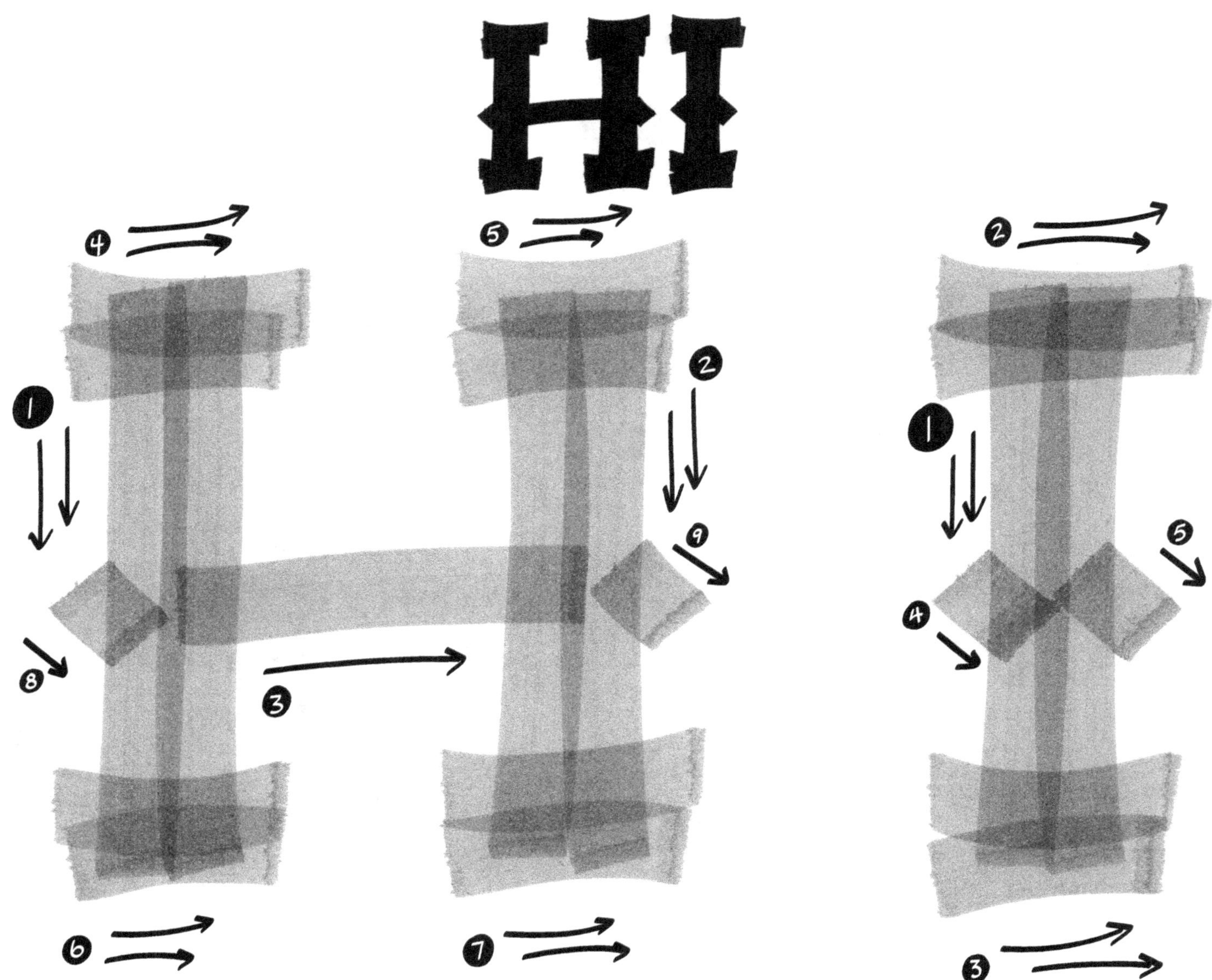

HI
THE DOWNSTROKES OF THE STEMS
CAN BE STRAIGHT OR HAVE A
SLIGHT CURVE — THE MORE CURVED,
THE MORE PLAYFUL & WACKY

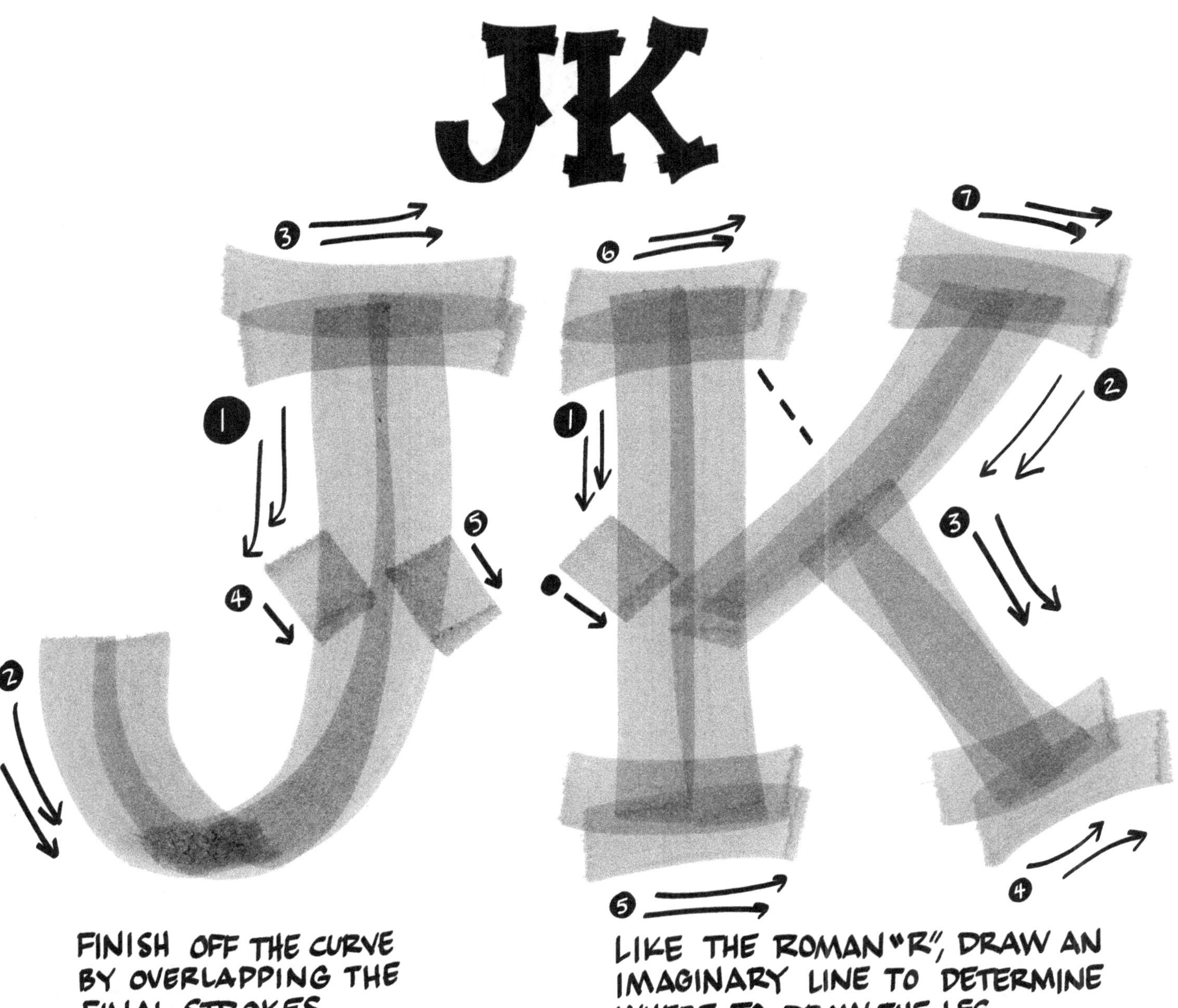


FINISH OFF THE CURVE
BY OVERLAPPING THE
FINAL STROKES

LIKE THE ROMAN "R", DRAW AN
IMAGINARY LINE TO DETERMINE
WHERE TO DRAW THE LEG

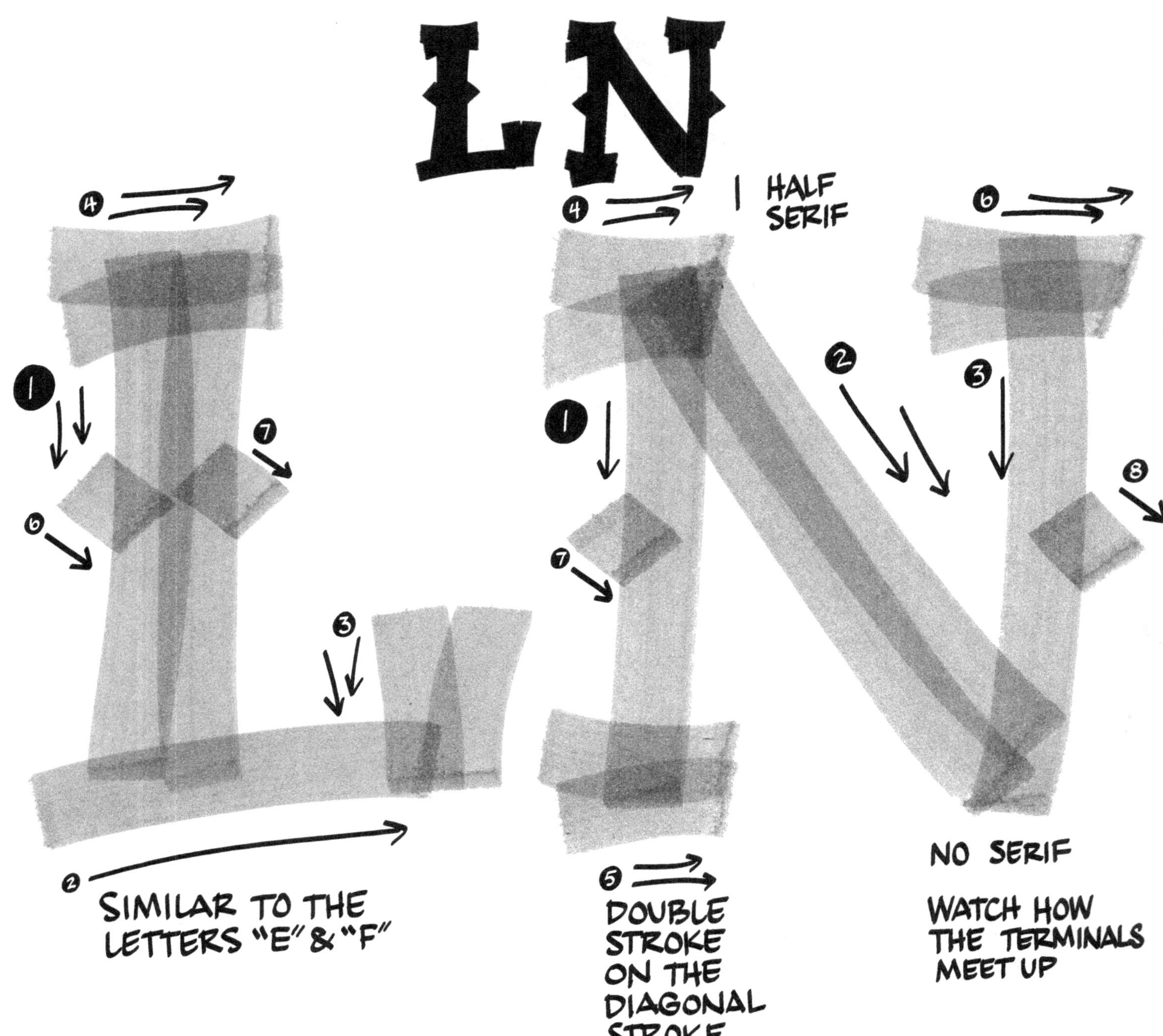

HALF SERIF
SIMILAR TO THE LETTERS "E" & "F"
DOUBLE STROKE ON THE DIAGONAL STROKE
NO SERIF
WATCH HOW THE TERMINALS MEET UP

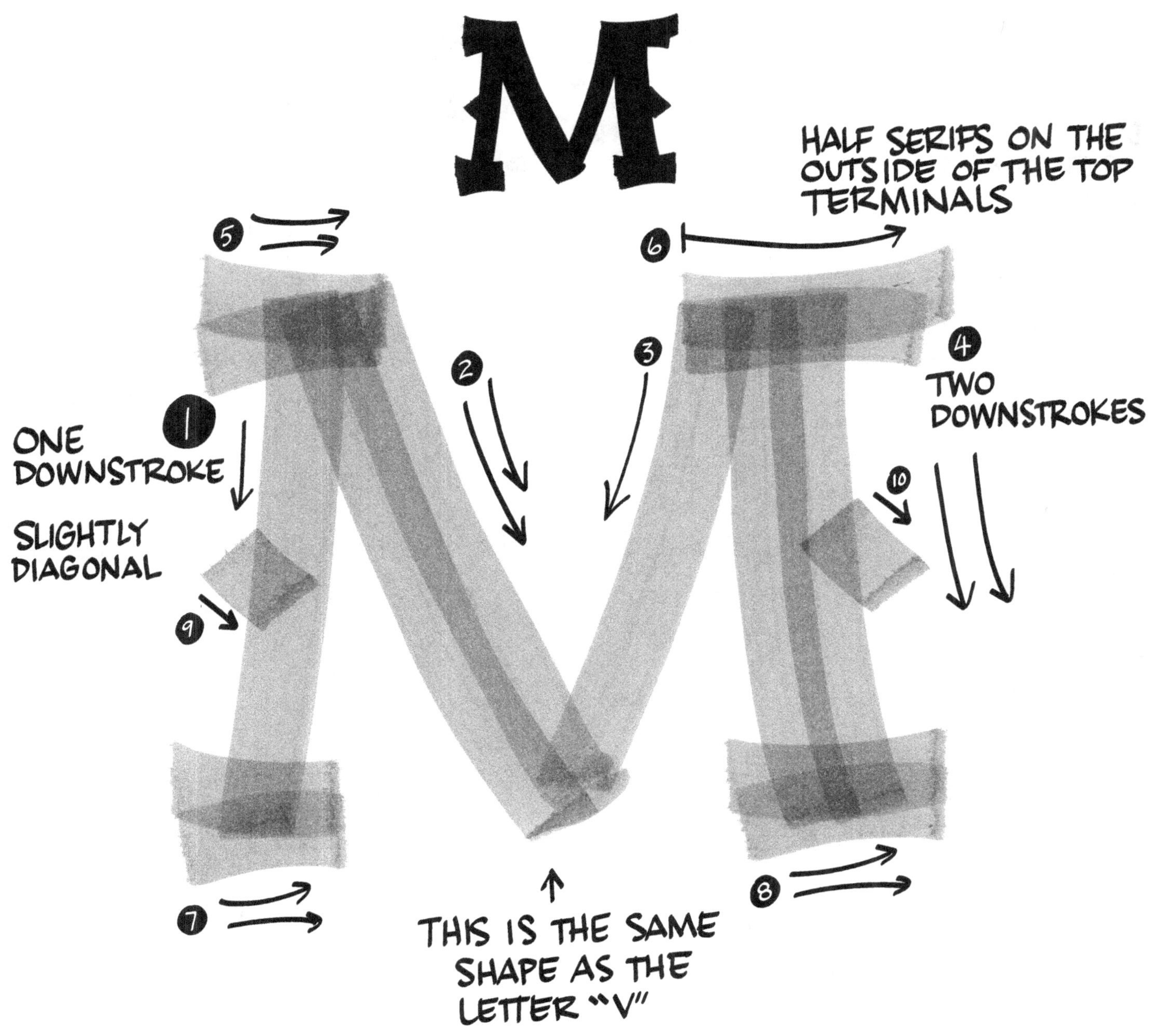

HALF SERIFS ON THE OUTSIDE OF THE TOP TERMINALS
ONE DOWNSTROKE
SLIGHTLY DIAGONAL
TWO DOWNSTROKES
THIS IS THE SAME SHAPE AS THE LETTER "V"
5
6
1
2
3
4
9
10
7
8

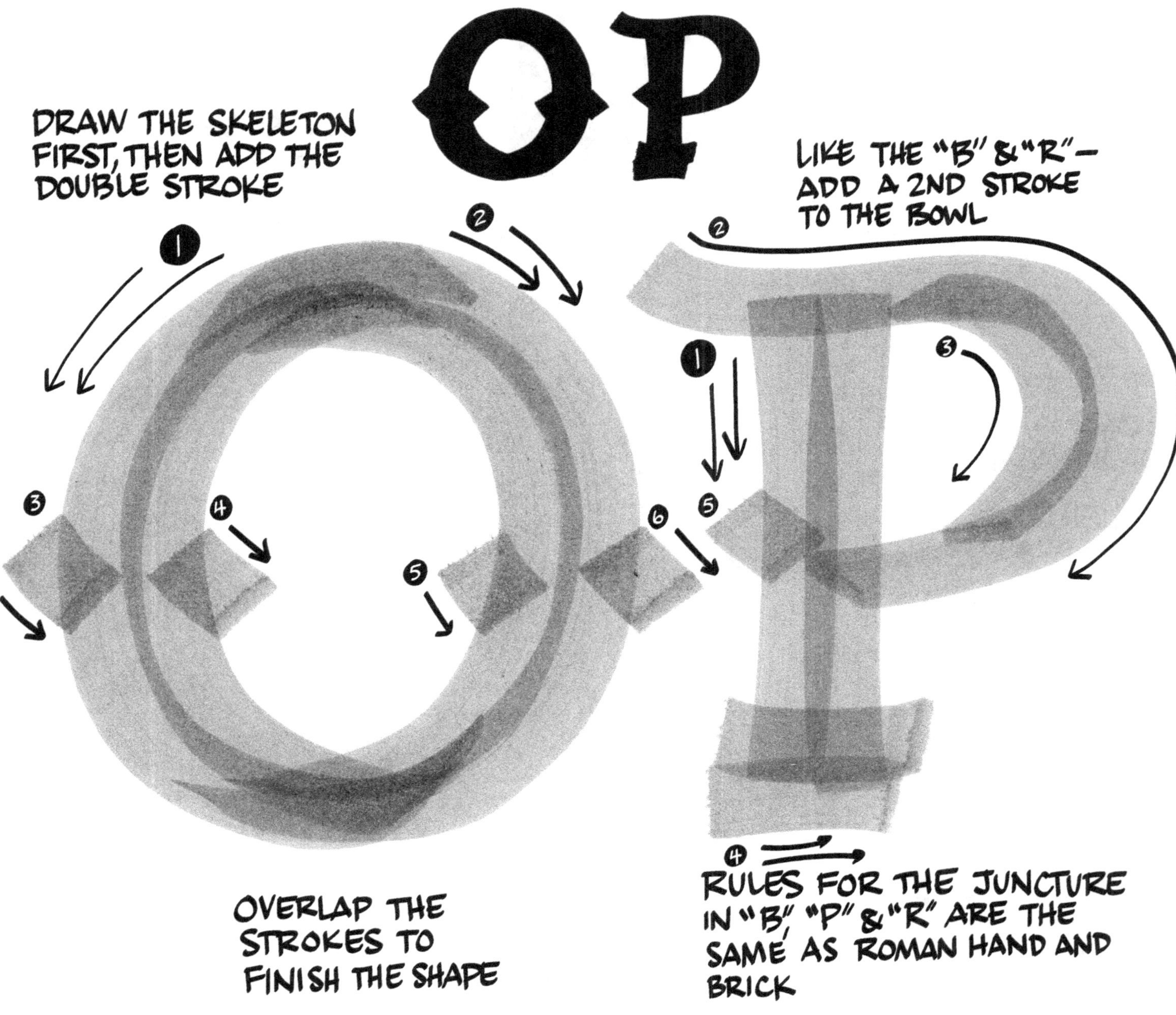
DRAW THE SKELETON FIRST, THEN ADD THE DOUBLE STROKE
LIKE THE "B" & "R"— ADD A 2ND STROKE TO THE BOWL
OVERLAP THE STROKES TO FINISH THE SHAPE
RULES FOR THE JUNCTURE IN "B" "P" & "R" ARE THE SAME AS ROMAN HAND AND BRICK

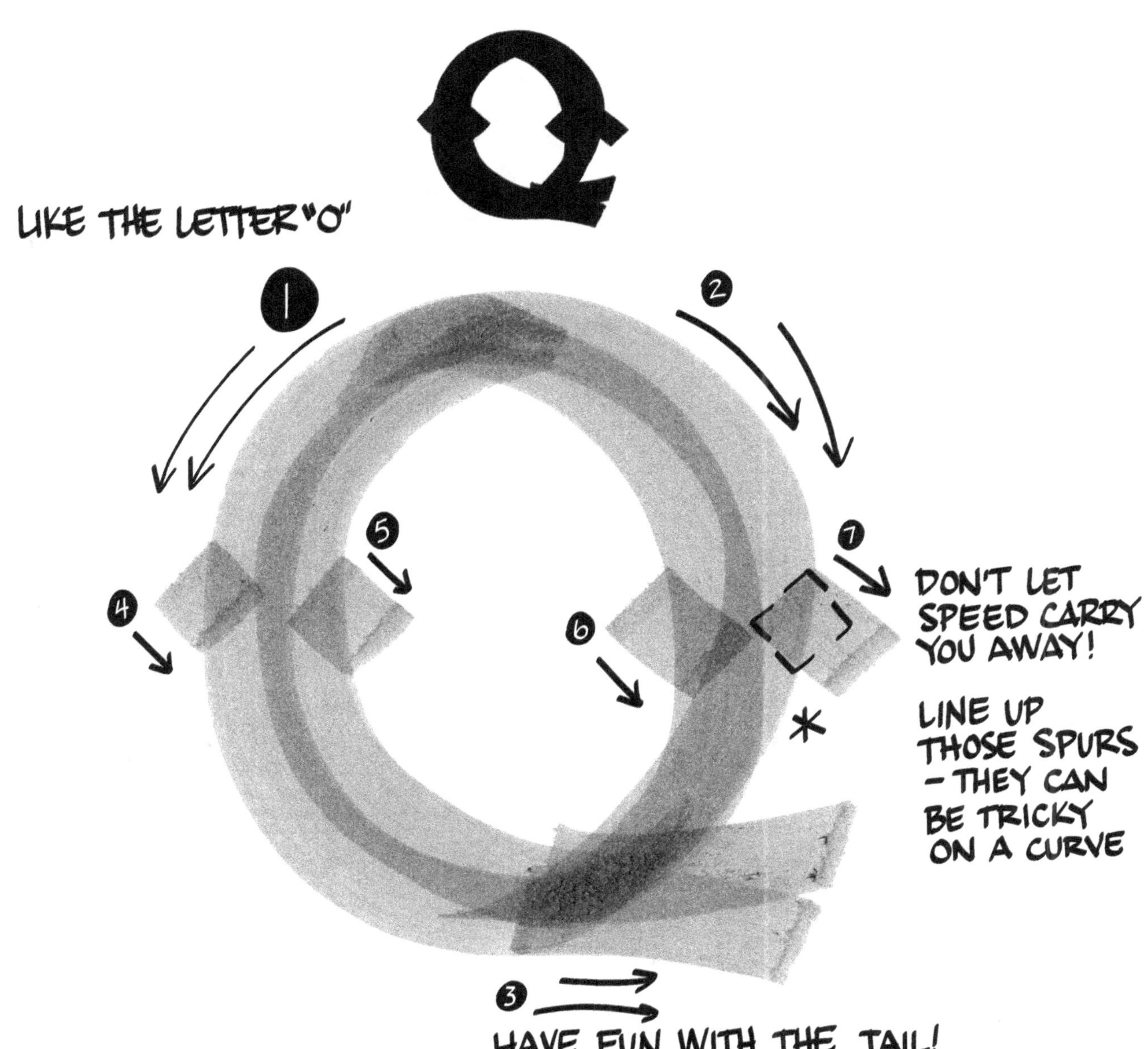


LIKE THE LETTER "O"
1
2
4
5
6
7
DON'T LET SPEED CARRY YOU AWAY!
LINE UP THOSE SPURS — THEY CAN BE TRICKY ON A CURVE
*
3
HAVE FUN WITH THE TAIL!

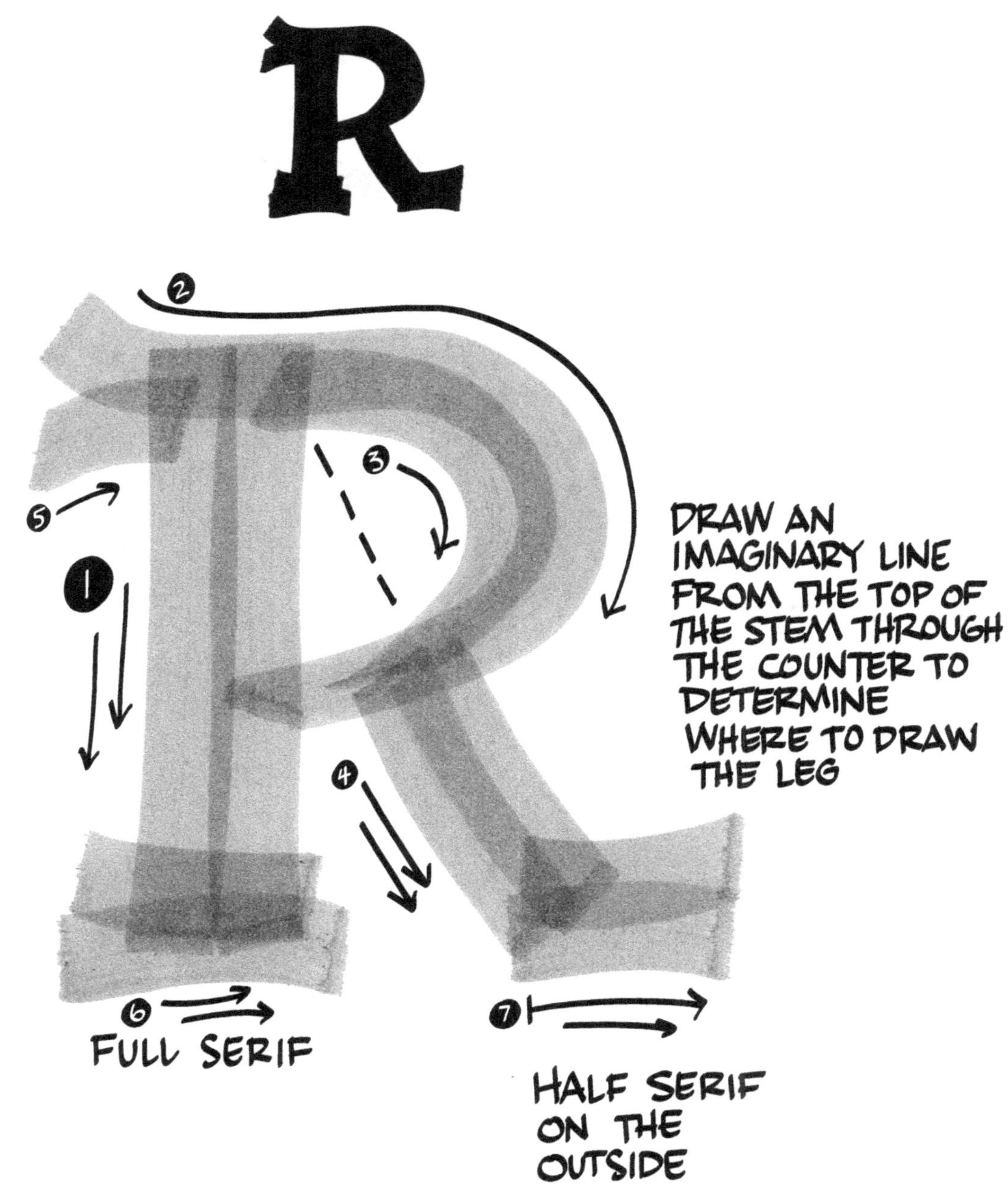

2
3
5
1
4
6
7
DRAW AN IMAGINARY LINE FROM THE TOP OF THE STEM THROUGH THE COUNTER TO DETERMINE WHERE TO DRAW THE LEG
FULL SERIF
HALF SERIF ON THE OUTSIDE

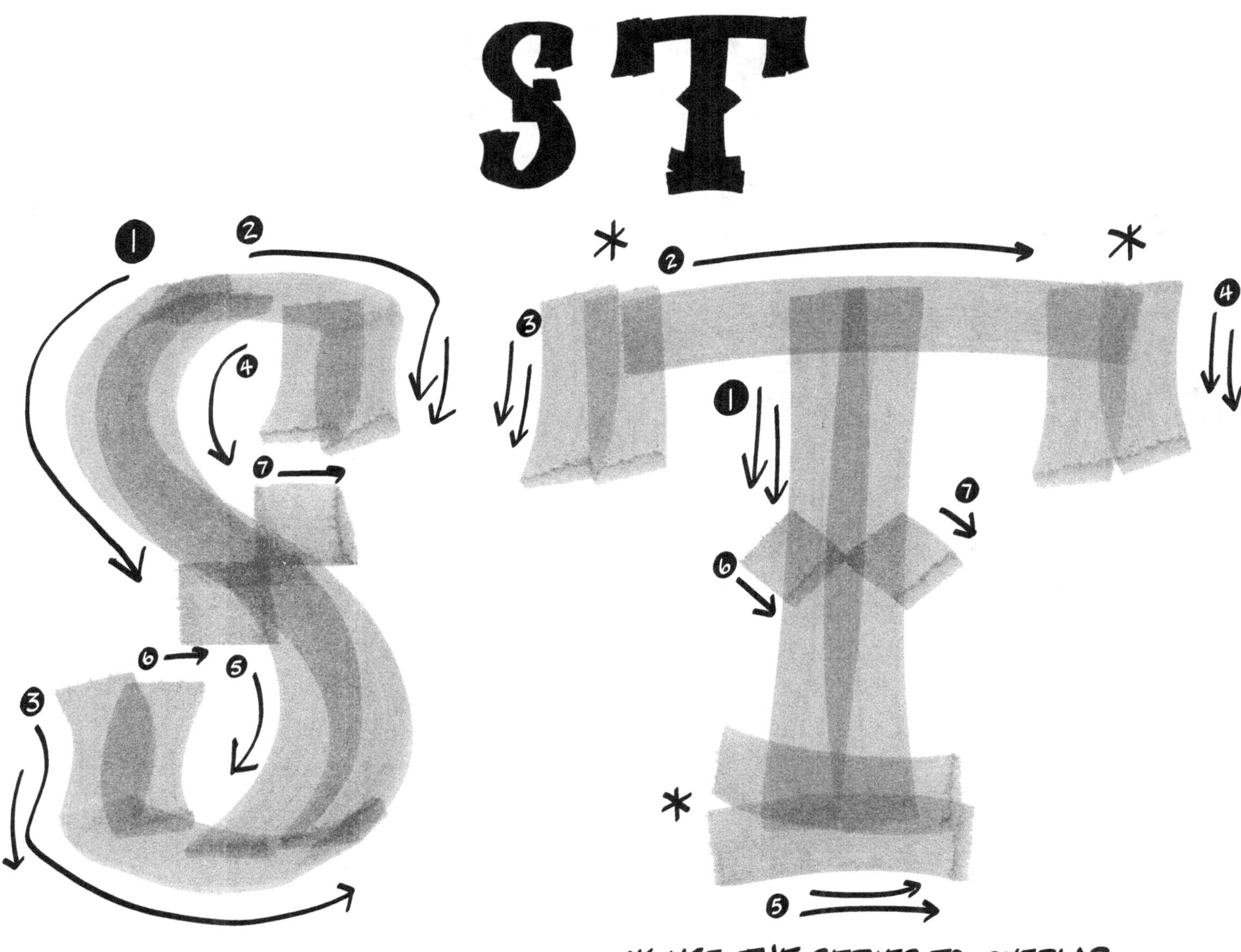


DRAW THE SPINE FIRST
FINISH THE FORM & ADD
SERIF IN A SINGLE STROKE—
TOP & BOTTOM

* USE THE SERIFS TO OVERLAP
AND CORRECT THE HEIGHT &
WIDTH OF MIS-DRAWN STROKES

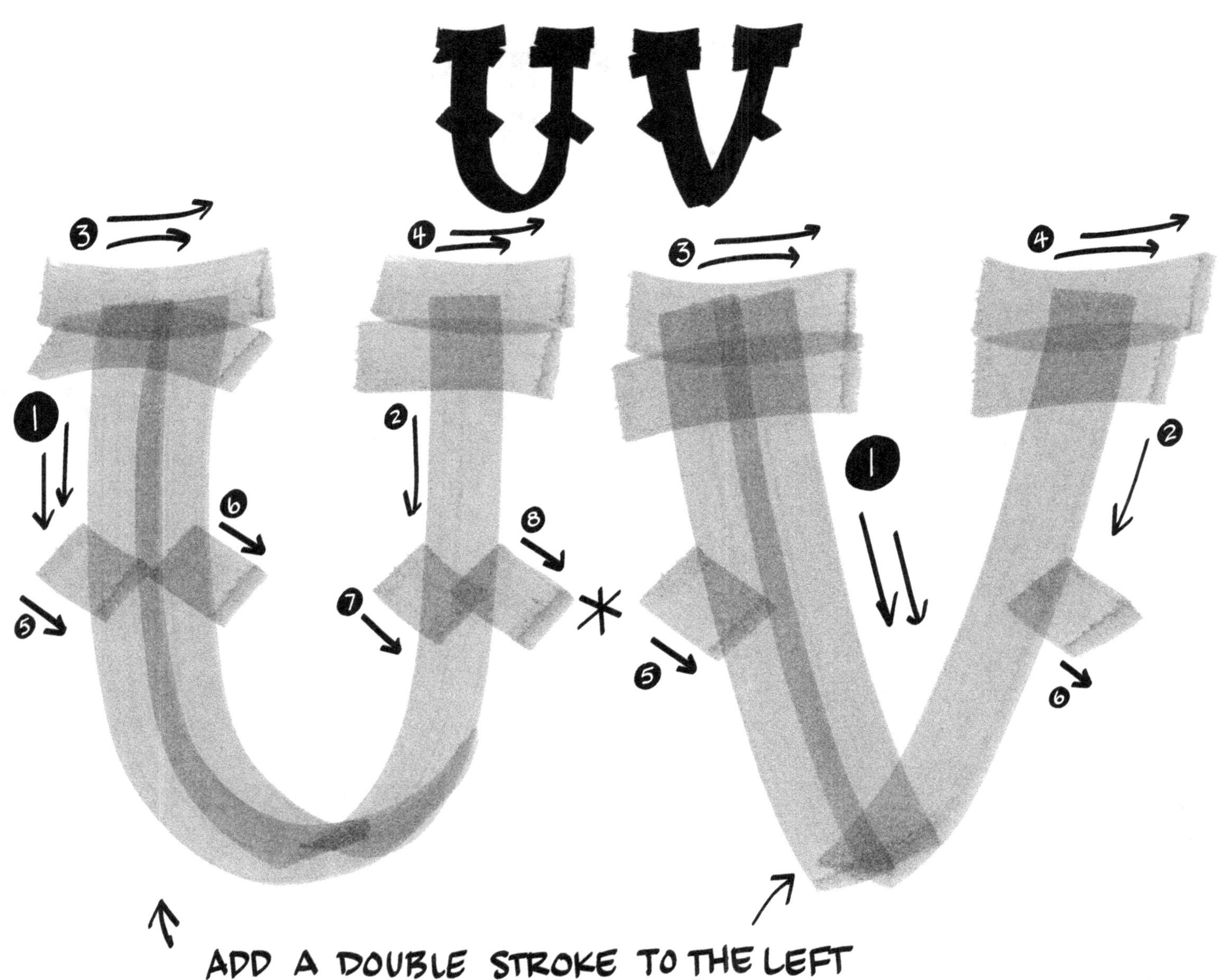

ADD A DOUBLE STROKE TO THE LEFT

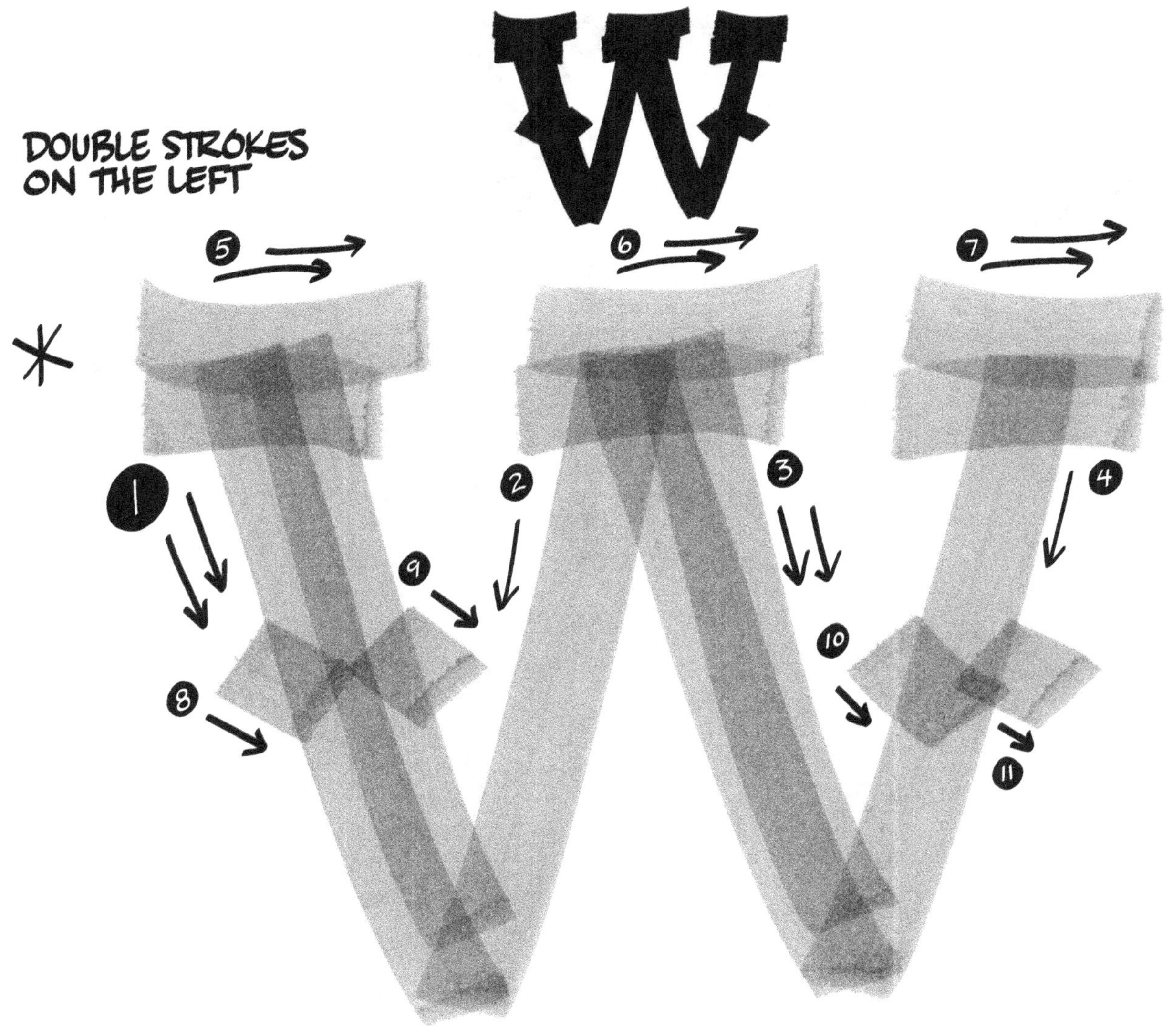

DOUBLE STROKES
ON THE LEFT
W
5
6
7
1
2
3
4
9
10
8
11
* SERIFS ON THE TOP ONLY
OTHERWISE IT'S TOO BUSY,
NOT AS LEGIBLE AND
LOOKS AMATEURISH

# XY

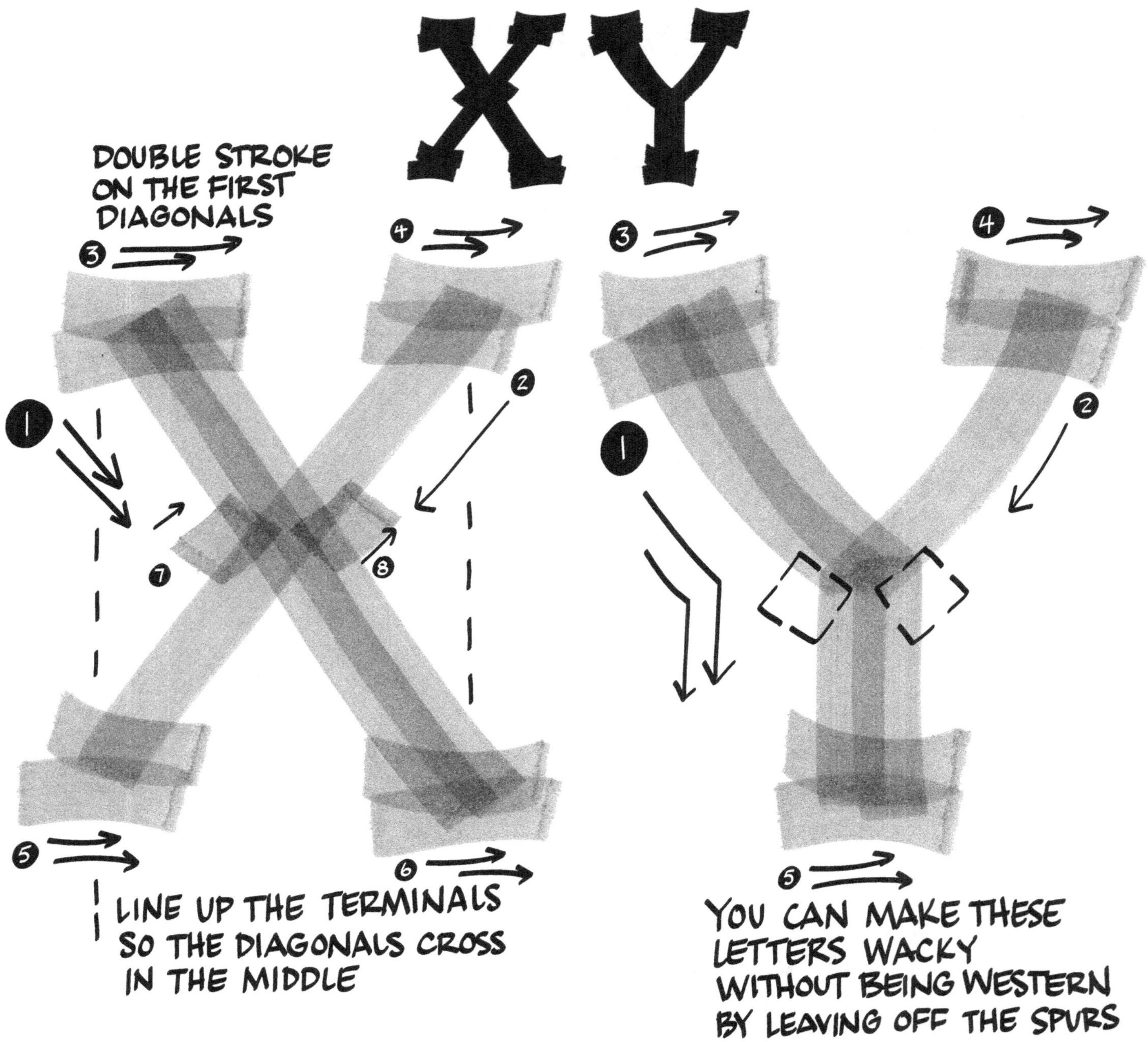

DOUBLE STROKE ON THE FIRST DIAGONALS
LINE UP THE TERMINALS SO THE DIAGONALS CROSS IN THE MIDDLE
YOU CAN MAKE THESE LETTERS WACKY WITHOUT BEING WESTERN BY LEAVING OFF THE SPURS

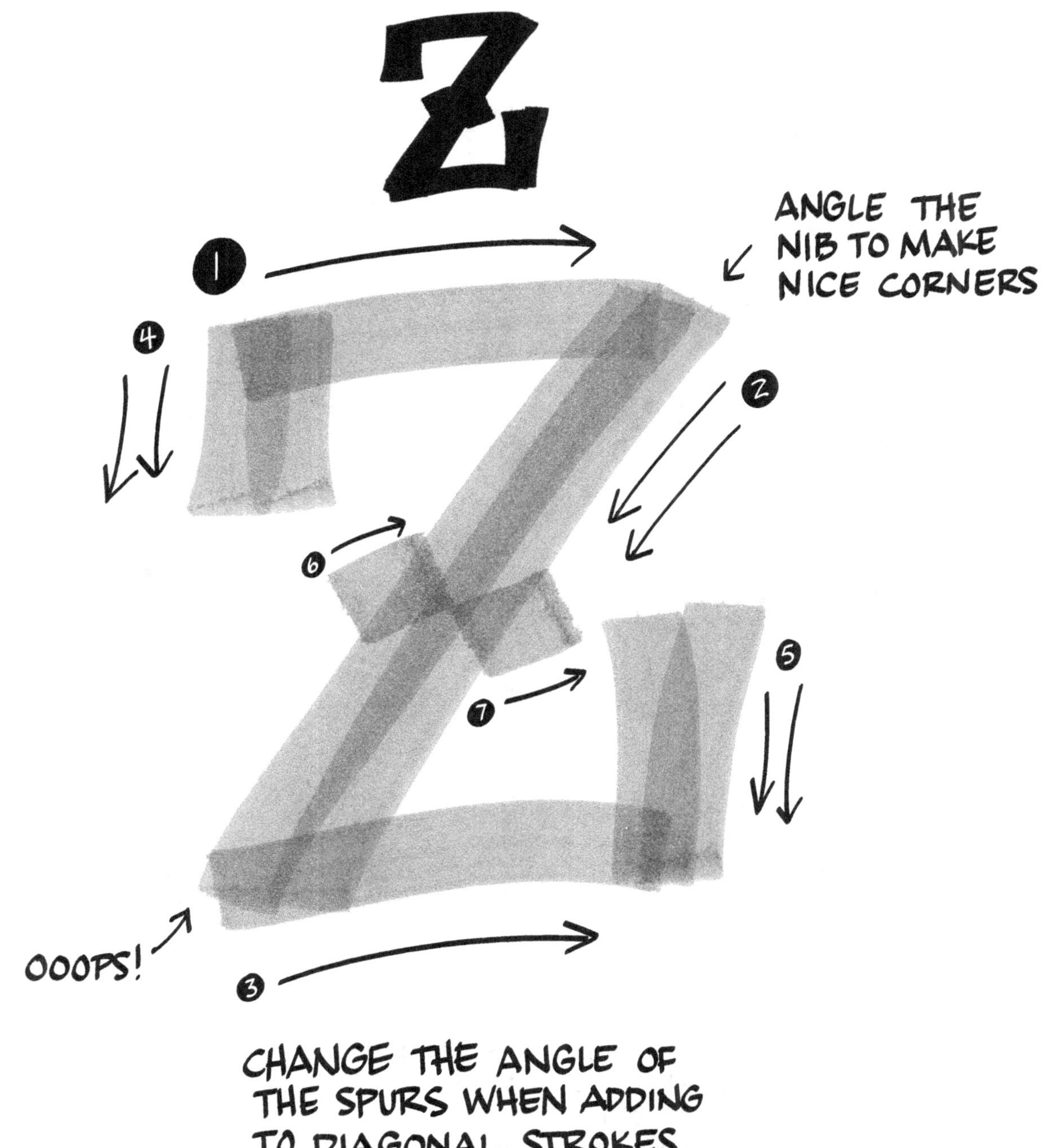
Z
1
2
3
4
5
6
7
ANGLE THE NIB TO MAKE NICE CORNERS
OOOPS!
CHANGE THE ANGLE OF THE SPURS WHEN ADDING TO DIAGONAL STROKES

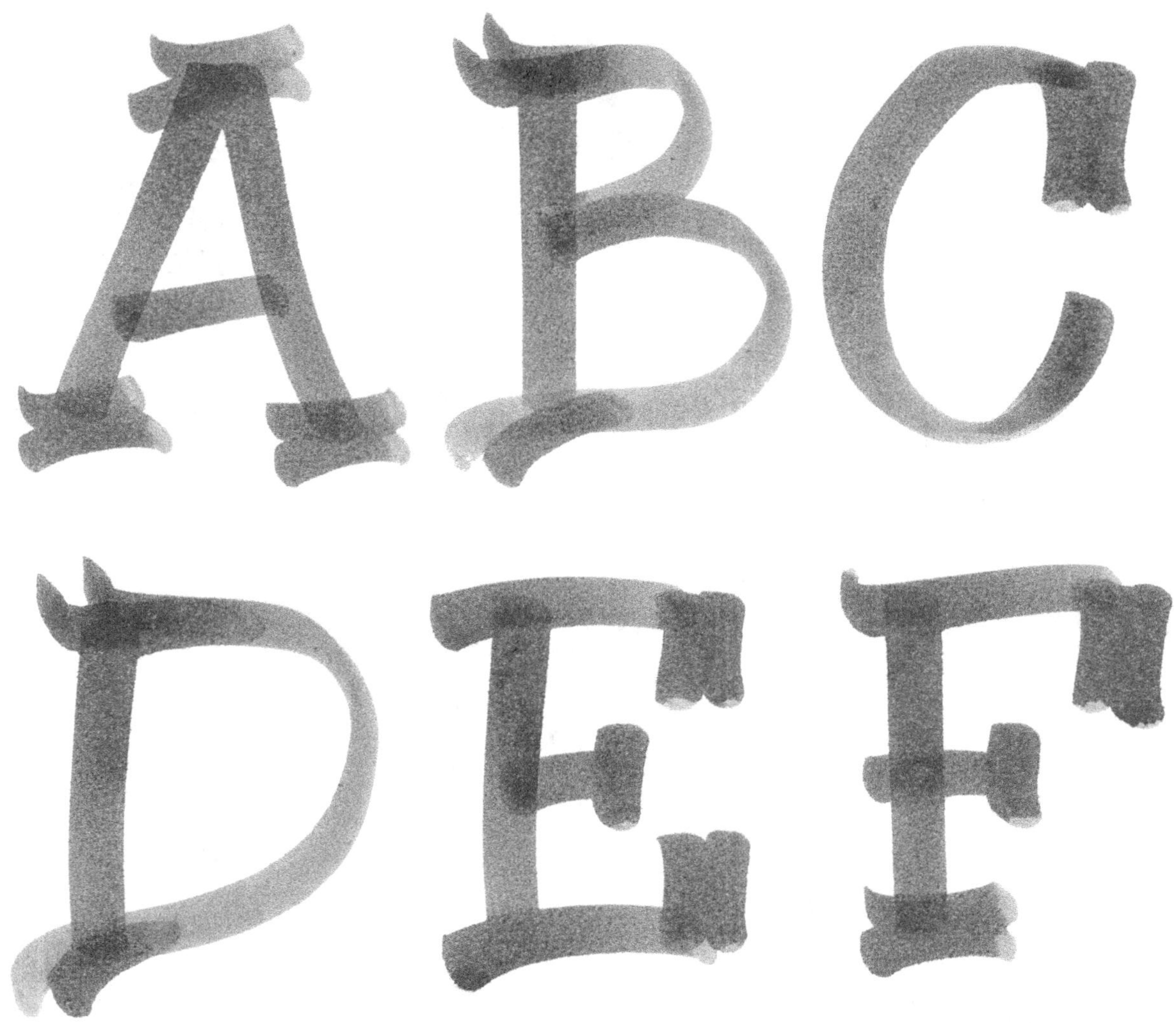

Double-slab serif written in a loose and fun Western style with a No.One Art. All of the letters in this chapter are printed at 100% so you can photocopy and trace them if it helps you get the letterforms or loosen up. This is a fun lettering style, so have fun with it!

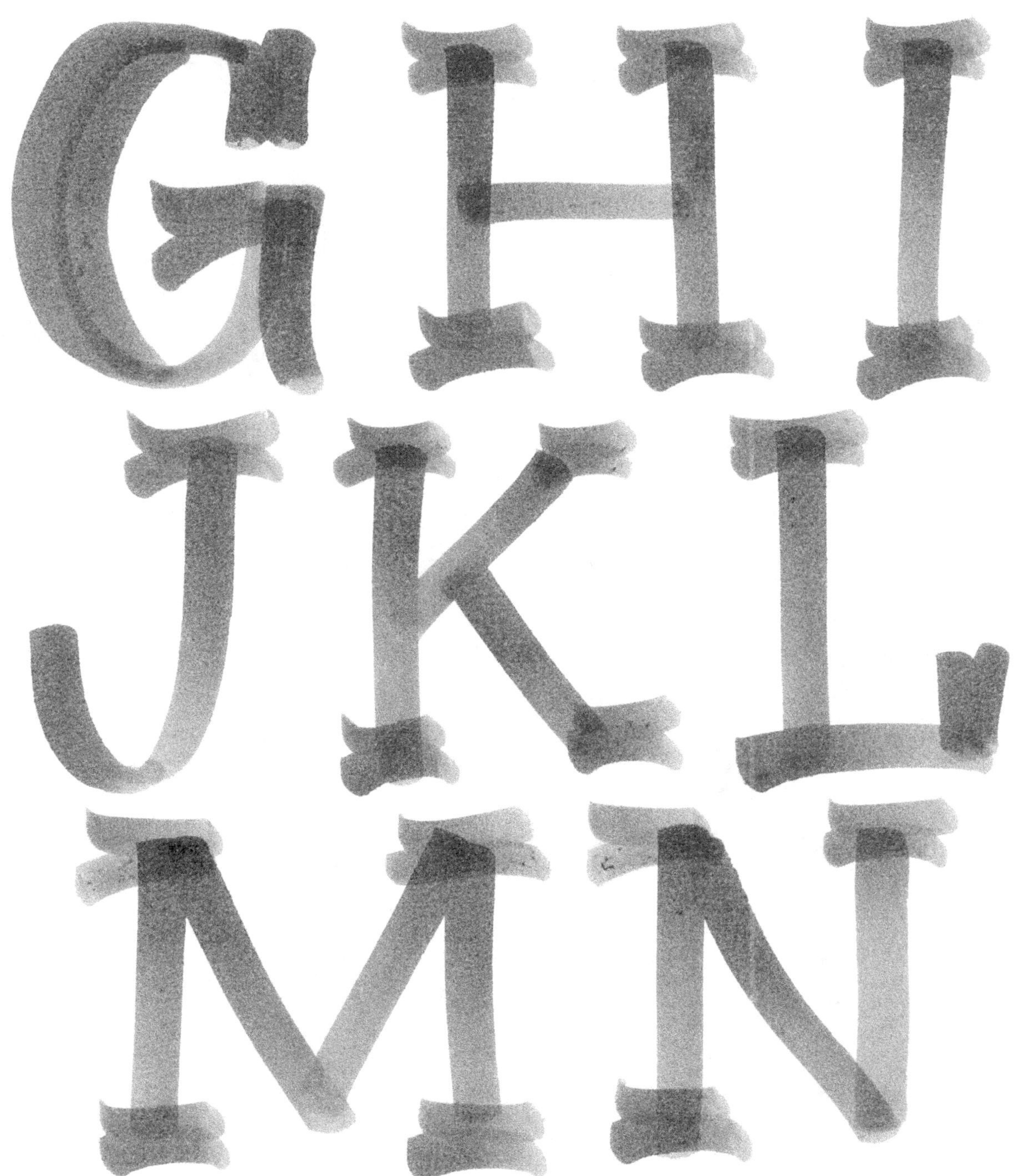

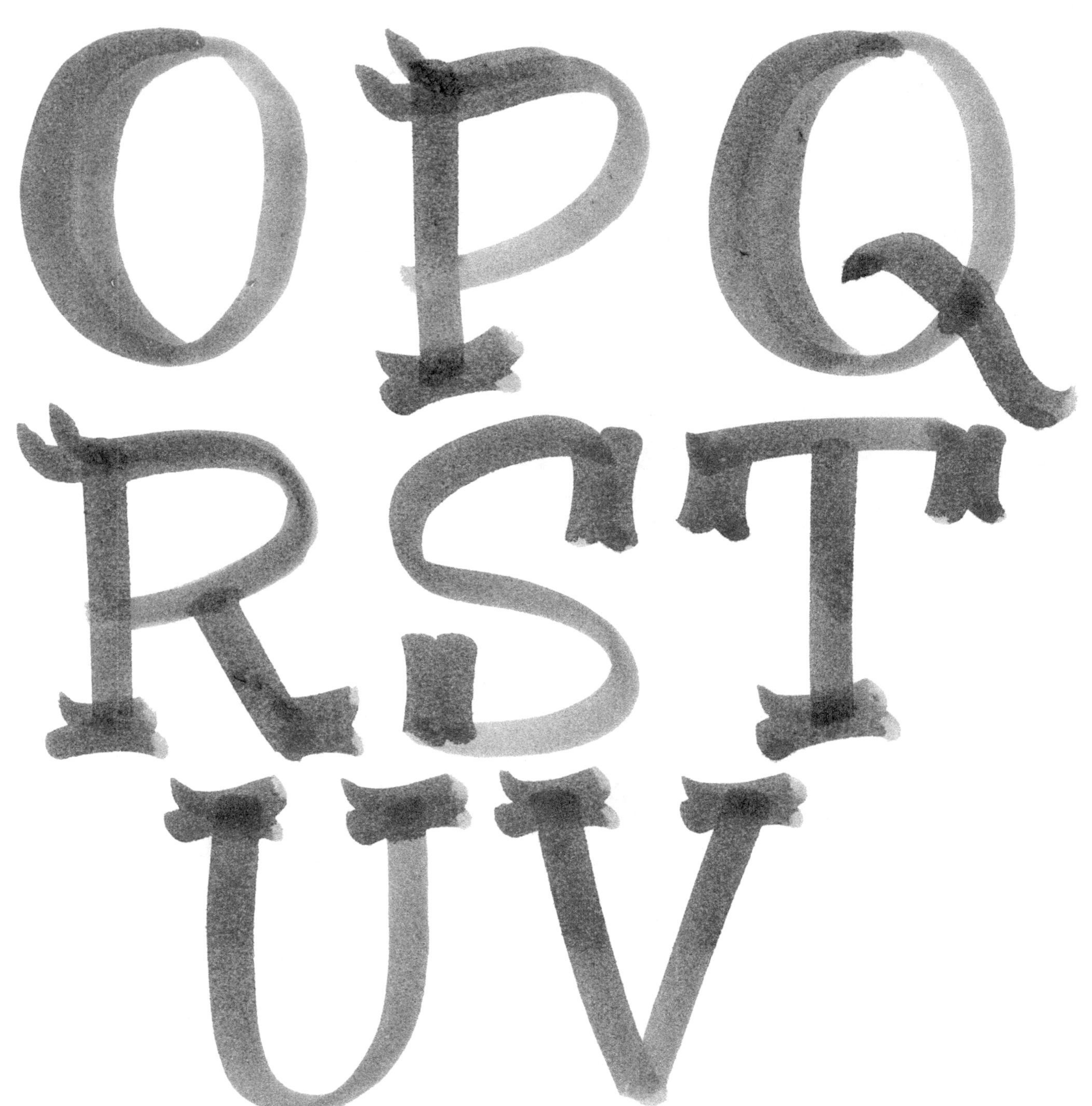

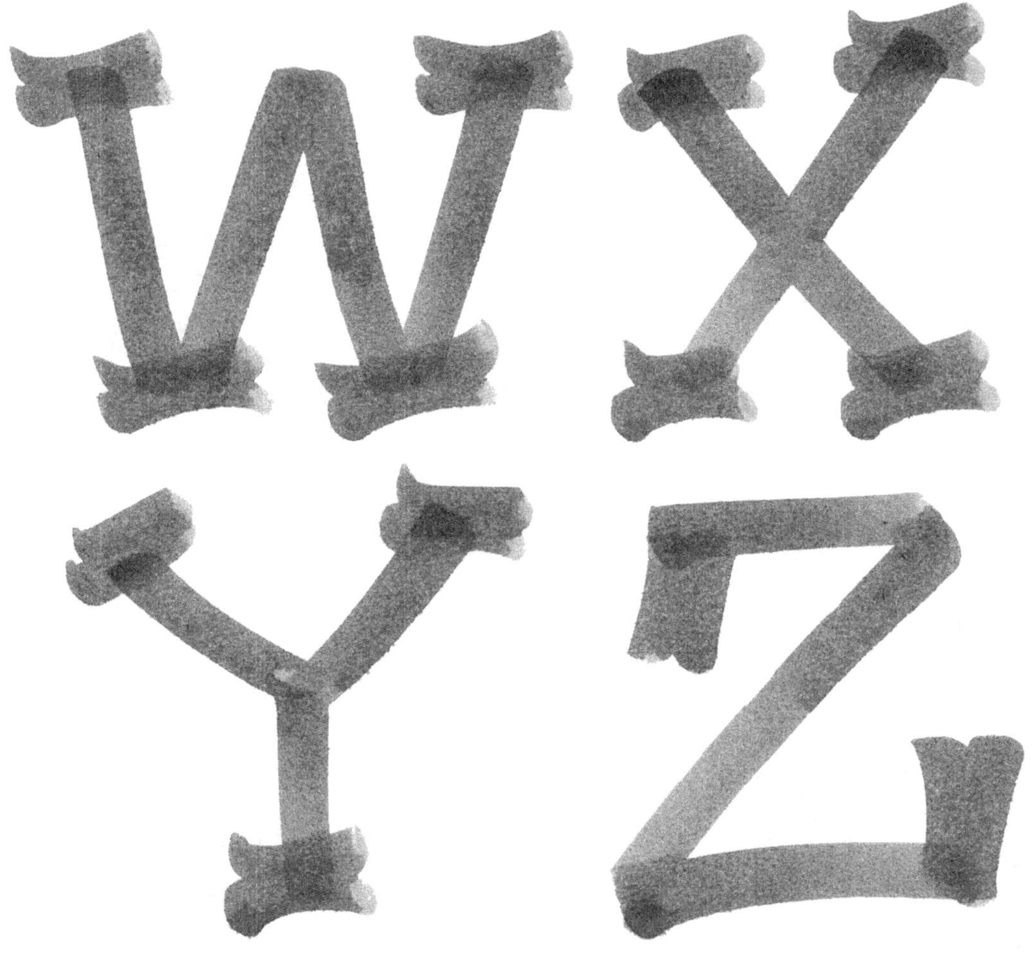

Now that you have written each letter, decide whether you want to make them more formal or even more wacky! Be sure to write some words or a pangram to practice spacing and bouncing baselines to see how the letters live in relationship to one another.

# LETTERING EXAMPLES

After some practice with serifs and fills, you can have all kinds of fun!

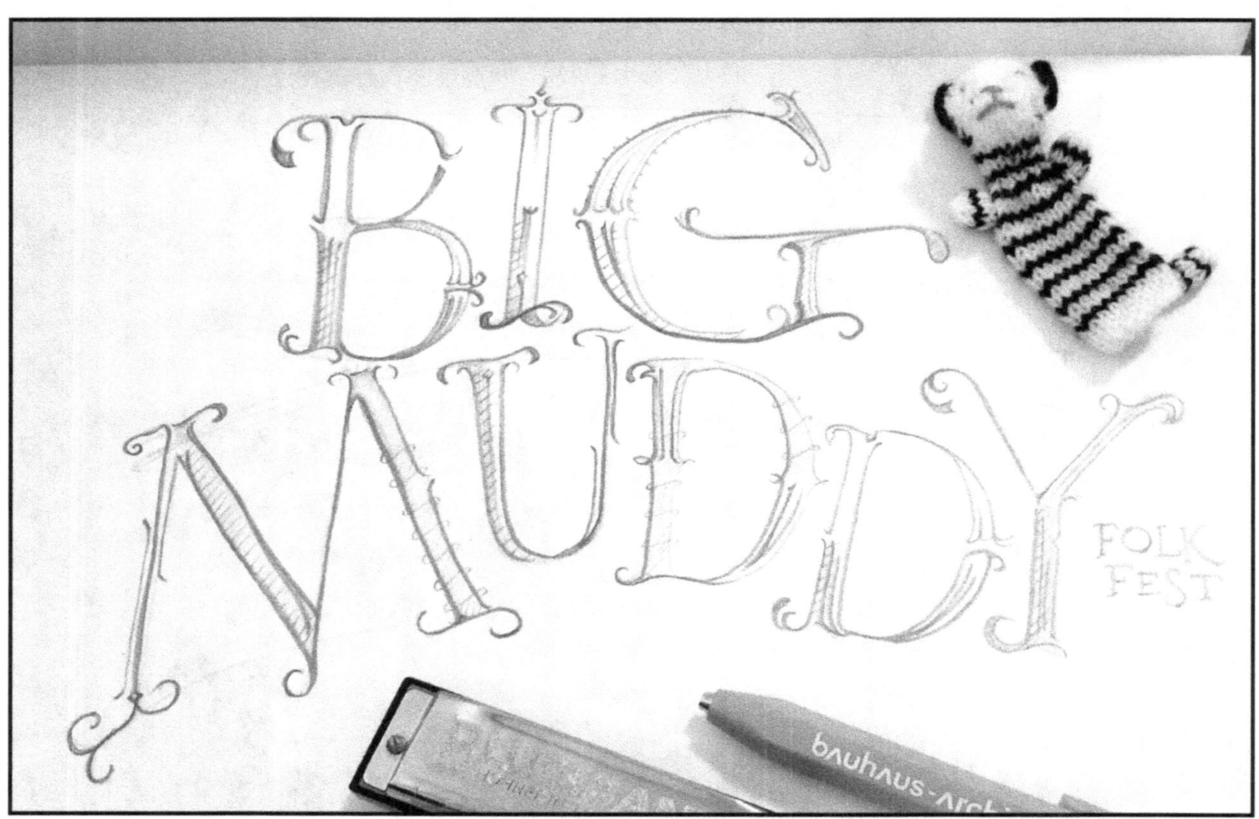


### Big Muddy

I drew this in my giant sketchbook while I was on the road. We stopped off at the Big Muddy Folk Festival for a harmonica workshop with my mom. I found a sample of this lettering style in an antique store, so I snapped a picture of it and sketched out some of the letters while sitting in a workshop of songwriters. They did their thing while I did mine, in pencil.

"Stripey" the finger puppet joined us in Chicago thanks to Brandy Agerbeck and travels in the Jeep with us to this day.

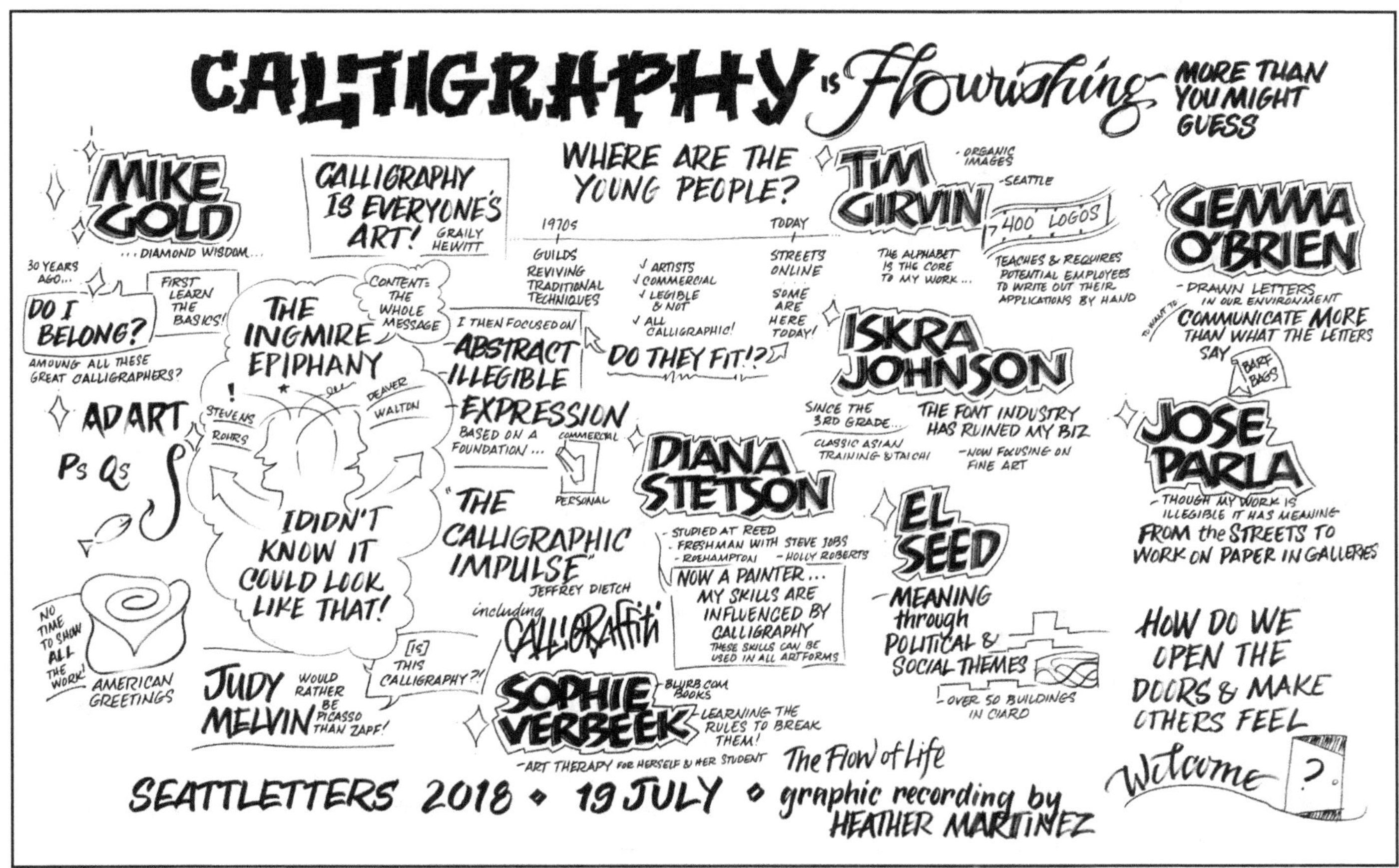


## Calligraphy is Flourishing

After a few days of lettering with Carl Rohrs at Seattletters, the 2018 International Calligraphy Conference, I was asked to graphic record a keynote lecture for Mike Gold. I used my interpretation of a lettering style learned in Carl's class for the word "Calligraphy" found here. It's a mix between Western and Eastern lettering styles. Other lettering styles used here include *Neuland Hand* written with a BigOne that has been hacked to write like a flat brush and *Sign Painter* written with a No.One Art marker.

You can see the entire chart and read an interview I had with the publisher, Christopher Calderhead, in *Letter Arts Review*, volume 32, number 3. He affectionately called me an "amanuensis"–a term I will take as a compliment.

# NATIONAL PARKS

Ahhhhh, the great outdoors!

Having lived in southwest Colorado on and off for the last 25 years, I thought I had earned my share of incredible mountain peak views, waterfalls and foliage. But never in my life had I seen so many shades of green as in the Hoh Rain Forest in Olympic National Park. Deemed one of the wettest places in the US, Ray and I enjoyed walking up the river trail to a bridge and waterfall, then sitting in the nook of a tree where we ate smoked salmon and avocado on crackers until we were overcome by ants at our picnic. While camping near Sol Duc Falls, we experienced the most magical and shortest hike of our lives in the Ancient Groves. The terrain changes from wetland to cliff-edge hiking, to a magically lit forest with such old growth and new growth forming that you feel as if you are surrounded by tree nymphs. I remember being compelled to skip about and bathe in the beauty.

From one of the wettest places, through the redwoods, to one of the driest and hottest, we made our way to Arches National Park in Utah. Those who know me well know that my melting point is 80°F. So no, I didn't make it to the arch, but we did manage to cover some great terrain and enjoyed seeing people rock climb.

The National Park Service celebrated its centennial in 2016. While we were traveling a year later, the remnants of the celebration persisted. Each time we stopped, I admired the classic posters for each park. While the lettering was different on each, there was one that really stood out. It was an Art Deco inspired lettering style that I finally landed on and enjoyed exploring.

I encourage you to study the typefaces found on the posters of the 58 National Parks. With a quick search online, you can find hundreds of examples. Studying posters is a good exercise because the bold lettering works well for chart and flip chart titles. And good design is always inspiring.

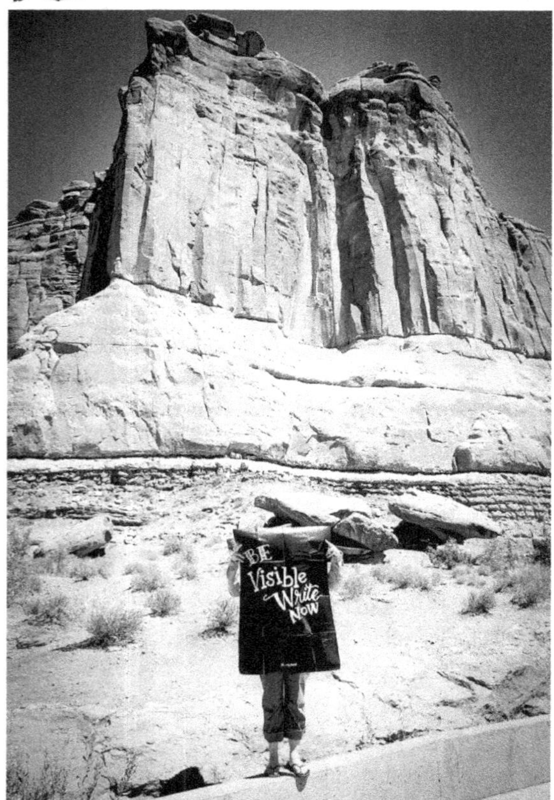


Arches National Park, Utah

# ATTRIBUTES



**Markers to use:**

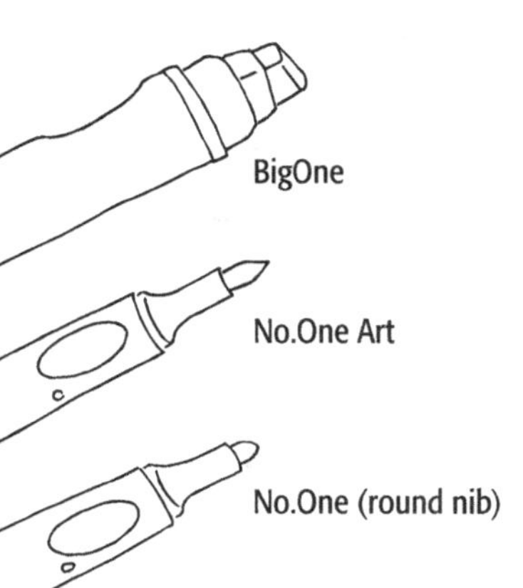

BigOne

No.One Art

No.One (round nib)

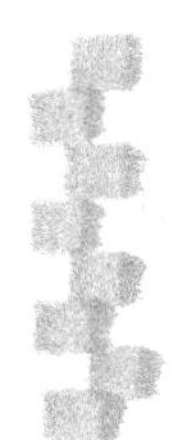

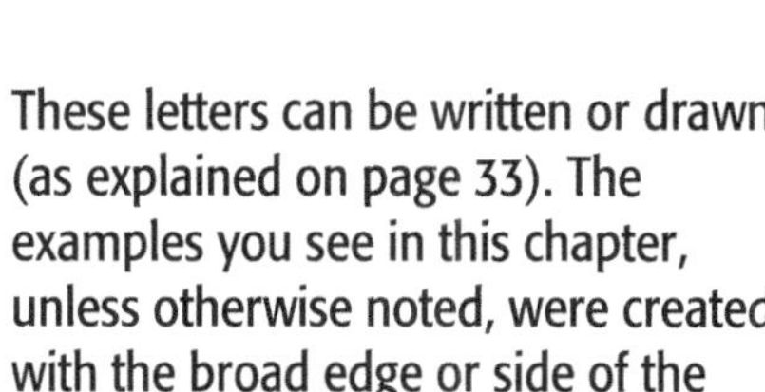



Note that the crossbars and junctures are either high or low. The only one that should be in the middle is the X.

These letters can be written or drawn (as explained on page 33). The examples you see in this chapter, unless otherwise noted, were created with the broad edge or side of the No.One Art.

**Lettering style attributes:**
- Inspired by Art Deco
- Condensed, mono-weight letters
- Taller than it is wide, ~8 nib widths, but can vary
- High or low x-height on crossbars
- Based on geometric shapes
- Blends well with historical and technology themes
- Can profoundly convey a mood or tone
- Formal
- Artistic

**When to use:**
- Titles
- Topics
- Emphasis
- Posters

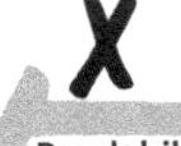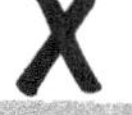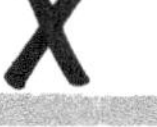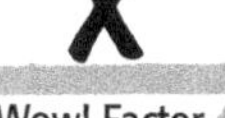

Readability    Emphasis    Wow! Factor

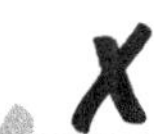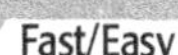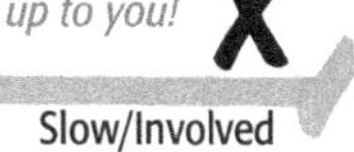

Fast/Easy    *Can be either. It's up to you!*    Slow/Involved

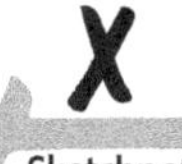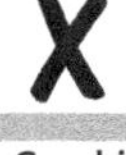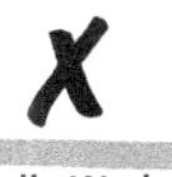

Sketchnotes    Graphic Recording    Studio Work

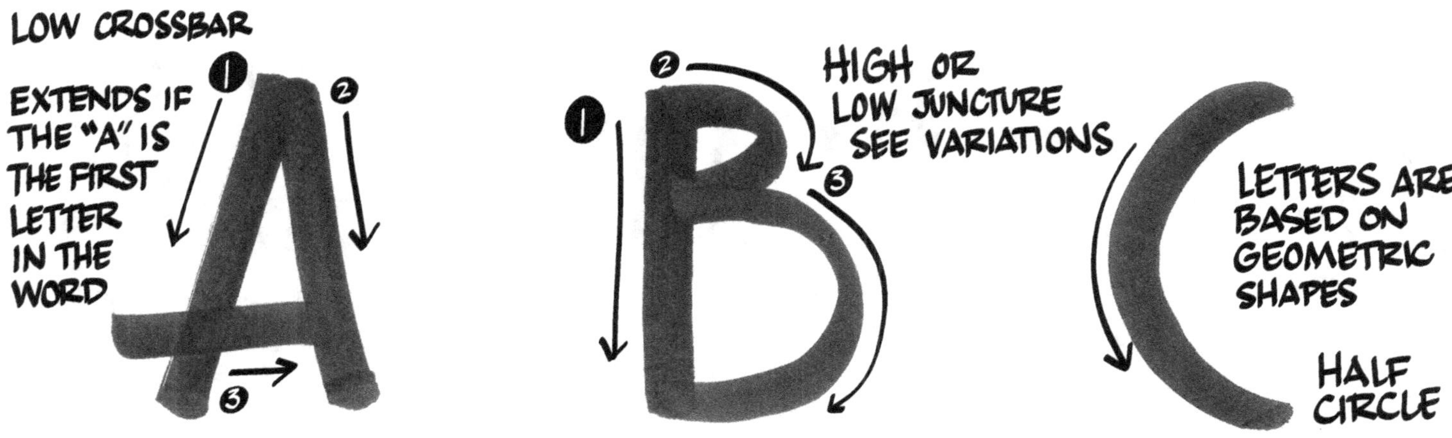


DRAW THE STEM FIRST OR FROM LEFT TO RIGHT

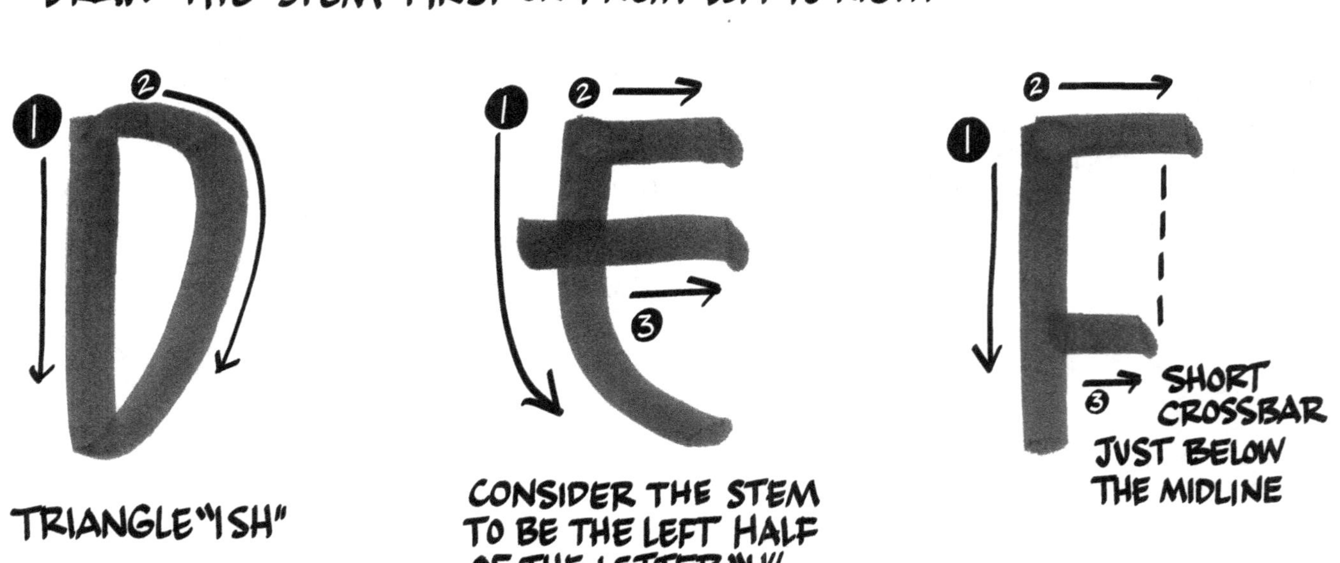

See page 19 for an important note about stroke order and direction.

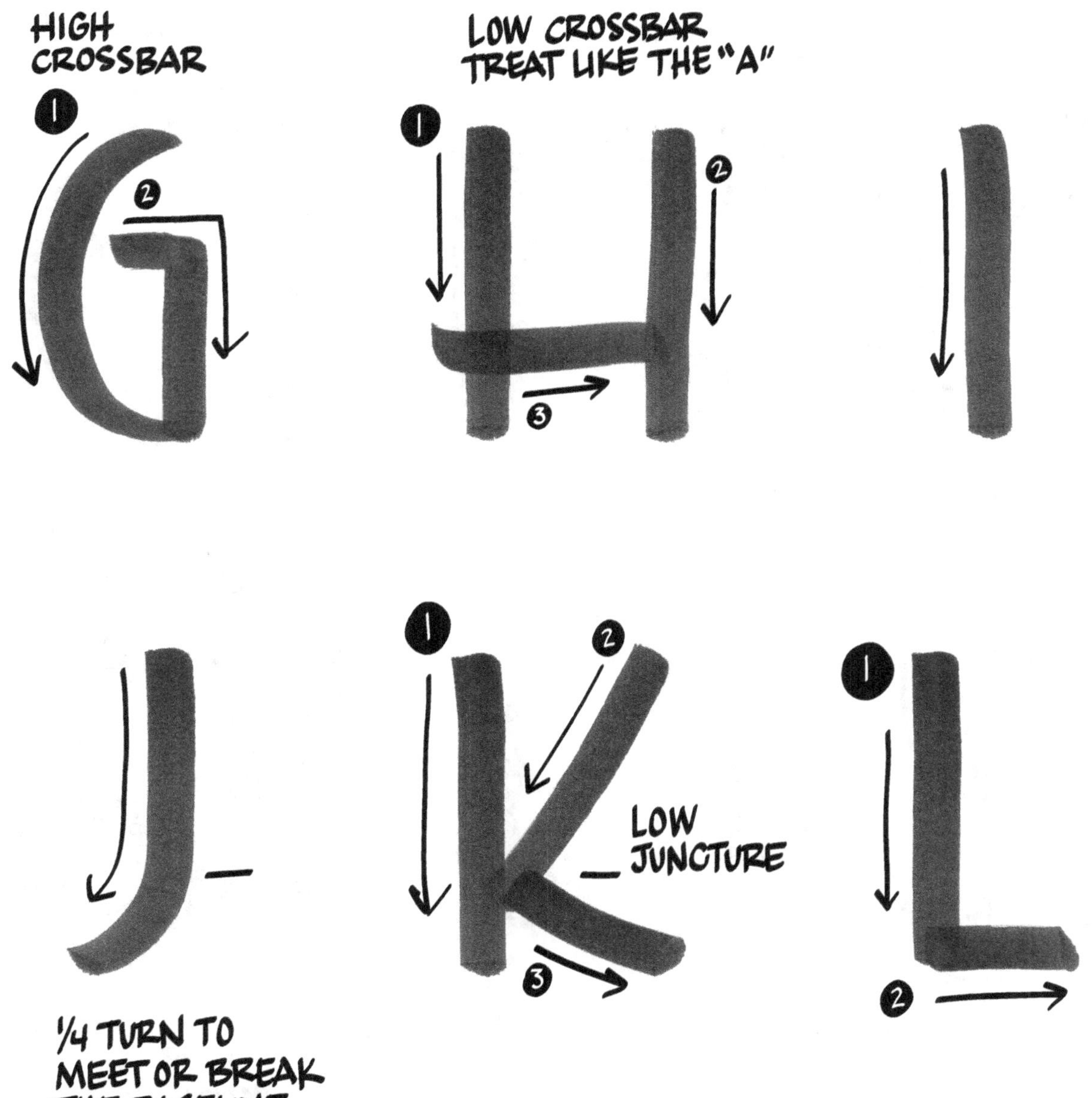

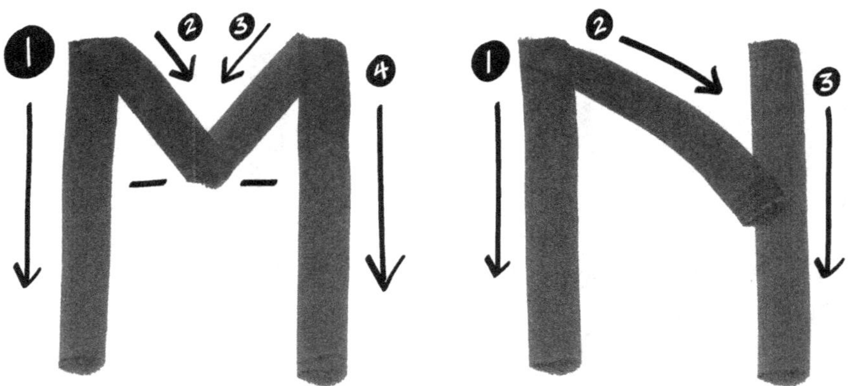
ALL DOWN STROKES
1
2
3
4
HIGH JUNCTURES

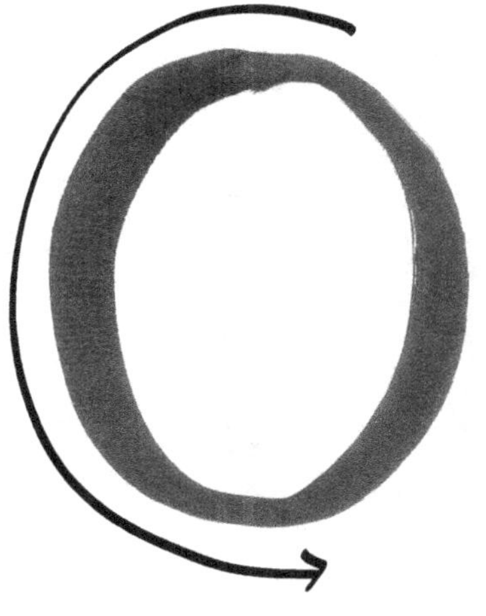
START A 1 O'CLOCK
& GO FULL CIRCLE
2
1
3

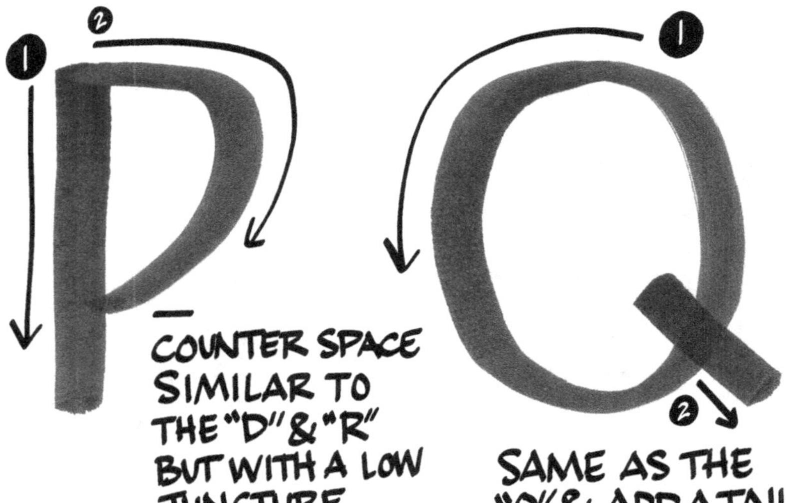
1
2
COUNTER SPACE
SIMILAR TO
THE "D" & "R"
BUT WITH A LOW
JUNCTURE
1
2
SAME AS THE
"O" & ADD A TAIL

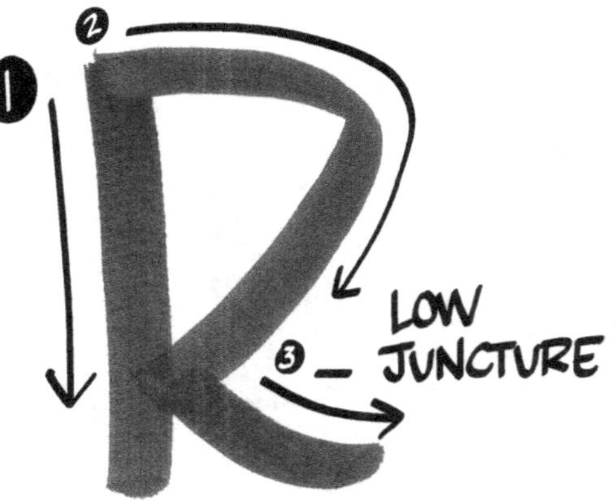
SAME AS THE "P"
& ADD A LEG
1
2
3
LOW
JUNCTURE
CHANGE THE ANGLE
OF YOUR NIB
THROUGHOUT

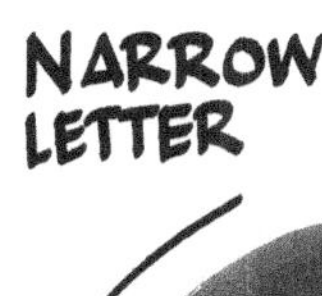


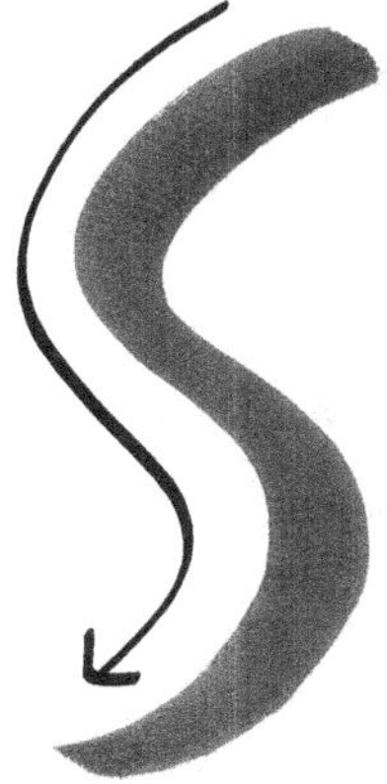

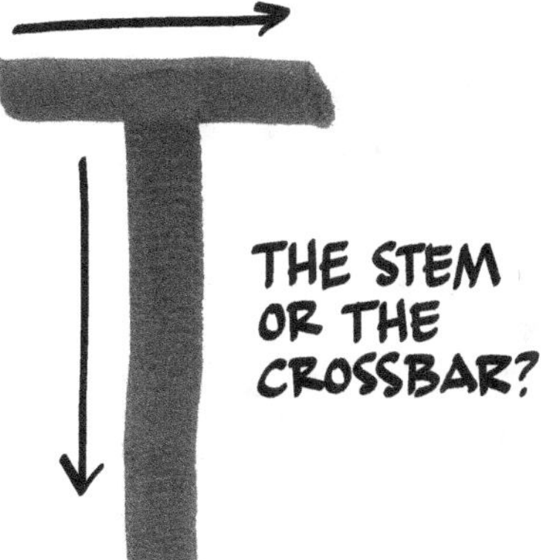


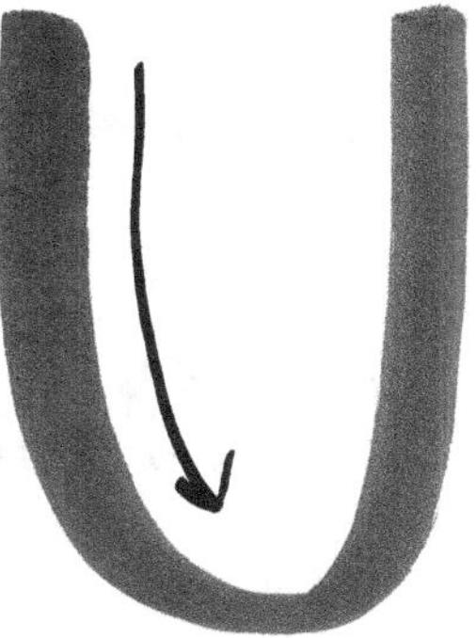


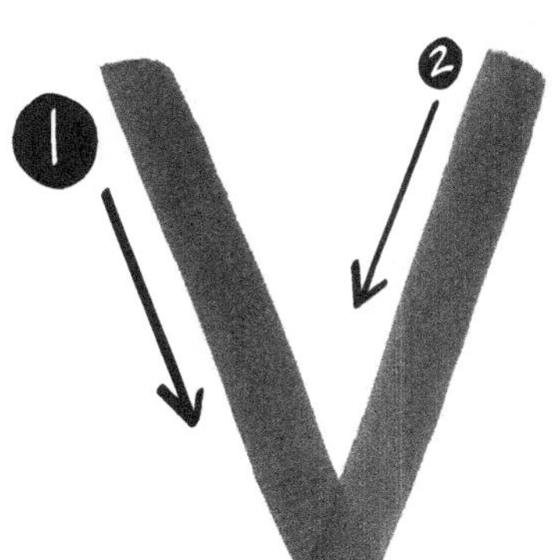


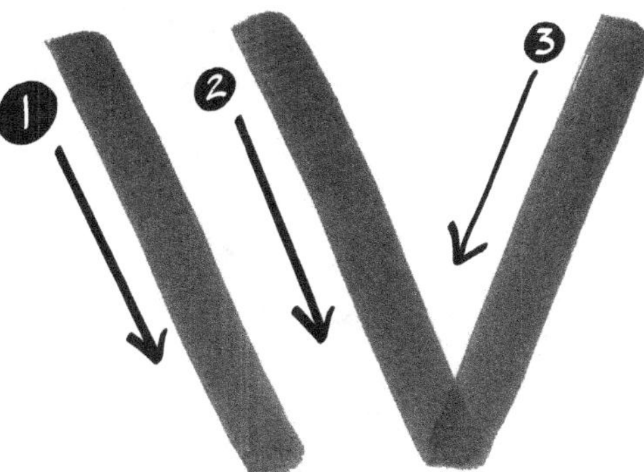


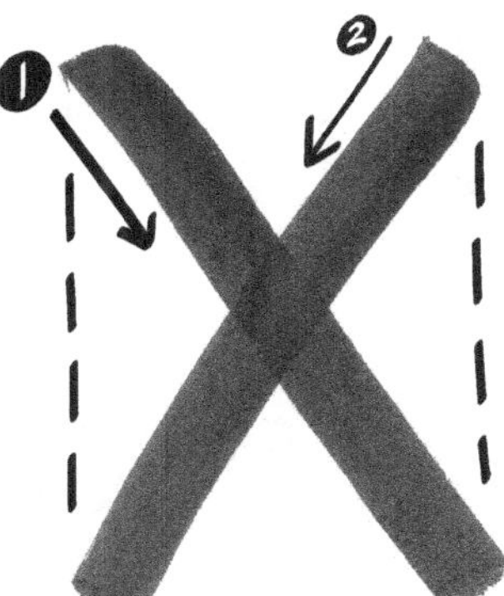


Keep the juncture in the middle!
This is true for most lettering styles regardless of where the juncture is in other letters.

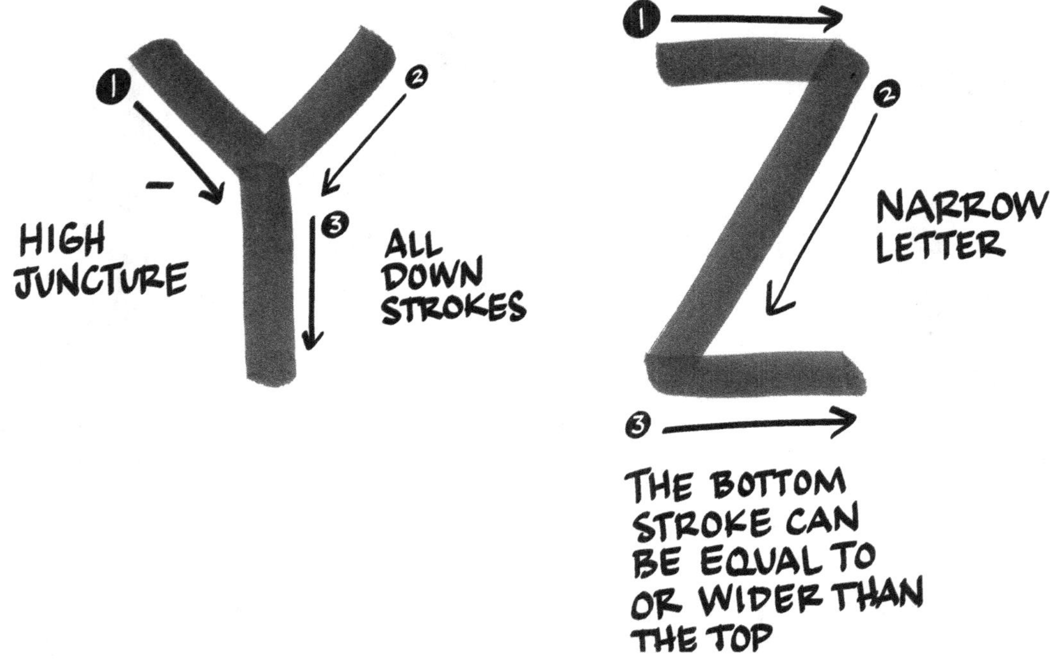


I don't know about you, but I feel taller just by practicing this lettering style!

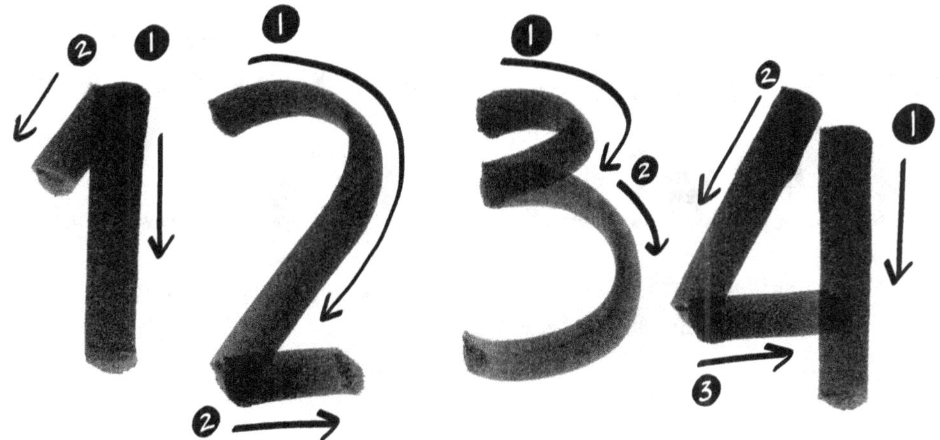

# VARIATIONS

# THE QUICK BROWN FOX SHOOTS LASERS

As soon as you learn the letterforms, start writing words! Thanks, Trent, for riffing off this well-known pangram to fit the theme.

## TRENT ART DECO VARIATIONS

AABCDEFGHIJKLMNO
PQRSTUVWWXYYZ

AABCDEFGHIJKHLM
NOPQRSTUVWWXYYZ

## TRENT TECH DEMO HAND

TECHNOLOGY
SAVES LIVES
TECHNO MUSIC
CAN BE DARK

Note how the high and low crossbars set a tone.

# TRENT HYPER TECH HAND

ABCDEFGHI
JKLMNOPQ
RSTUVWXYZ

Initially presented in the September 2018 session of *Lettering with the Masters*, this hand by Trent Wakenight adapts half of an Art Deco inspired lettering style to reflect a "technology" style. This means you only have to learn 13 of the letters: A, B, E, H, K, M, N, P, R, T, W, Y, and Z. This highly stylized letterform can be used to emphasize words and slow down the reader. And these "interruptions" could force greater comprehension and memory.

# VARIATIONS

A A A A B E F F
G G H K K M N N O P
Q U V W X Y & & G

Have fun finding your own variations!

# LETTERING EXAMPLES

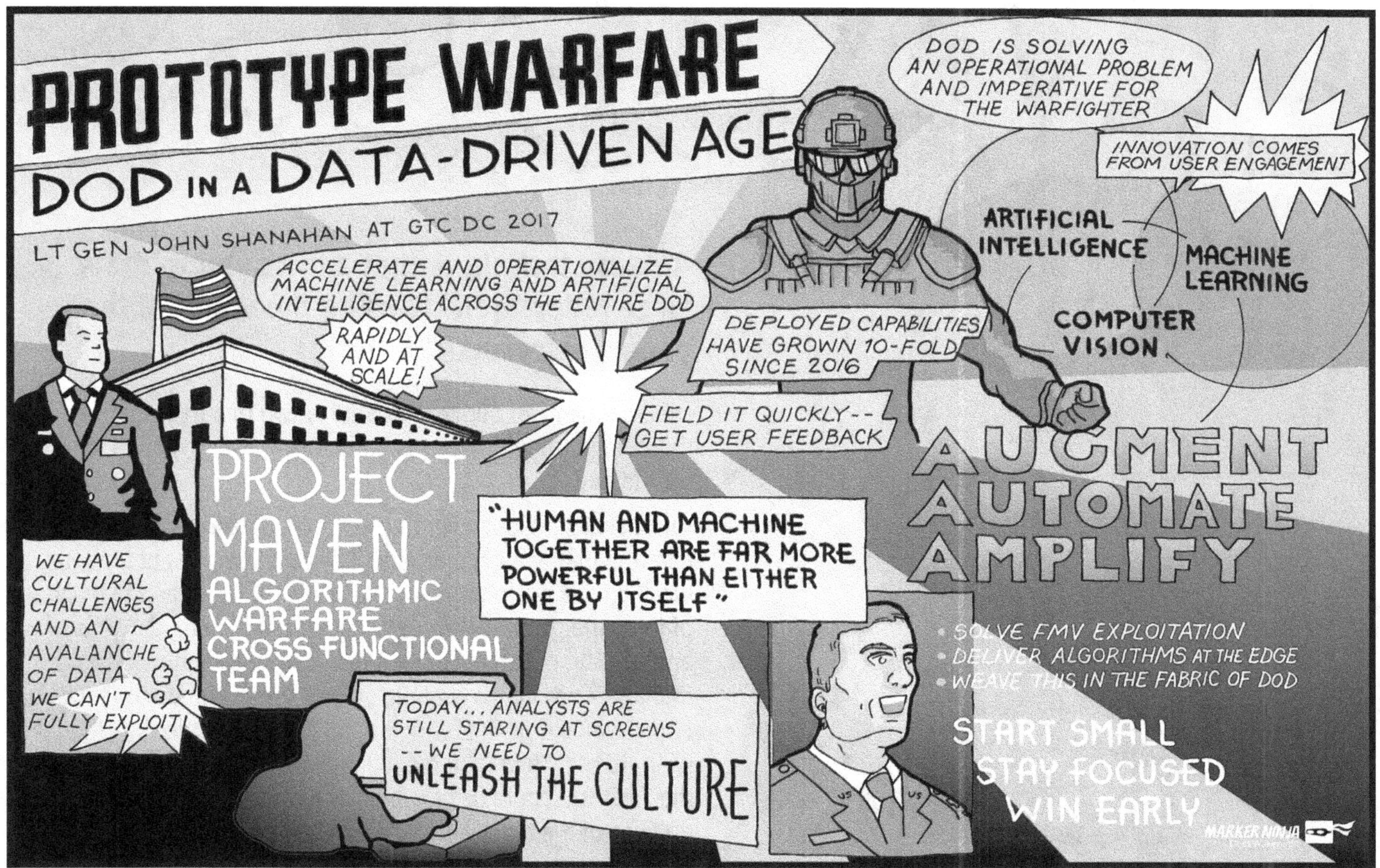



*pictured above*

**Trent Wakenight** of Lorton, Virgina, drew this graphic as a single 11x17" poster in black ink and then colorized it in Adobe Photoshop.

The Art Deco lettering style was used to convey futurism and technology while exploring security and defense.

# HARBOR

**An easy technique that allows you to draw large letters quickly using the white of the paper as "reverse" lettering.**

I was sitting in an auditorium on day two of a three-day gig thumbing through my notes and looking over my chart layouts for the day.

While sketching out a lighthouse, I was thinking about the lettering that would go around it. I really didn't want to write black on yellow–to represent light beams. I wanted the white of the paper to show through. With a pencil behind my ear and my 30mm FatOne in my hand, I wondered how I would manage. Certainly, a big bold yellow line would do the trick. But I don't enjoy drawing block letters! They always look rushed and weird to me. Then it hit me, if I taped a pencil on both sides of the FatOne, I could use the pencils to quickly and easily create outlines of the block letters.

I was pleased with the result of this hack, so naturally, when Ray and I came across this lighthouse in the Pacific Northwest, I asked him to snap a picture because I had to include the technique in this book. And a few days later when I spotted this massive ship anchor outside of the Columbia River Maritime Museum in Astoria, Oregon, I considered how the spaces in this lettering style can be eliminated to create a "chain" of letters.

While this technique is in no way original and I couldn't source who first thought of it, I can say that it is a handy tool to keep in your kit for when you need it. Or just "MacGyver" it on the fly!

Lighthouse, Pacific coast
Anchor, Astoria, Oregon

# ATTRIBUTES

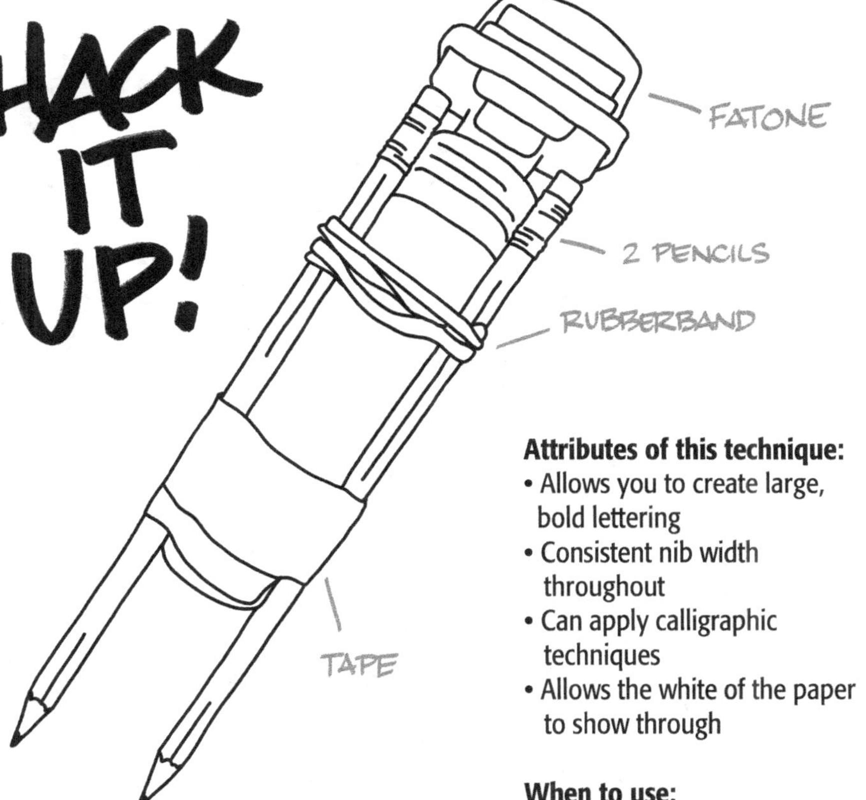


## Do you ever wonder how to get white letters with a color background?

I get asked that question a lot! I use this technique and then color around the letters to let the white of the paper show through.

This technique allows you to write letters faster than it takes to draw them. They tend to be more accurate in shape and you can make the stroke width consistent.

You can use other mark-making tools as the spacer in between the pencils. Be sure to position your tools facing opposite directions so you can use both. You can use tools already in your toolkit when assigning hierarchy by using the tools as spacers. And a word of advice, use a rubber band to secure the back end first. It will hold the pencils in place while you ensure they are exactly parallel and across from one another and the tips are at the same height before you tape them into place.

**Pro-tip:** Use two new pencils so they are the same length.

**Attributes of this technique:**
- Allows you to create large, bold lettering
- Consistent nib width throughout
- Can apply calligraphic techniques
- Allows the white of the paper to show through

**When to use:**
- Titles (FatOne hack)
- Topics (smaller hack)

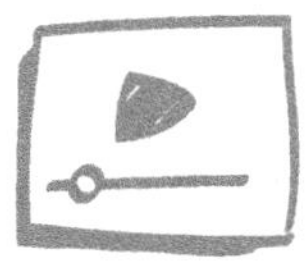

Learn how to create this silly-looking contraption by visiting the online resources page for this book at www.LetsLetterTogether.com.
I also teach this technique in my in-person workshops.

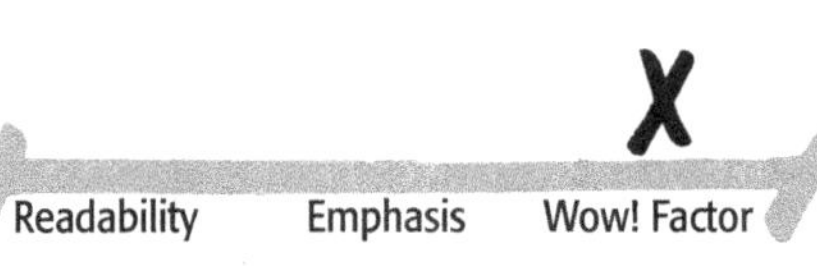


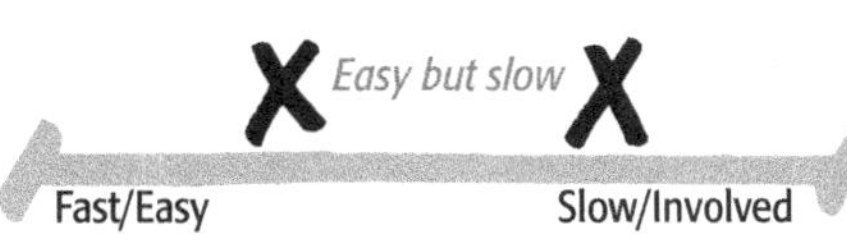


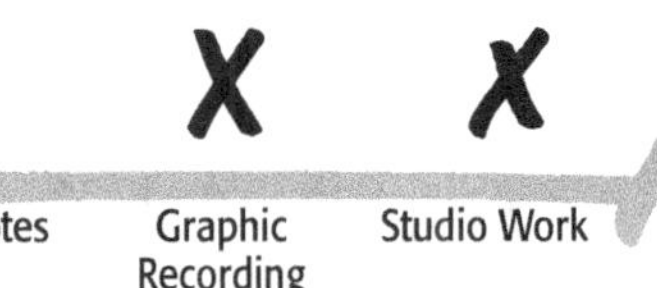

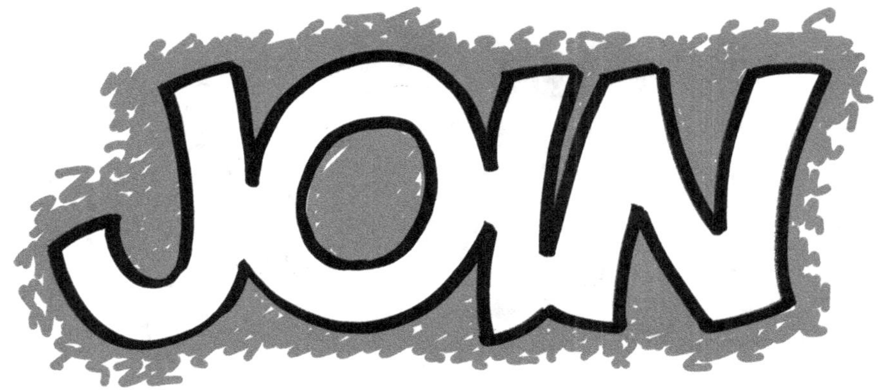


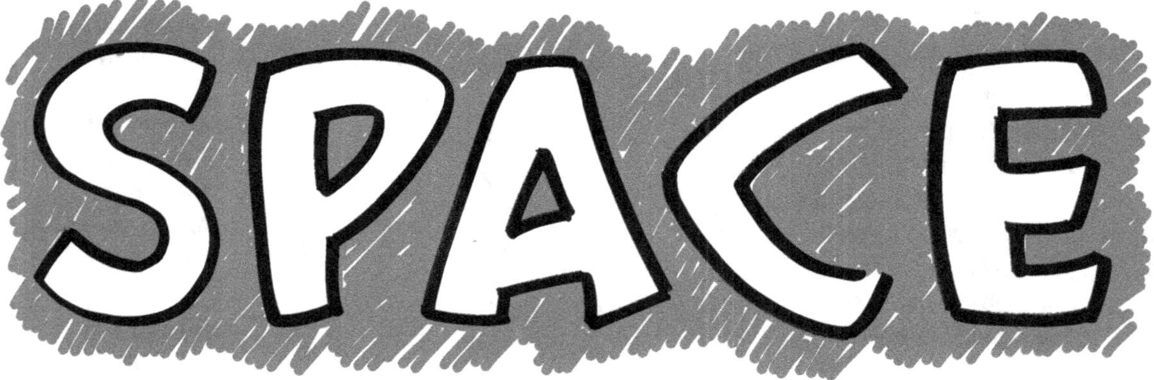


*Harbor* is about the linking of letters, so relationship is key.

You can choose to create more space between letters, allowing the color to show through more.

Joining letters is fun and looks cool but isn't always very readable. Test it out before you commit as some letter combinations are easier to read than others. Use this technique for short words or one word in a title if you are in a hurry because it can be time consuming to fill in all that negative space!

# A VARIETY OF LETTERING STYLES ALL IN ONE TOOL!

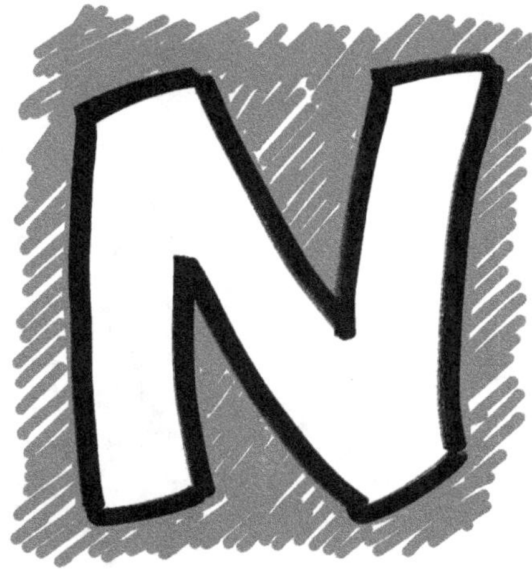

### *Neuland Hand 2.0*
Great for bold styles and easy to learn.

Note: I use a very round and bouncy variation of this lettering style. Why? Because these are the marks I naturally make when writing at speed in front of the client.

Here are just two lettering styles I use with this tool. You may discover and design your own. Keep in mind that it is like a broad-edge tool and angle will be very important.

And guess what? You don't have to follow your pencil lines exactly. They are there as a guide only. When you outline your letters, take the opportunity to define them the way you want them to look.

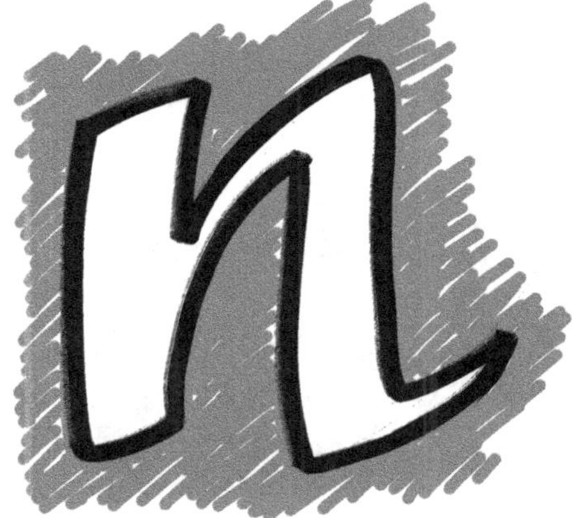

### Italic
Stylized and elegant, connecting the letters and outlining them is the ultimate in faux calligraphy. Hold the tool at a 30 to 45° angle and keep it at that angle throughout each stroke as you write.

# LETTERING EXAMPLES

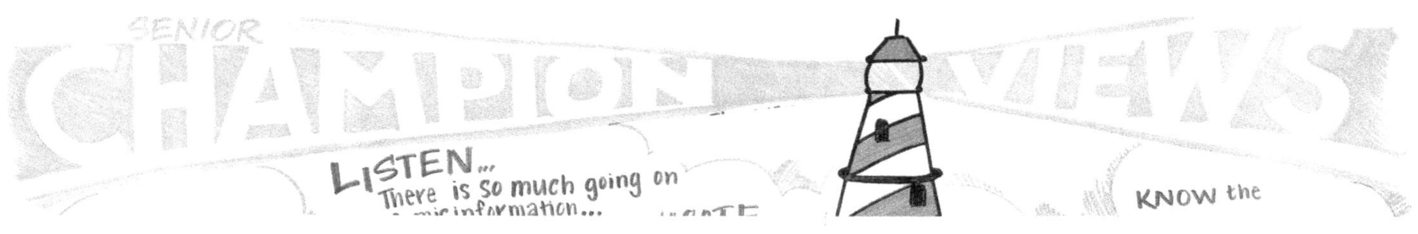


### Lighthouse
The original title that inspired this hack. Keep in mind that this is NOT a studio piece but my first attempt at using this hack just moments before the talk began.

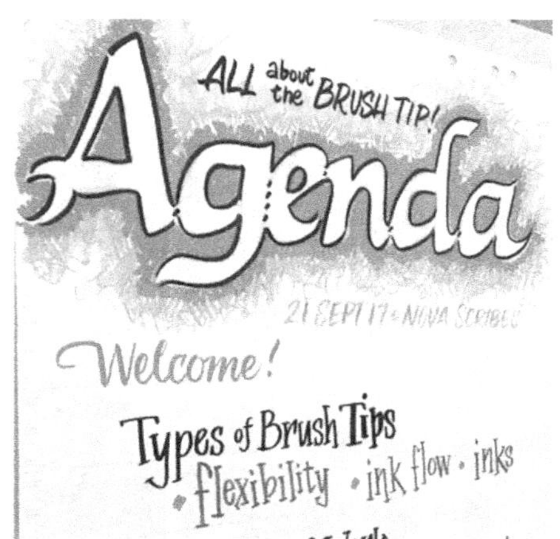


### Agenda
One word on a flip chart is a great way to draw attention.

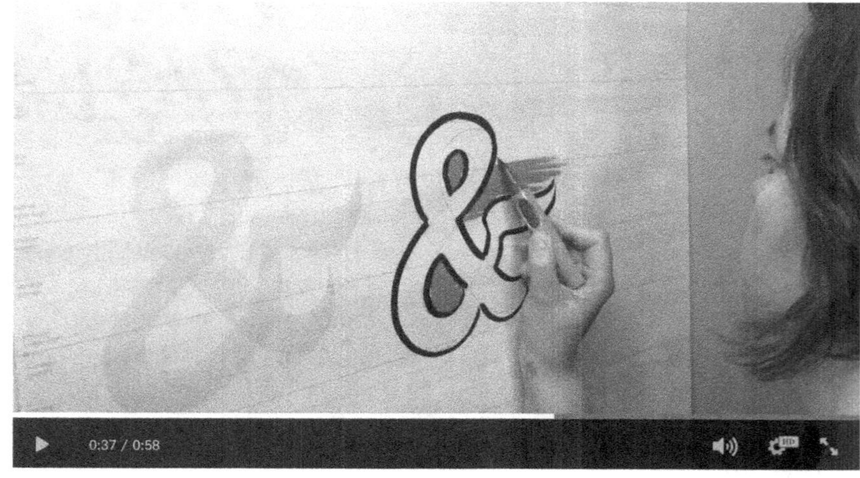


### Ampersand video
In this video, the first ampersand was drawn with a 30mm FatOne with Neuland's 500 brilliant yellow ink. The second one was drawn with the hack and outlined with a No.One Art Outliner. Note how I didn't follow every pencil line drawn, just the contour lines.

# PLANNING FOR THE FUTURE



**Sam Bradd**, from Vancouver, BC, Canada

Sam used the hack to create this title for a workshop where a health center was defining their unique model of holistic, culturally safe, wrap-around wellness care. Sam shares, "I don't usually work with big titles in the middle of a two-day session, but I noticed something interesting. This was a group made up of mostly front-line health workers, who were being invited to design policy that directly affects them. And policy-making for almost everyone is out of their comfort zone! So having the big title called 'planning for the future' and then a 'model of care' poster (not pictured) made it very clear what two tasks we were working on. One great question we used was 'what would you want clients to know about our new model of care?'"

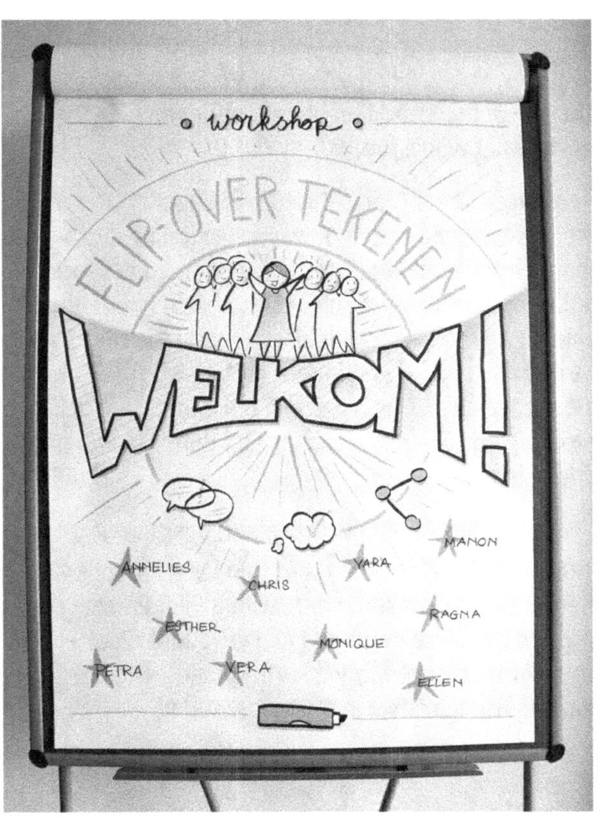


*pictured left*

**Birgit Smit,** from the Netherlands, always makes a personalized poster for people to feel welcome when entering her workshops. It's functional too: She puts a little sign like a star next to their name when they come in so she can track whether the group is complete.

Here she used the hack with two pencils attached to a No.One Art. It worked great! For the background color, she used Pan pastel.

# CLOCK FACE

## A thick-and-thin lettering style inspired by centuries-old hand-painted clock faces.

The pendulum clock was invented in 1656 by Christiaan Huygens and is known as the most precise type of mechanical timekeeper. The face of the clock is the backdrop of its measurement. While many different lettering styles have been used in clocks over the centuries, it is the Roman numerals that have me most intrigued. Compressed and condensed, the numbers are almost unreadable, but the variations as a handwritten lettering style are practically endless. In the following pages, you will find a few different approaches to inspire the use of thick and thin lines in your work. Play with it and discover what works for you!

While the Conger Street Clock Museum in Eugene, Oregon, is now closed, the day we visited, it was transitioning into a clock repair shop, giving these treasures a dry home to tick tock. We planned the trip so that we would arrive before noon, hoping they would all strike at once. But alas, none of the clocks were set to the current time. At first I thought that was nice to be able to hear each clock's unique tone. But with all the ticking and the tocking and the random chimes, I think I would go mad working in a space like that!

Instead, I took the inspiration with me and over the next few months, I began to see thick-and-thin lettering styles everywhere. I even spent some time with a Pilot Parallel pen, which inspired the piece on page 118. I've taught *Clock Face* in my *Level Up Your Lettering VIRTUAL* courses, and several of those students use that style in their work today.

Conger Street Clock Museum
Eugene, Oregon

# ATTRIBUTES

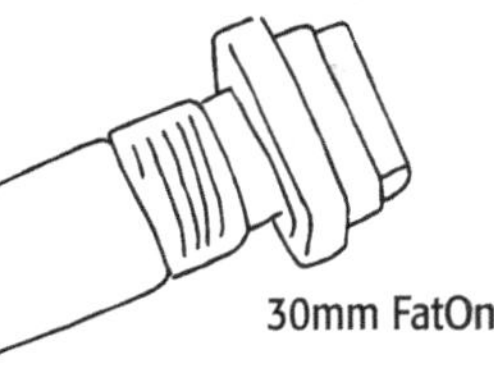

**Markers to use:**

30mm FatOne

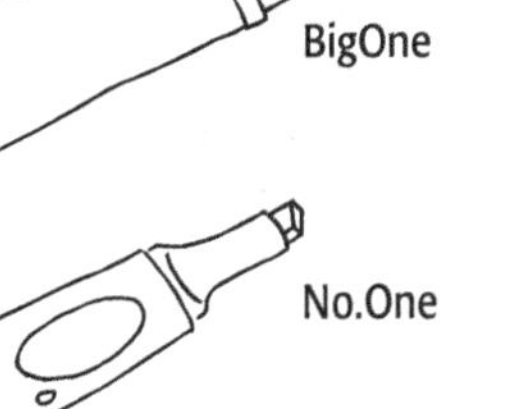

BigOne

No.One

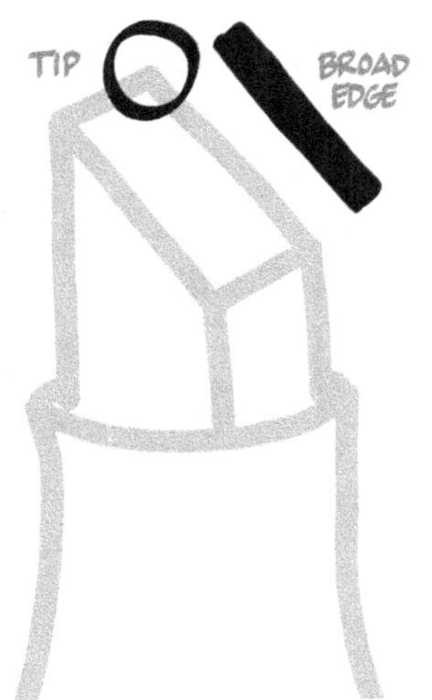



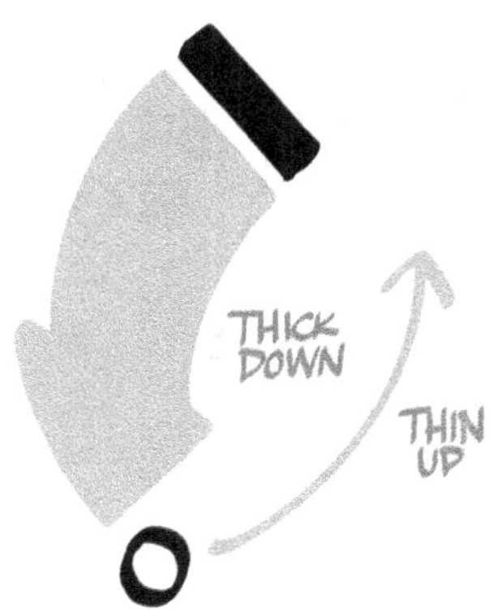



Like in brush lettering, most down strokes will be thick and most upstrokes and cross strokes will be thin. Once you know the stroke order and direction, with a "flip of the marker" the technique is easy to apply to script and print versions of this lettering style.

**Lettering style attributes:**
- Can be used with any tool that has a broad edge and a functional tip
- Serif style can be varied
- From fun/whimsical to formal
- Easily scaled
- Variations are endless!

**When to use:**
- Short titles for flip charts
- Short topics for large charts
- For emphasizing a word

I consider the use of thick and thin lines to make letters a technique because there are so many different styles you can create by using the broad edge and a corner of the tip of the nib. The trick is knowing where to put the thicks and thins and turning the marker to make the intended marks. Like with any new lettering style, start slow to get the form in your hand, then find ways to make this your own!

Like with *Brick* in the first chapter, take a few moments to refer to the exemplars on the following pages. They are based on *Roman Hand* and printed at 100% using a BigOne so that you can make a copy of the pages and trace the letterforms if you want. Once you get them down, be sure to have fun and adapt them to fit your style preferences.

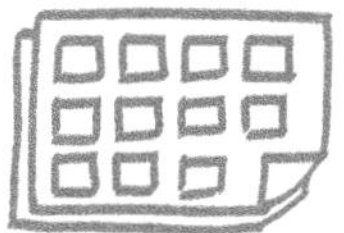

You can download a PDF template to help you learn the letterforms in the following pages.

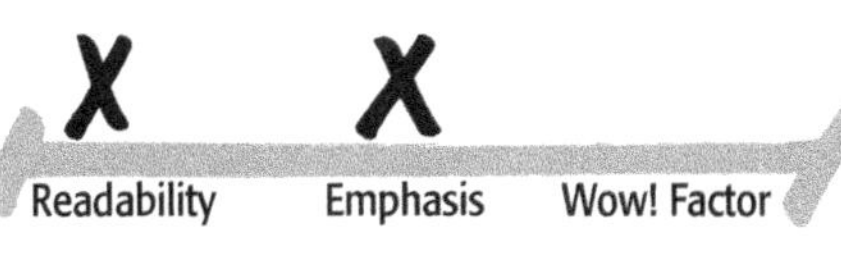



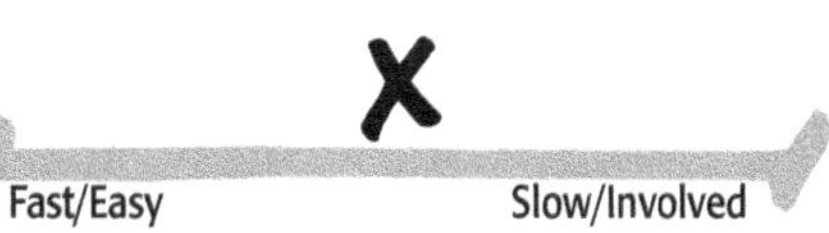



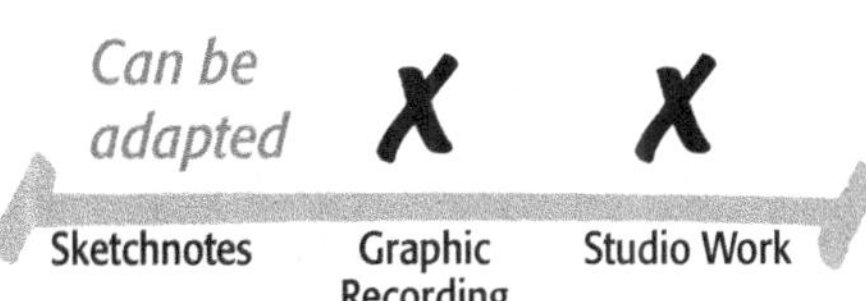

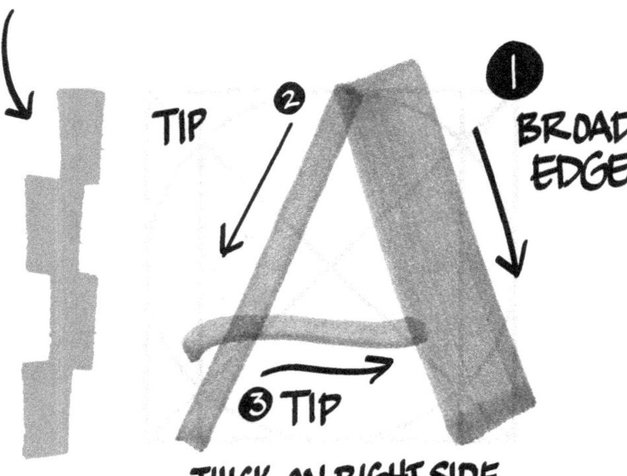


START BY MAKING
A 4-NIB-WIDTH SCALE

TIP

2

1
BROAD
EDGE

3 TIP

THICK ON RIGHT SIDE

FOLLOW THE INSIDE OF THE
CIRCLE FOR THE SMALLER
TOP COUNTER & THE
OUTSIDE OF THE CIRCLE FOR
THE LARGER
BOTTOM
COUNTER

2

1

3

REMEMBER:

"FAT-BOTTOMED
GIRLS, YOU MAKE
THE ROCKIN' WORLD
GO 'ROUND!"

- BRIAN MAY,
QUEEN


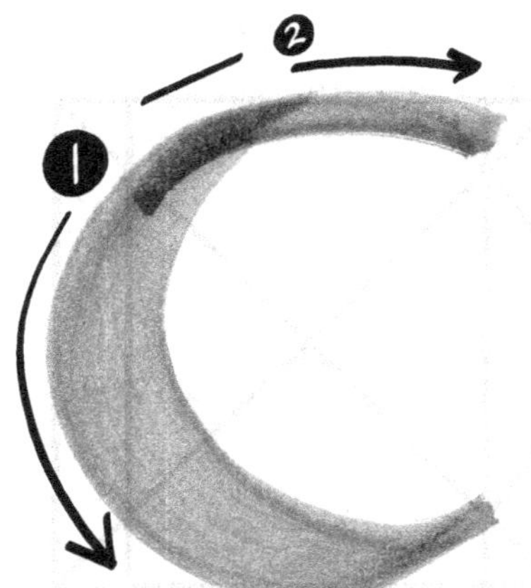

2

1

NOTE THE ANGLE OF
THE BROAD EDGE
STAYS THE SAME AS
YOU FOLLOW THE
CIRCLE


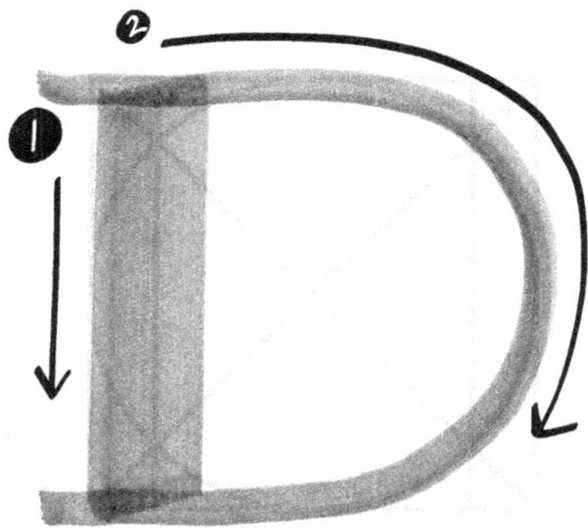

2

1

FOLLOW THE CIRCLE

See page 19 for an important note about stroke order and direction.

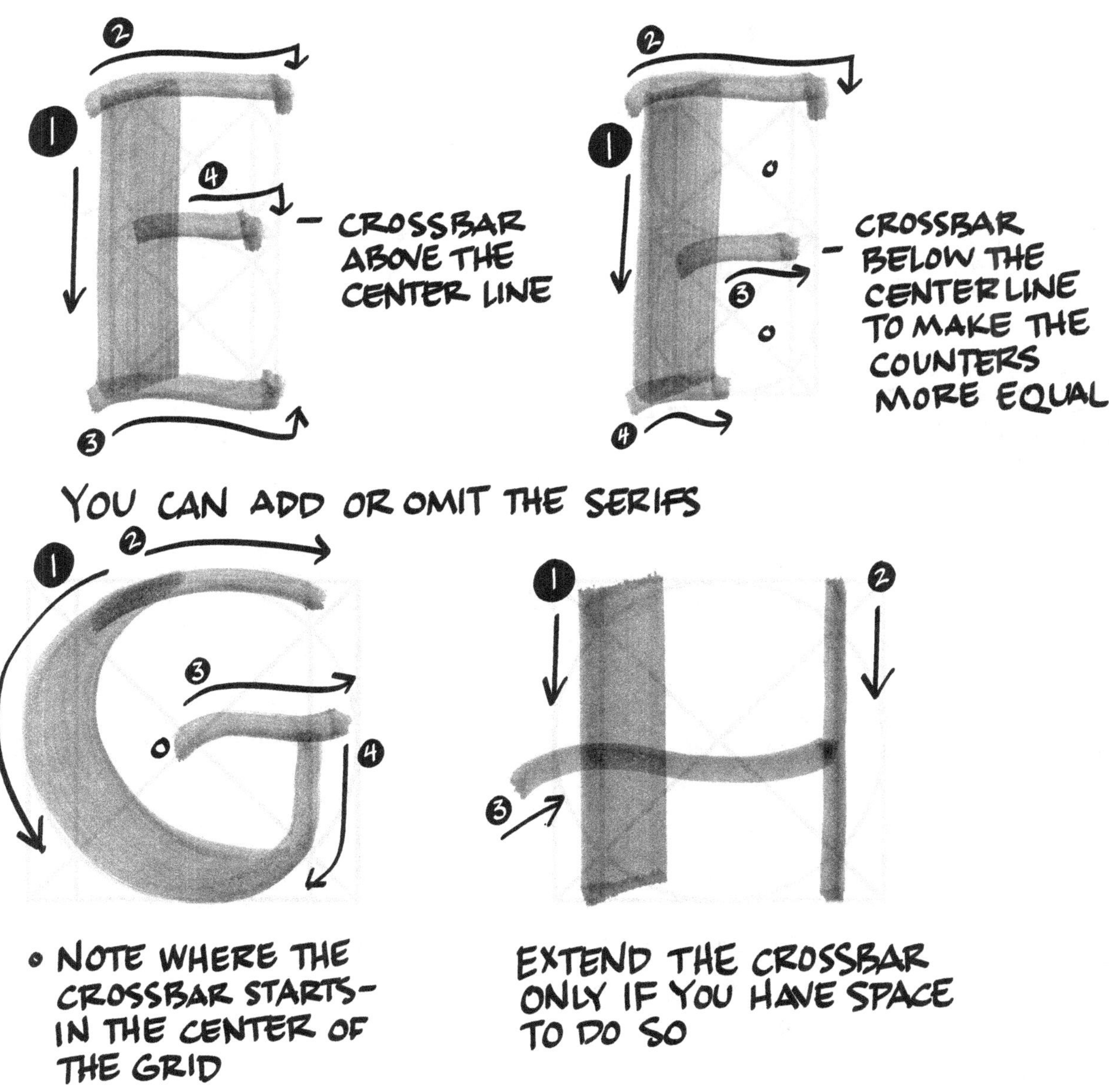



• NOTE WHERE THE CROSSBAR STARTS— IN THE CENTER OF THE GRID

EXTEND THE CROSSBAR ONLY IF YOU HAVE SPACE TO DO SO

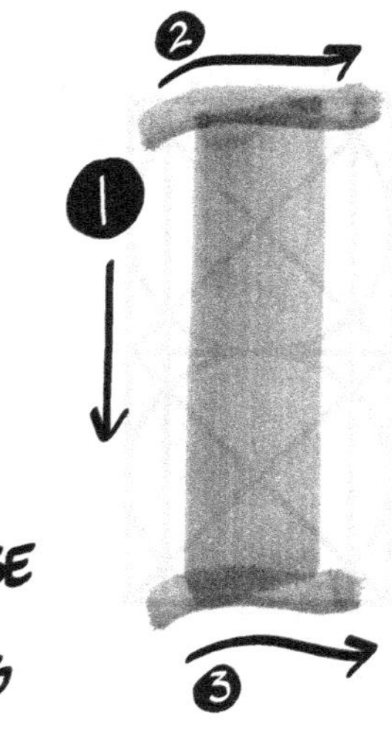

LETTERS CAN BE
SIMPLIFIED BY
NOT INCLUDING
SERIFS

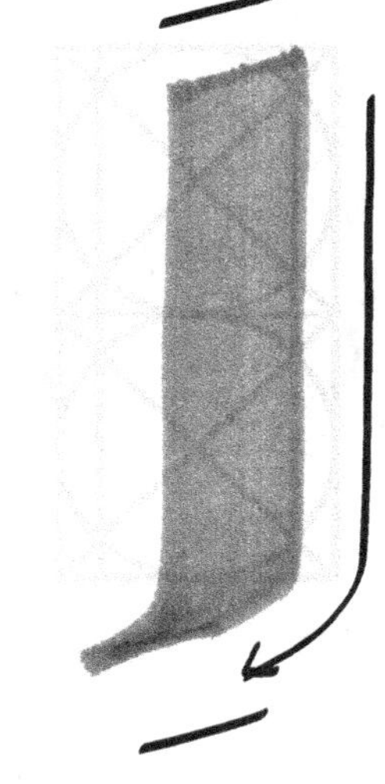

KEEP THE
SAME ANGLE
THROUGHOUT

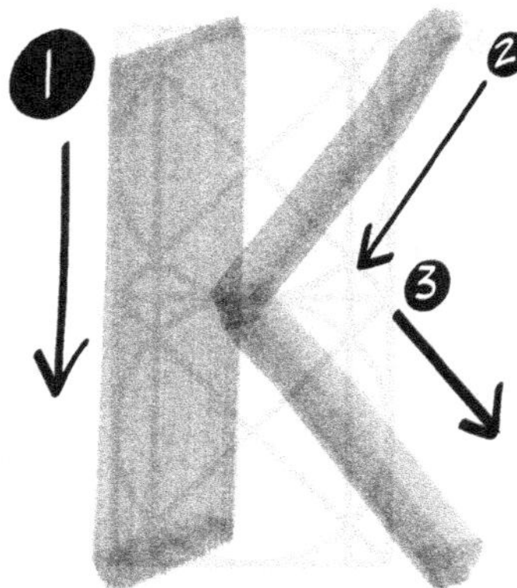

JUST "KISS" THE
STEM IN THE
MIDDLE

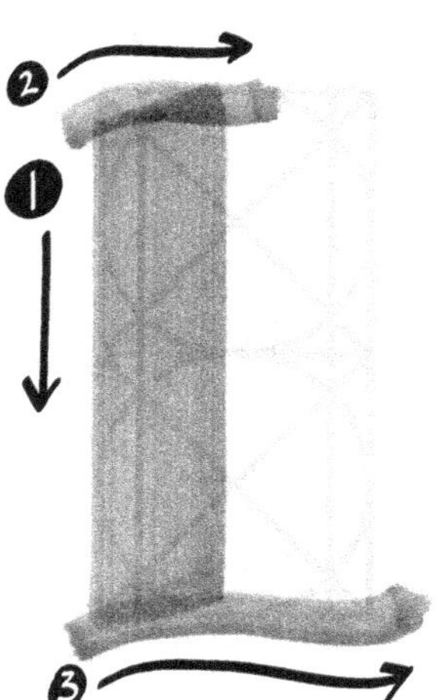

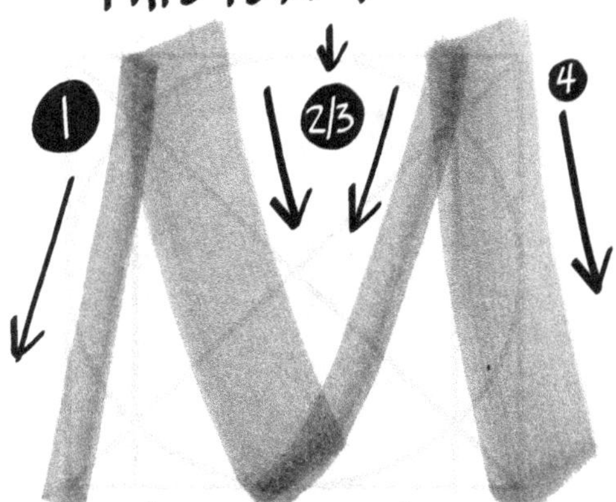

ALL DOWN STROKES
THIS IS A "V"
1
2/3
4
MAKE THESE SPACES EQUAL


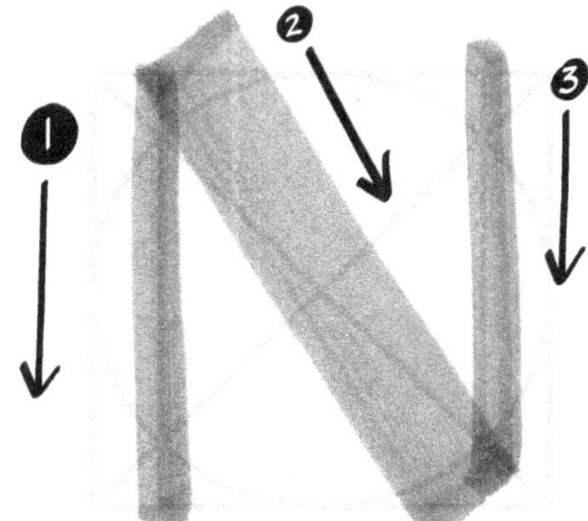

1
2
3
MAKE SURE YOUR STROKES MEET


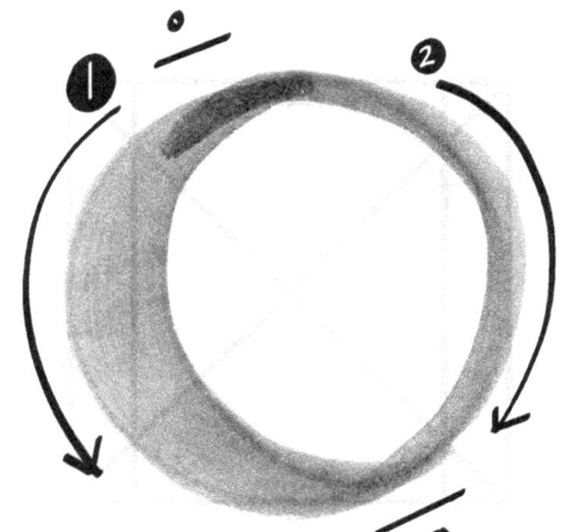

1
2
OVERLAP STROKES TO MAINTAIN A ROUND SHAPE, AVOID MAKING AN "EGG" O
LIKE THE "C", KEEP THE ANGLE OF THE BROAD STROKE CONSISTENT


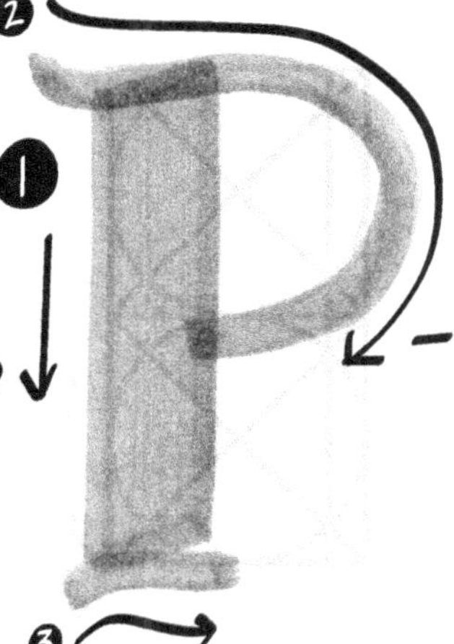

1
2
3
CONNECT THE JUNCTURE BELOW THE CENTER LINE, LIKE FOR THE "F"

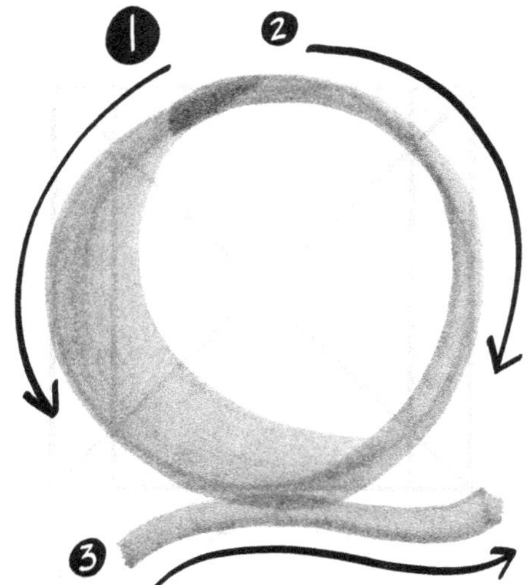

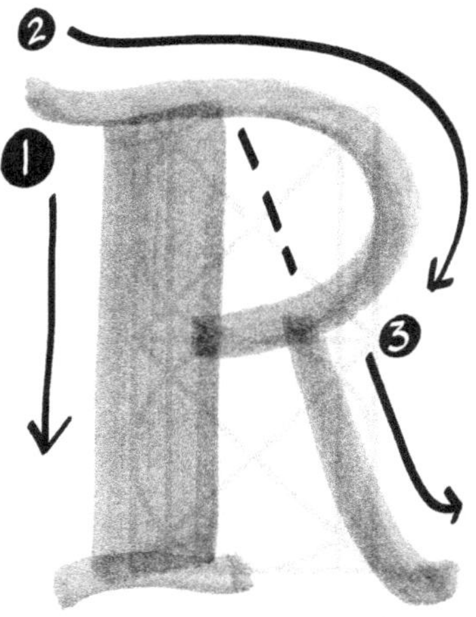

THE TAIL CAN BE VARIED—
HAVE FUN & EXPERIMENT!

DRAW AN IMAGINARY LINE
THROUGH THE COUNTER TO
START THE "LEG STROKE"

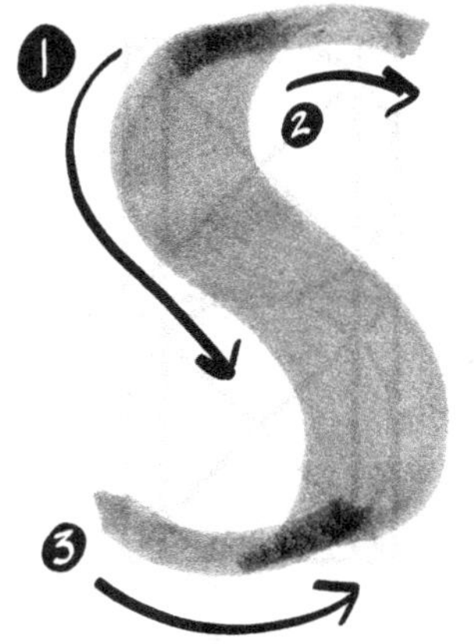

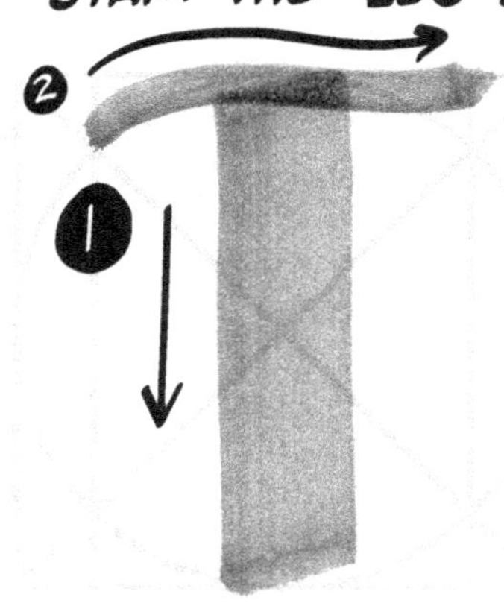

DRAW THE "SPINE"
FIRST!

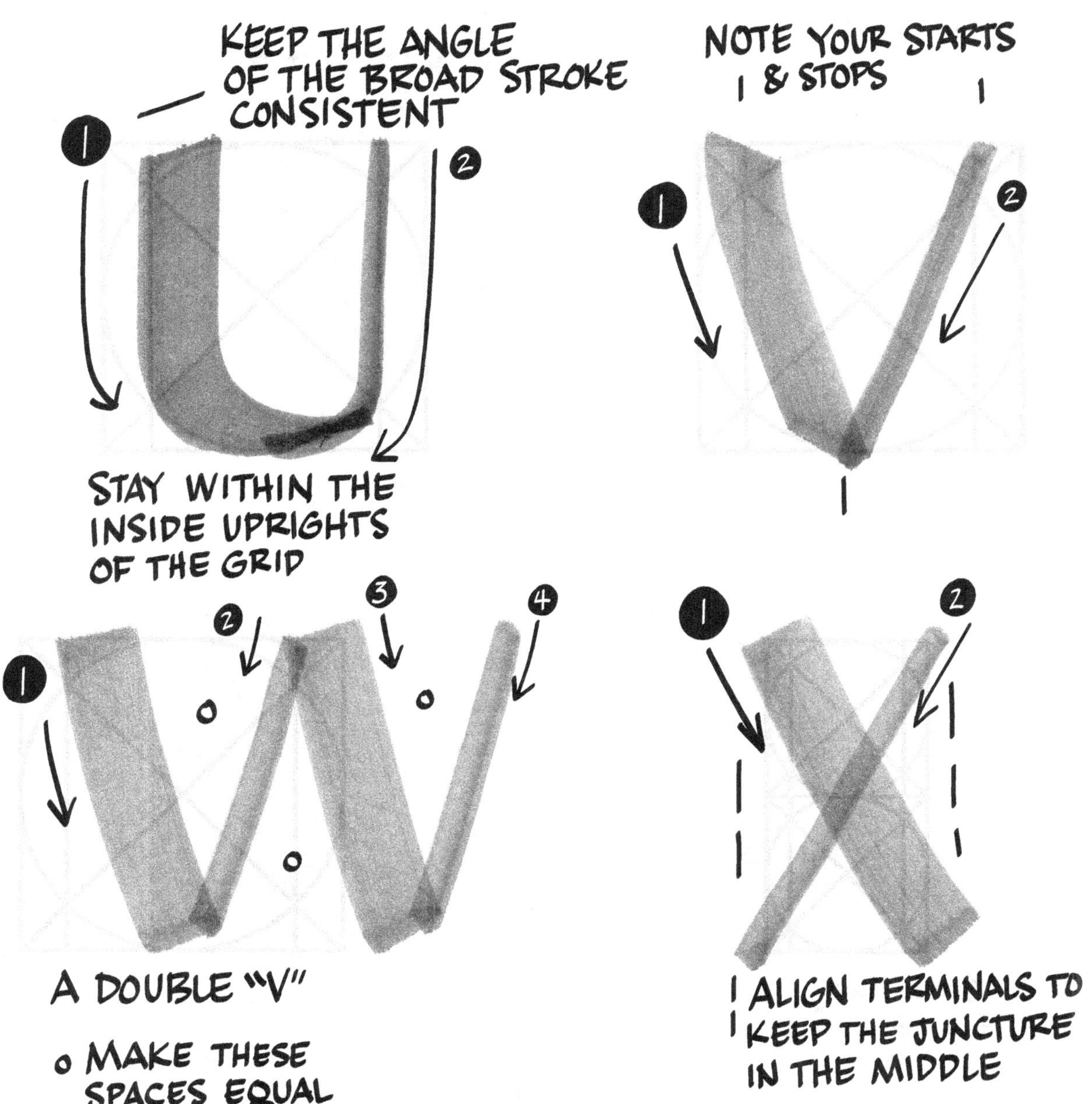


KEEP THE ANGLE OF THE BROAD STROKE CONSISTENT
NOTE YOUR STARTS & STOPS
STAY WITHIN THE INSIDE UPRIGHTS OF THE GRID
A DOUBLE "V"
o MAKE THESE SPACES EQUAL
ALIGN TERMINALS TO KEEP THE JUNCTURE IN THE MIDDLE

TRY DIFFERENT
VARIATIONS OF THE "Y"

YOU CAN START WITH THE
TOP HORIZONTAL OR THE
DIAGONAL STROKE —

IT'S UP
TO YOU!

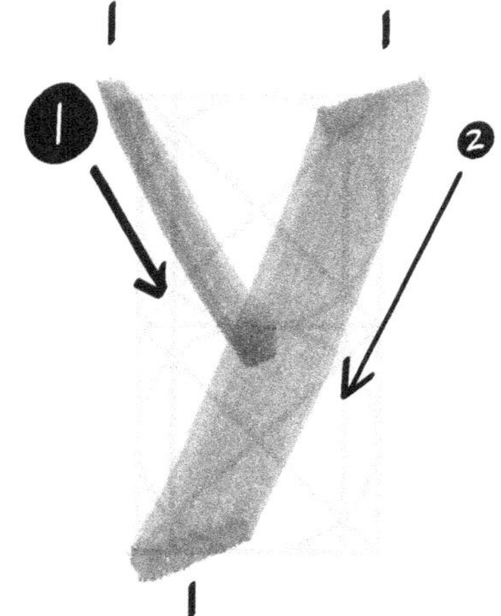

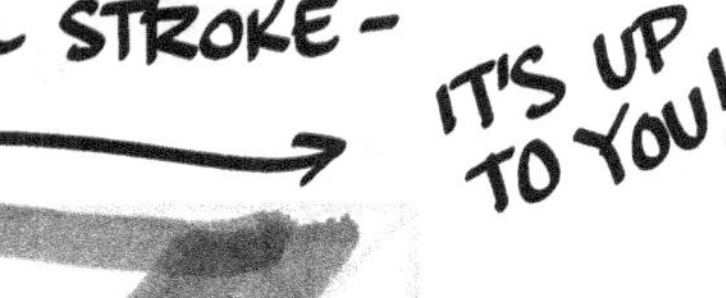

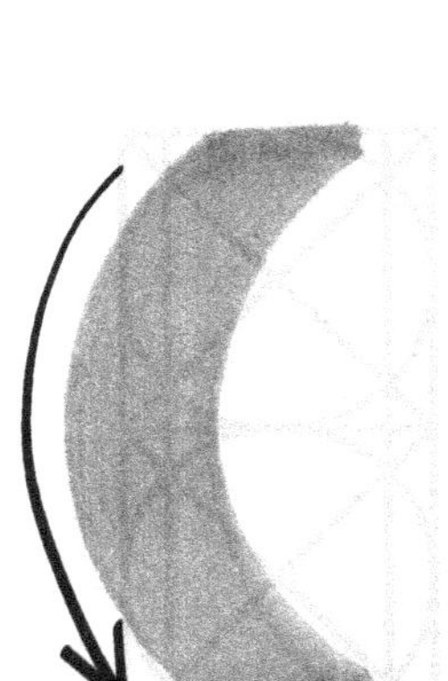

THINK ABOUT CREATING
THE COUNTER/NEGATIVE
SPACE WHEN DRAWING
CURVES

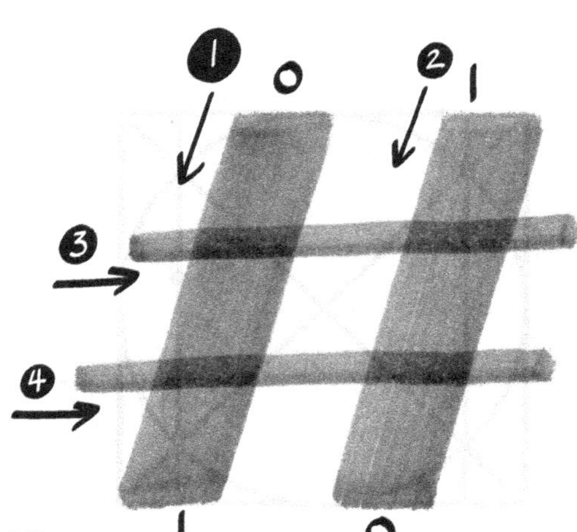

NOTE WHERE THE
LINES LIE ON THE
GRID & START/STOP

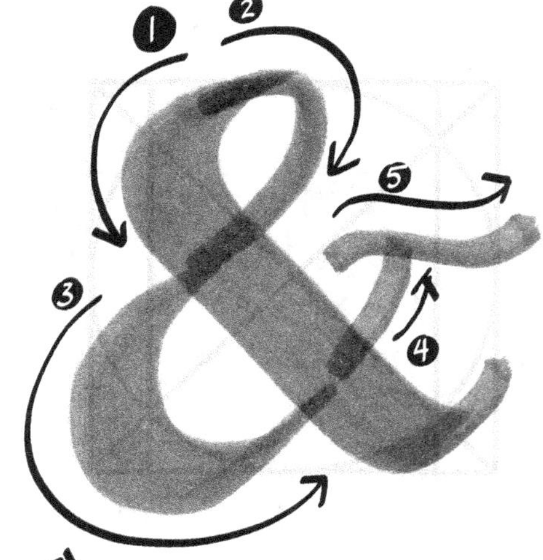

YEP!

THAT'S 5 STROKES FOLKS!
AND TOTALLY WORTH IT!

NOTE THE ANGLE OF THE NIB
KEEP CONSISTENT THROUGHOUT


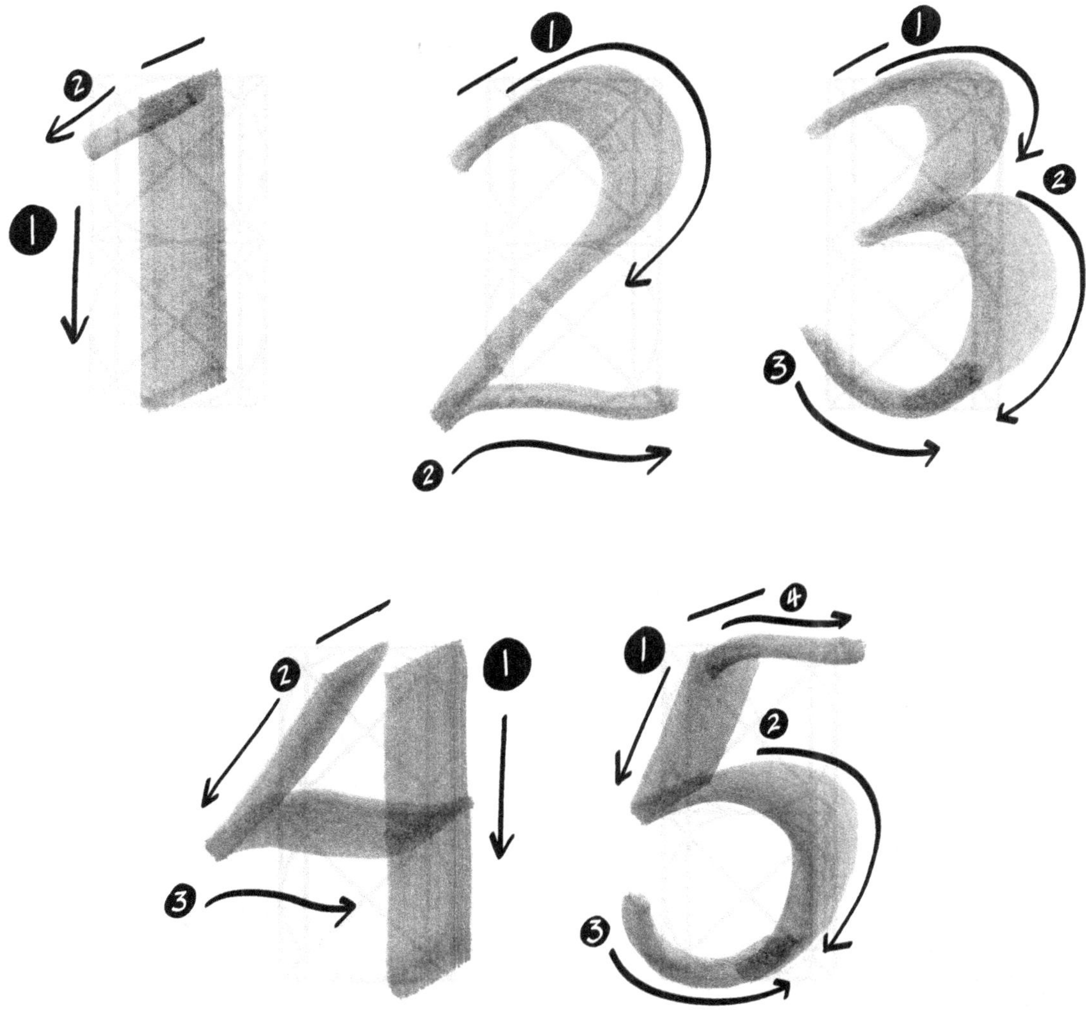

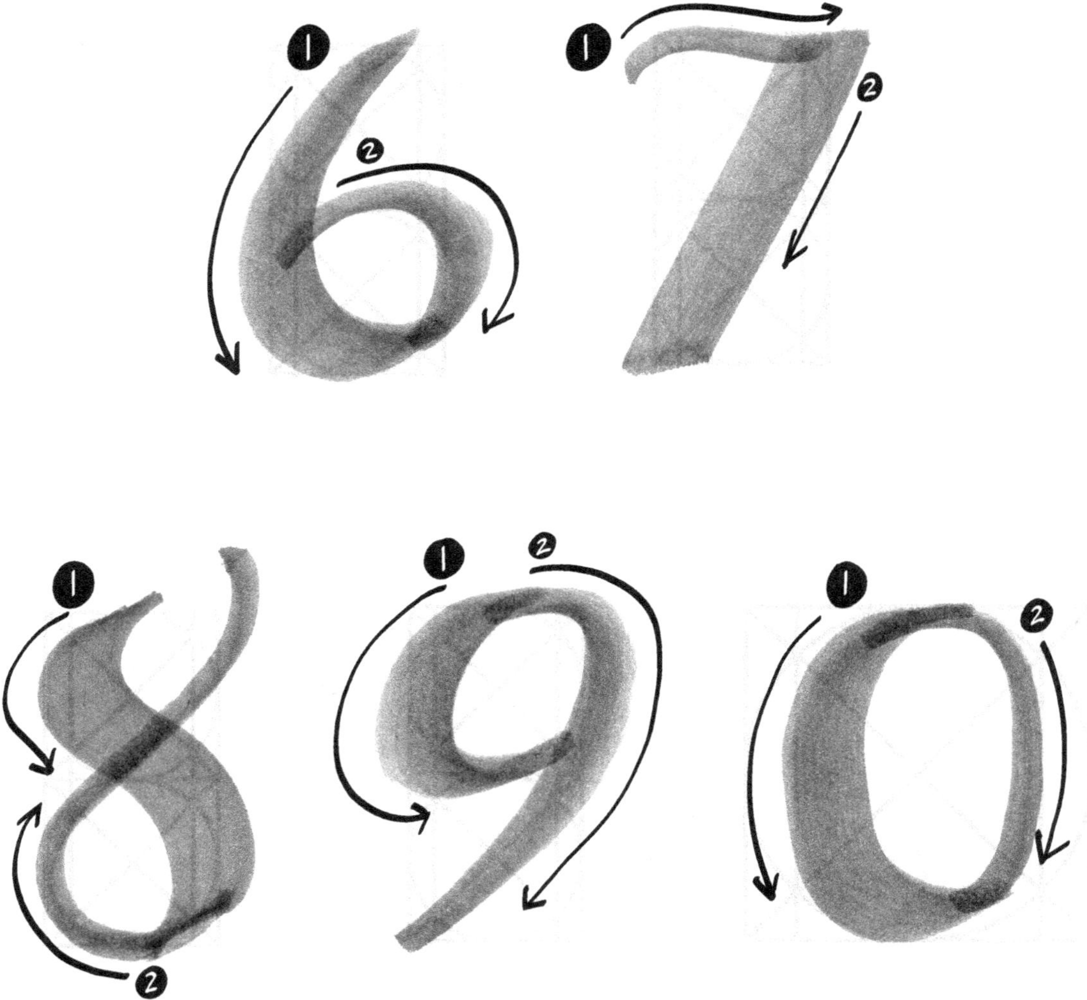

# VARIATIONS

abcdefghijk
lmnopqrst
uvwxy&z

*Thick-and-Thin script* written with a No.One wedge nib.
While not practical at this size for rapid capture, this
script has its applications in beauty and can be scaled
up in size using a BigOne or FatOne.

I taught this lettering style as part of Sandra
Dirks' Winter Session. The video and practice
sheets are available on her YouTube channel.

# VARIATIONS

A A B B C D E E
F F G H H I i i j K
L M N O P R R S
T U V W X Y Z

Thick-and-thin style inspired by Ben Shahn's letters, which are frequently found on his iconic protest posters. Note that you have the freedom to vary it as you wish!

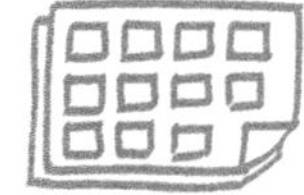

ABCDEFGHIJKL
MNOPQRSTUVW
XYZ & ALT FILLS
& SERIFS

abcdefghijk lmno
pqrrsstuvwxyz

Hand-drawn version with a mono line. Great for chalkboards and other uses
where faux calligraphy is warranted.

# LETTERING EXAMPLES

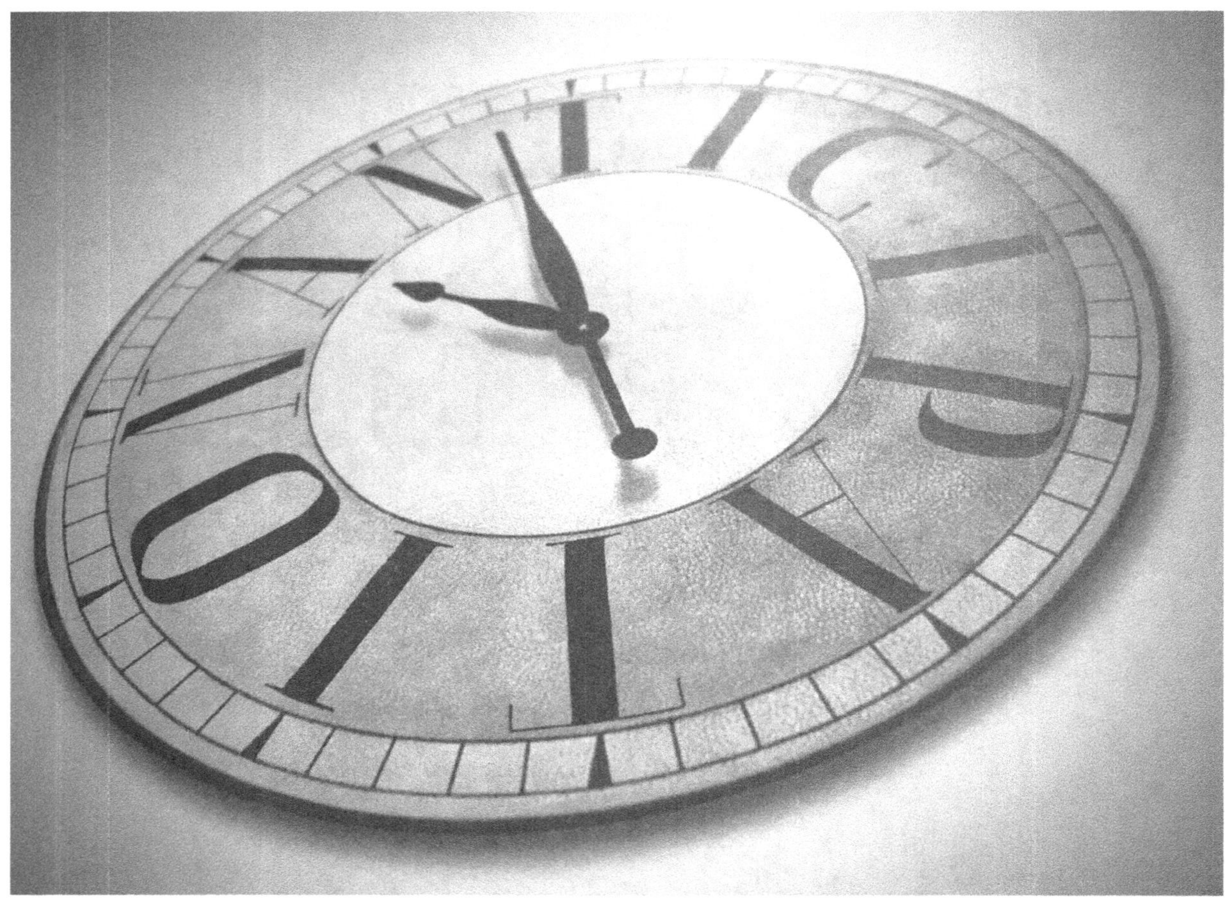



*pictured above*

With much anticipation and inspired by a weekly creative prompt by the same name, I participate in a secret Facebook group of calligraphers called "Scribbled Lives." Each week, a different member posts a prompt and we respond with a piece of art. My submissions often take many forms. Some are traditional ink-on-paper calligraphy, while this one was mixed media.

First, I drew out the letters with a Pilot Parallel pen and scanned them into the computer. Then I took a stock photography photo of a clock face and removed the numbers. I superimposed the twelve letters into place: A N T I C I P A T I O N.

Finally, I printed out the graphic I had created and took a picture of it at an angle to give it a forced perspective.

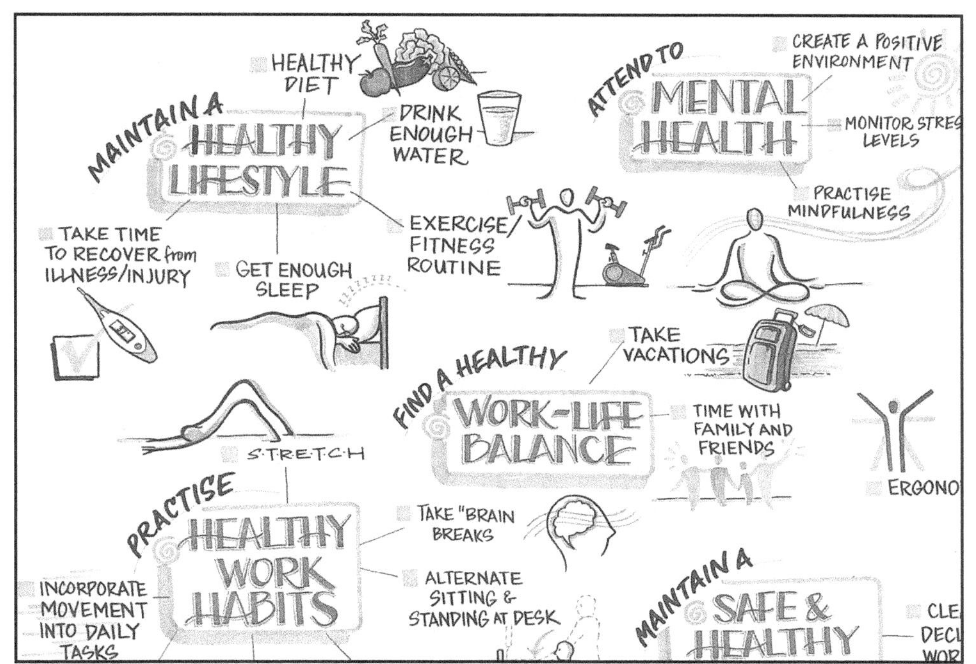



*detail pictured left*

**Avril Orloff,** from Vancouver, BC, Canada, used *Clock Face* in this chart to write in Scan or topic level size. She also added a drop line to the left, framed it with a container, and balanced it with drawings. She maintains a clear hierarchy with her lettering and creative use of colour to help the reader distinguish top-level topics from supporting text and to aid the flow of the content. Notice how her Read/ content is written in *Sign Painter* and *Architect* lettering styles. She often adds text on an angle or a curve to break the horizontal pattern of the page.

*pictured right*

**Sandra Dirks,** from Braunschweig, Germany, has a YouTube channel where she shares flip chart tips and tricks. Every year, she invites artists from around the world to letter and draw as part of her holiday series. This is what she created from the session we had together using *Thick-and-Thin script*. Here, she used Neuland's metallic markers to adorn a black box to serve as a holiday decoration.

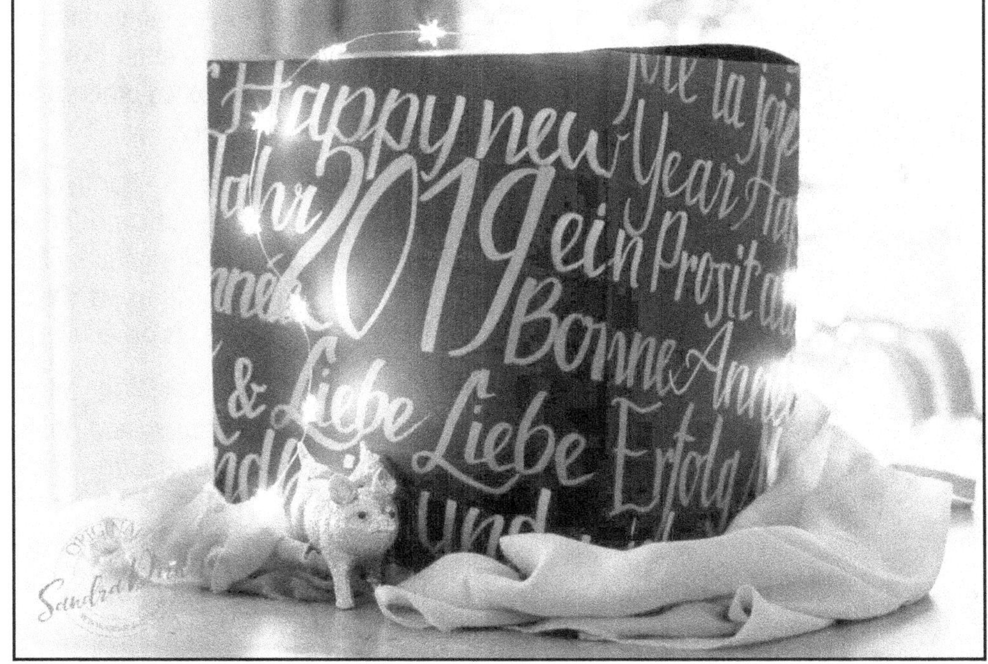





Clock Face | Lettering Journey

# ARCHITECT

**A fast lettering style to learn and use that can be scaled to any size.**

I was deep into my art-making processes in Albany, New York, when Ray bought me the book *Lettering for Architects and Designers,* by Martha Sutherland. It felt like the book was the "missing link" from the handout *How to Write Like an Architect,* which I created for a breakout session I offered at the International Forum of Visual Practitioners DC Conference in 2016.

I didn't crack the book until we got to British Columbia, Canada, where I started to build my lettering website and designed the *Unlock Your Neuland Markers* online course. I was considering the types of lettering styles that would work for rapid capture of content while graphic recording. I started studying the letterforms in the book and loved that there were many different variations. I immediately felt confident that I could letter like an architect even if I wasn't one. And I felt that if I could teach others, they could use it in their work and make it a style of their own.

It was the Price Tower in Bartlesville, Oklahoma, that inspired me pick up my pencil again and consider the letterform. This is the only fully-realized skyscraper designed by Frank Lloyd Wright. We took a tour of the building and museum, where I had the opportunity to see Wright's lettering in a few of his original architectural drawings of the building.

In the fall of 2017, I taught the lettering style in the online *Level Up Your Lettering* course and redesigned the templates to include sketchnoters and bullet journalists as well as graphic recorders and those working on flip charts. In January of 2018 I launched the online course.

This lettering style works well at any size given you are using the right tool to keep it in proportion. And because it's easy to learn, it's great for those who want to use it to tandem record, too.

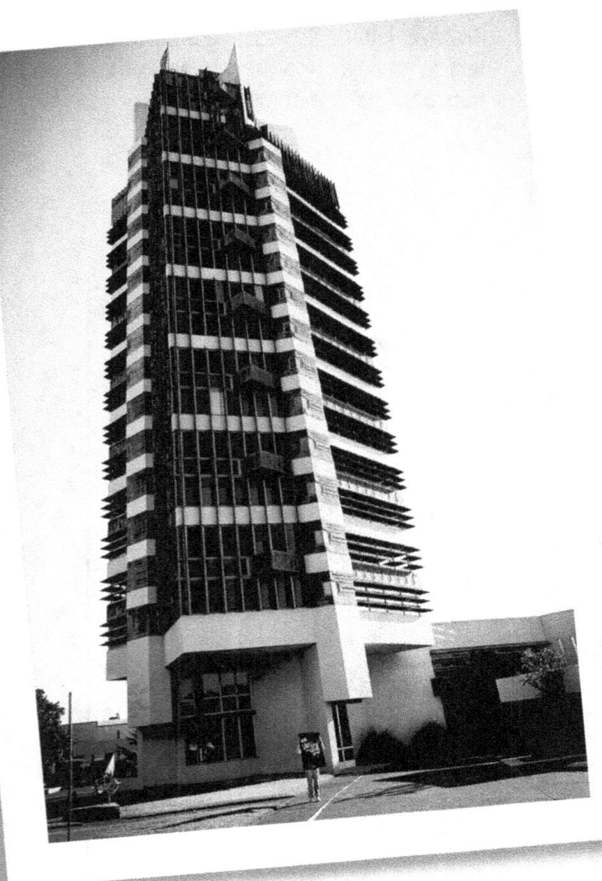

Price Tower
Bartlesville, Oklahoma

# ATTRIBUTES



ALL MAJUSCULE LETTERS ARE APPROXIMATELY SQUARE EXCEPT "I"

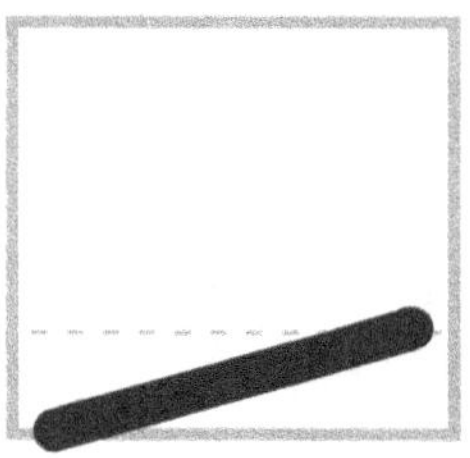  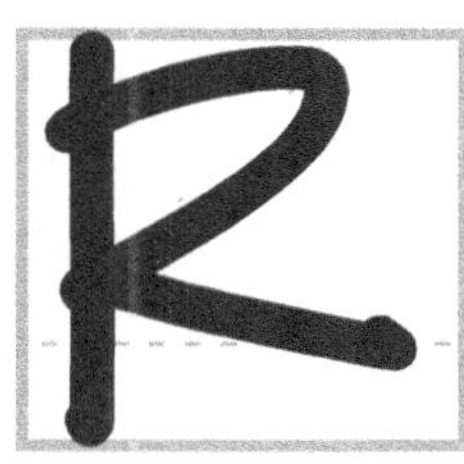 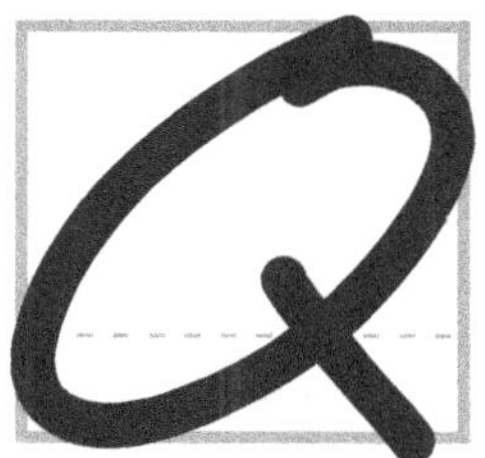

Excerpt from the 6-page PDF download, part of the *How to Write like an Architect* online course.

## Are you an architect?

Well, you don't have to be in order to write like one!

I love writing like an architect because it makes me feel planful and design savvy. While architect students take entire semesters just on lettering, I learned the basics by watching videos and studying hand-drawn blueprints.

## Lettering style attributes:

- Based on the square
- Crossbars are slanted up and to the right
- Round letters are based on a tilted oval
- Second stems and legs are higher than the baseline

**WARNING:** This letterform is close to handwriting. It's actually dangerous to copy someone else's handwriting so please find your unique hand in this. Also, I have found that I have far too much information to share than can be shared in this book. I'm sharing the attributes to offer some guidance and some examples to inspire you. For more information, you can download templates that accompany the videos in *How to Write Like an Architect* available at www.LetsLetterTogether.com.

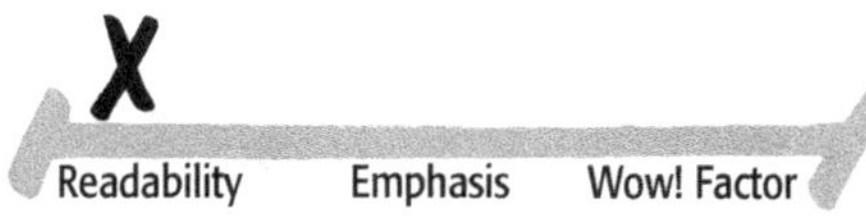

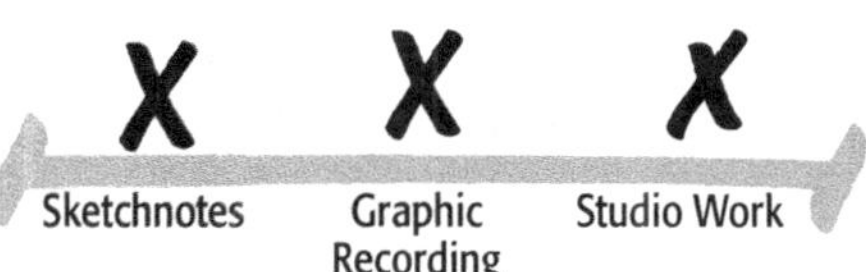




Architect | Lettering Journey

# LETTERING EXAMPLES

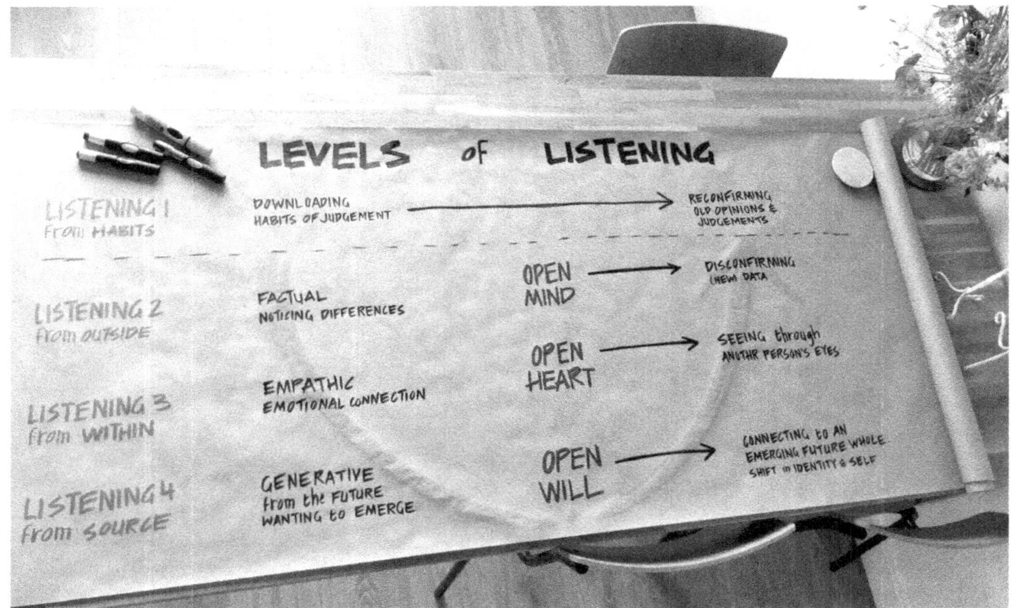



*pictured left*

**Tamar Harel** is a freelance visual facilitator who collaborates with purpose-driven individuals and organizations. Here, she writes in *Architect* on kraft paper. This poster, which is inspired by the work of Otto Scharmer and Kelvy Bird, was commisioned by Except Integrated Sustainability for their five-day journey with leaders in nature conservation and preservation in South Africa.

*pictured right*

**Amy Sparks**, a graphic recorder from Minneapolis, Minnesota, had an opportunity to graphic record a thesis presentation in under three minutes. She spent time practicing *Architect* in advance so she could capture it as well as possible given the time constraints. She used Procreate on her iPad to create this graphic.

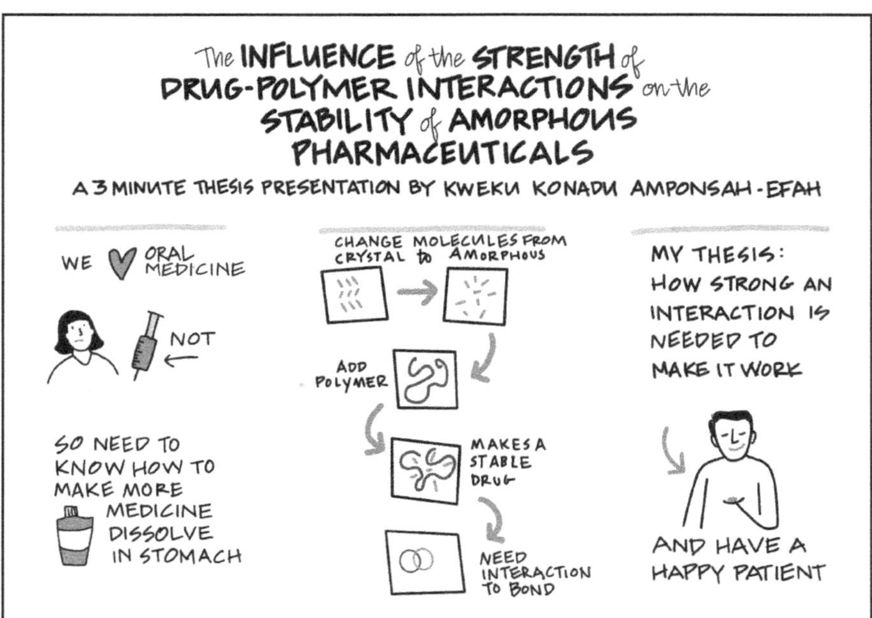

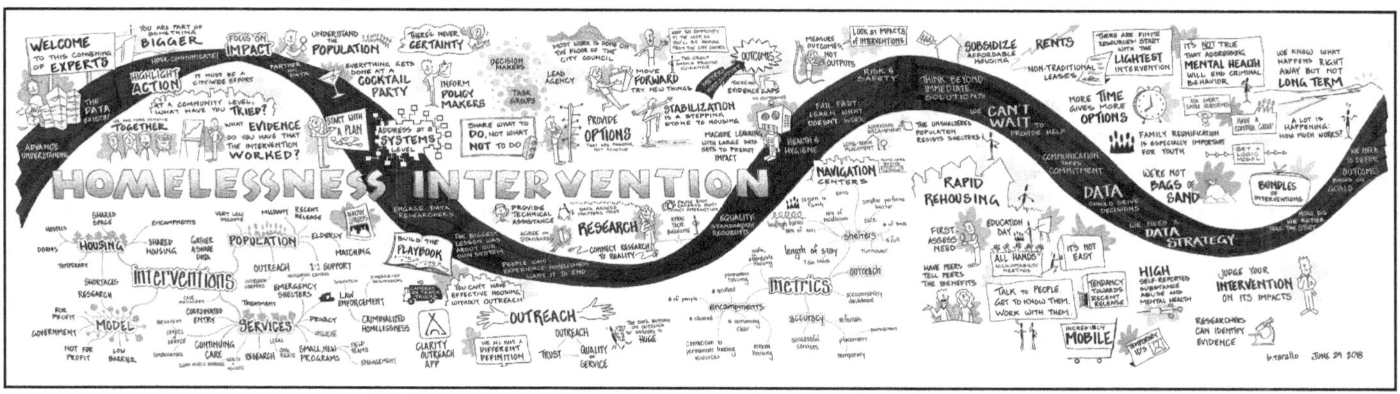



*pictured above*

**Brian Tarallo** of Herndon, Virginia

"This chart was the result of a day-long facilitated event with a very open agenda. Below the black line, I mindmapped two brainstorming sessions, one on the nature of homelessness interventions, the other on success metrics. Above the black line, I captured highlights from a series of breakout sessions and plenary discussions. Inside the black line, I captured key learnings and themes. The chart captured content from right to left as the day progressed. Given the loose agenda, I wasn't sure I'd have any reset time, so I used only one chart to harvest content. I chose to use architect's hand for most of the text because it's fast, clear and shows up well with various marker nibs. Text was written in real time as participants reported after their breakouts; the little illustration there was drawn during the breakouts. The day also went long, by nearly three hours! I spliced in more paper just to the right of the metrics mindmap.

For this chart, I drew inspiration from Kelvy Bird and the way she draws flows and connections, Nevada Lane and the way she draws figures and color splashes, and Heather Martinez for her lettering and color theory."

You have been making marks since before you started making memories. But are your letterforms correct? Legible? Stylistic? Do you feel confident about writing every letter? Changing the way to write is akin to changing how you breathe. It takes conscious effort and you will see the results each time you practice with intention. I often tell people not to practice a letter more than three times in a row if you aren't getting it. Build good muscle memory by having a keen eye for form and command over your hand coordination. Take advantage of the feedback you are receiving and apply that to your learning loops.

### Know your letterforms

While most of the lettering styles in this book are inspired by environment and some are merely techniques, most all lettering styles have a lineage or bear a resemblance to other scripts such as *Roman Hand* or italic. By studying these and treating them as "skeletal" forms, we can be designers of the letters we create. Paying homage to the masters who came before us by studying and practicing their techniques will improve our muscle memory and give us the ability to learn many styles (like learning multiple languages), which in turn will help us grow our "lettering library."

### Know your tools

Use the right tool for the job and know what kind of marks it makes.

Let bigger markers do the heavy lifting when writing larger letters for chart titles. Use a nib width scale to scale your letterforms appropriately for their intended use.

Nearly every lettering style used in calligraphy and sign painting can be translated into the markers we use. Look for clues and attributes about the lettering style and what type of tool it took to create it: broad edge, brush, or round nib.

### Have command over your tools

Establishing command and control will help you build confidence in your writing. You can increase your marker manipulation skills by

- learning pressure techniques by practicing brush lettering,
- understanding when to keep a constant angle, as used in italic versus changing the angle to keep a consistent broad edge width, as found in *Neuland Hand*, or
- twisting the marker as you work to create a "waist" on long strokes or to finish off a terminal in a unique way.

### Test your tools

Notice what kind of marks each tool naturally makes and experiment with what else it can do. Can you use a wedge nib to create a thick/thin style like in brush lettering? Can you use the broad edge of the brush to create *Neuland Hand*?

Writing in grey ink makes assessing your progress easier as it helps you see how your strokes cross or come together.

### Want to write in a straight line?

Lined practice sheets are a great way to build the muscle memory necessary for good lettering. You can create your own with baselines or purchase pre-lined practice sheets. Neuland carries the Hand Lettering Learning Pad in both flip chart and A4 sizes.

### Finding your own style...

I often get asked, "If many visual practitioners take your courses or use your lettering styles, what will differentiate us?" My response: "Your hands! And your creative minds!" Each person's hands are different. Our handwriting is unique to us, so even if you try to letter like me or someone else, you won't! We all have different types of marks that we each make and various skills levels, so we will each have unique lettering. While we may practice similar forms, when we introduce rhythm, our true styles will emerge.

Now leverage that one-of-a-kind ability of yours and find your style!

> "Hope is not an action plan,
> critical practice is."
>
> – Carol DuBosch

When I heard Carol say this in a workshop I was taking from her in 2016, my ears perked up. As a visual practitioner, action plans are a big part of my work and likely of yours, too. What do we know about the execution of them? It takes critical means to make them happen. Setting your intentions to improve is important.

### Set goals

What do you want to accomplish in your practice session? Write it down on your actual practice page or on a sticky note and attach it afterward. Make sure it's measurable and attainable in the time you are allotting. This will help you focus and give you the criteria for success.

### Appreciative Inquiry approach

I don't believe in looking at problems and solving them. That is an antiquated paradigm that I simply don't subscribe to. I look for what works and gives us vitality. I base my aspirations on my strengths and what I'm passionate about and hope that you will too. To apply that to lettering, reflect on the letters on your practice page and choose the ones you like. Notice what attributes those letters have and use them to improve similar letters. For example, if your "n" looks good, apply what works to your m, h, u and y. If you like your "o," use it as a model as you practice your a, c, d, e, g and q.

### Challenge letters

If you insist on putting energy into what's not working, do yourself a favor and really look at the forms you are wanting to emulate and write the challenge letters alternately between vowels. For example, if you want to work on your b, g, s, r and v, write them in this order: abegisoruv. After doing this a few times, write a pangram so you can see how the letters look in relation to other letters.

### The most common letters in the English language

When all else fails, at least master the most common letters.
They are ETAOIN (eh-tay-oh-in) SHRDLU (shird-loo)
What are the most common letters from the Latin alphabet in your language?

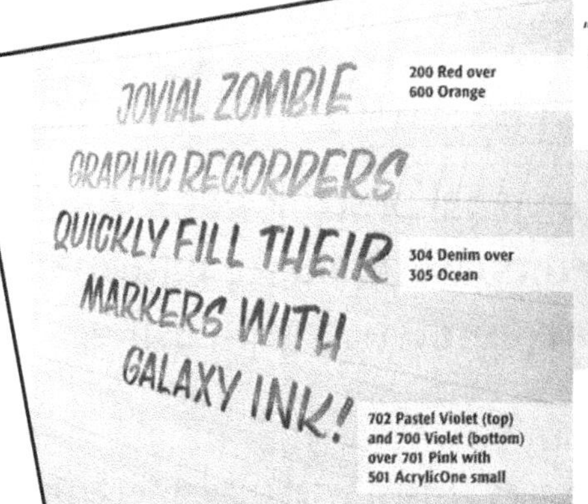


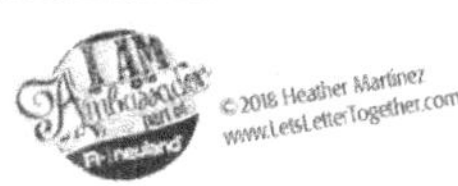

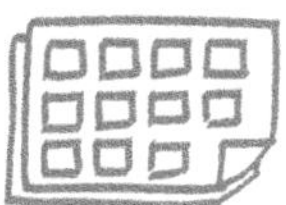

A pangram is a sentence that contains every letter of an alphabet. Practicing them allows us to write letters in relationship to one another to improve form and spacing. You can download this PDF at www.LetsLetterTogether.com.

# HIERARCHY

As a visual practitioner, creating a formula for hierarchy will allow you to compartmentalize information, making your charts easier to read, more aesthetically pleasing, and more decipherable for the viewer.

Now that you've learned seven new lettering styles to use for titles, what about the rest of the page?

Just as you would practice drawing to build your icon library, create a What-you-see-is-what-you-get (WYSIWYG) hierarchy chart using the lettering styles you have learned here or brought with you from other sources. It's great practice and it helps build the muscle memory of creating different styles at different sizes when recording live. Using all of the markers you have and working at the size you normally work (flip chart, sketchbook, or full-size wall chart), divide your chart into four sections:

- Glance (for titles)
- Scan (for topics)
- Read (for main content)
- Study (for details and "fine print")

**Pro-tip:** Reserve about half of your chart for Glance, about 1/4 of it for Scan and split the remaining 1/4 between Read and Study.

Notice that some lettering styles are slow and deliberate while others are faster. Ask yourself "How many of these lettering styles can I write smaller and faster? Can I use them for emphasis within my content?" And always remember to use the right tool for the job. For example, use a bigger marker for bigger letters and a wedge nib to get all thicks or a mix of thick and thin strokes.

Creating your own formula/system will help you manage your lettering styles and size while working with color on the fly!

**How many lettering styles should be used in one chart?**
With a background in graphic design, I say keep the variety of styles to a minimum. But many people like variety and want to show it off. So, try it out and see what approach works for you. If you feel two lettering styles is too limiting, then add some variations to your existing lettering styles: Bold, oblique and x-height variations are all fast ways to write and show emphasis using the lettering styles you are currently working in without slowing you down.

**What lettering styles look good together?**
I like to pair the following styles:

*Neuland Hand* and *Architect* are my absolute favorites and what I use most frequently.

Other good pairings: *Marquee* and *Sign Painter, Brick* and any mono line, or *National Parks* and *Architect*.

Sometimes I start with all the same style and use variations, size and color to show variety and create emphasis. *Neuland Hand* has more variations than one can count: bold, compressed, extended, light, thick/thin, etc. *Architect* and *Sign Painter* are two that I highly recommend for rapid capture. They are great for improving legibility and are fast. They can also be scaled up and down to give you hierarchy. Any lettering style can be scaled, just remember to use the nib scale or attributes when scaling. Keep in mind, however, that some lettering styles aren't fast when scaled down, so don't expect to be able to write fast in *Neuland Hand* or *Clock Face*. They weren't designed to be fast.

# LETTERING EXAMPLES

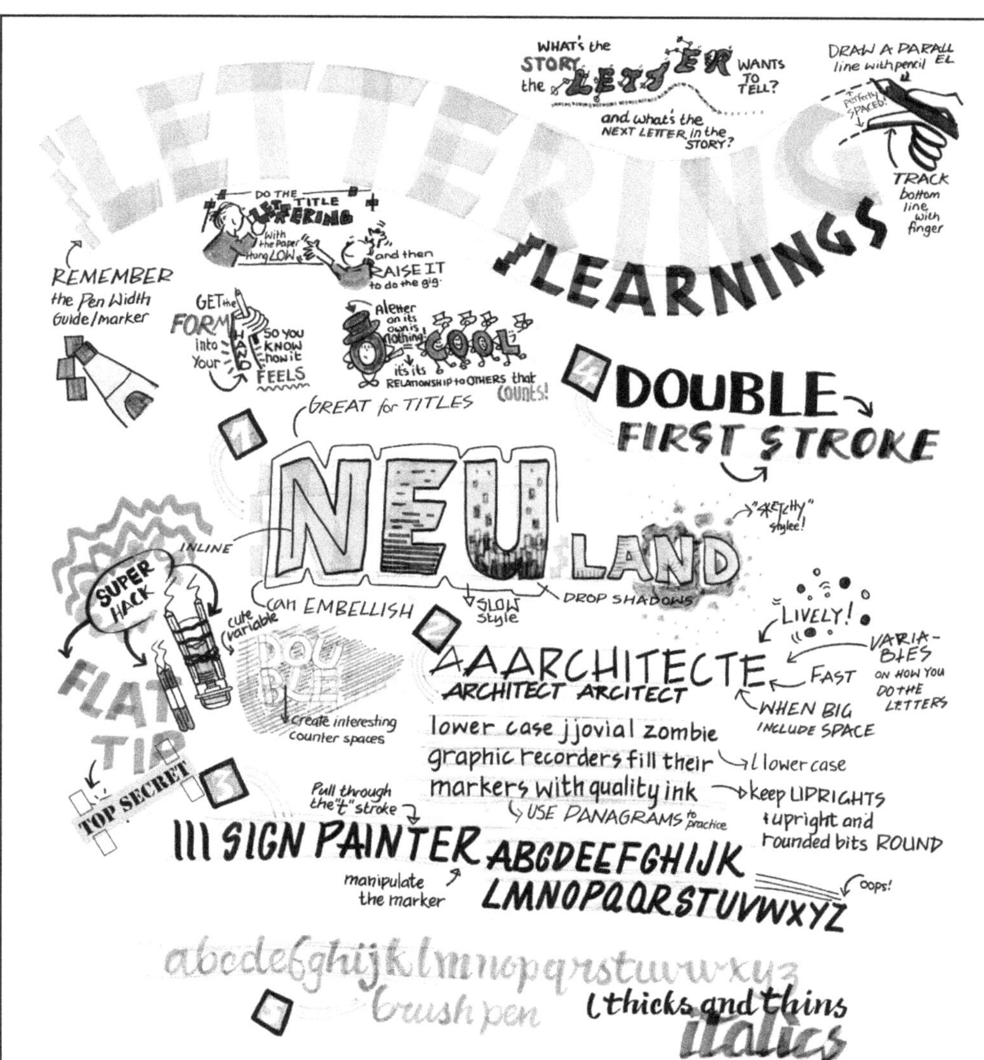


As part of the *Level Up Your Lettering* in-person workshops and online course, participants are encouraged to create a WYSIWYG chart to help them see the lettering styles they have within them. It serves as a lettering library they can refer to and is an excellent way to practice and begin to find their own style as they formulate how to use lettering hierarchy.

**Caroline Chapple**, a UK Graphic Recorder, took note of the different styles she'd learned in one of my workshops, along with some tips I'd shared, and created this lettering hierarchy chart. She then practiced the styles at home to further embed her learning. I recommend making a new chart at least once a year to refresh your library of available lettering styles. It's great practice and can inspire your next project.

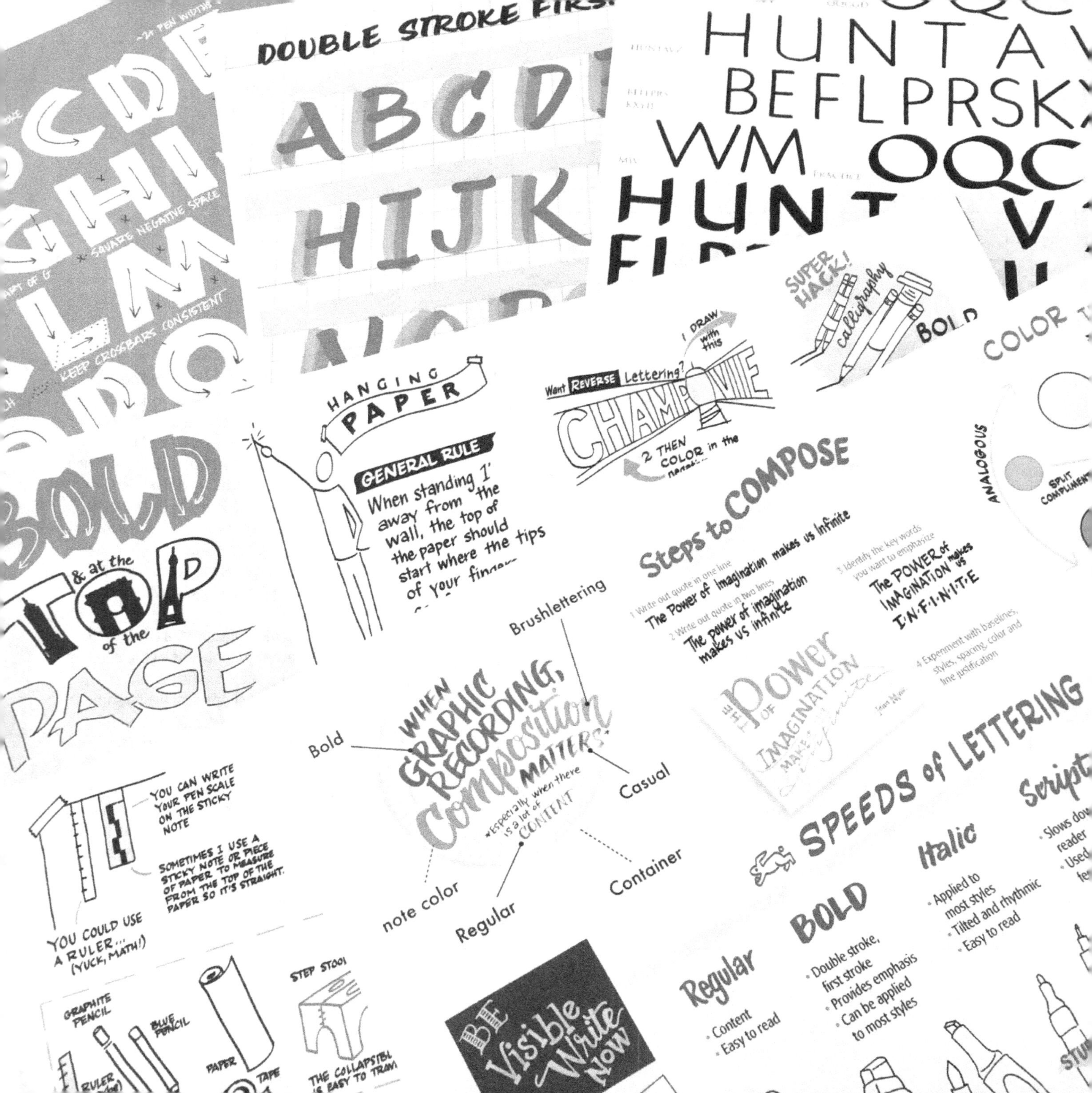
DOUBLE STROKE FIRST
ABCD
HIJK
KEEP CROSSBARS CONSISTENT
SQUARE NEGATIVE SPACE
~24 PEN WIDTHS
HUNTAV
BEFLPRSKX
WM
OQC
HUN
FIRS
SUPER HACK!
calligraphy
BOLD
COLOR
BOLD
& at the TOP of the
PAGE
HANGING PAPER
GENERAL RULE
When standing 1' away from the wall, the top of the paper should start where the tips of your finger
Want REVERSE Lettering?
CHAMPAGNE
I DRAW with this
2 THEN COLOR in the negative
Steps to COMPOSE
1 Write out quote in one line
The Power of Imagination makes us Infinite
2 Write out quote in two lines
The power of imagination makes us infinite
3 Identify the key words you want to emphasize
The POWER of IMAGINATION makes us I·N·F·I·N·I·T·E
4 Experiment with baselines, styles, spacing, color and line justification
the Power OF IMAGINATION MAKES
ANALOGOUS
SPLIT COMPLIMENT
YOU CAN WRITE YOUR PEN SCALE ON THE STICKY NOTE
SOMETIMES I USE A STICKY NOTE OR PIECE OF PAPER TO MEASURE FROM THE TOP OF THE PAPER SO IT'S STRAIGHT.
YOU COULD USE A RULER... (YUCK, MATH!)
WHEN GRAPHIC RECORDING, COMPOSITION MATTERS!
*Especially when there is a lot of CONTENT
Brushlettering
Bold
note color
Regular
Casual
Container
SPEEDS of LETTERING
Script
Italic
BOLD
Regular
Slows down reader
Used for
Applied to most styles
Tilted and rhythmic
Easy to read
Double stroke, first stroke
Provides emphasis
Can be applied to most styles
Content
Easy to read
GRAPHITE PENCIL
BLUE PENCIL
PAPER
RULER
TAPE
STEP STOOL
THE COLLAPSIBLE IS EASY TO TRAV
BE Visible Write Now

# MORE LETTERING RESOURCES

**A variety of resources to meet your learning style**
We all learn differently...some learners are kinesthetic and need a hands-on experience, like that found in my in-person workshops. Others would prefer to learn at their own pace or simply can't attend in-person workshops due to budgetary or geographic constraints. That's why I offer online courses to meet your schedule and budget.

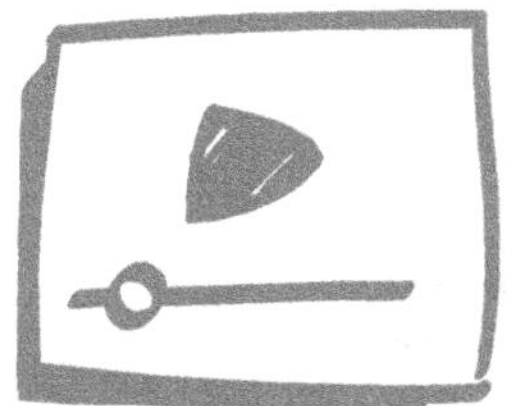 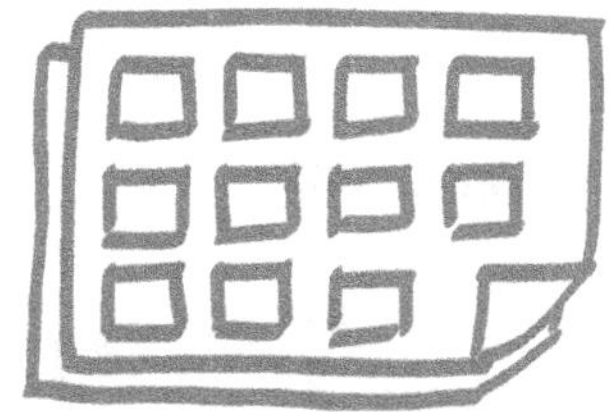

Throughout the book, you may have noticed the video and template icons.

If you find that you need more support than what's found in this book, check out www.LetsLetterTogether.com/resources. There you will find a free resources page that offers
- Free PDF downloads of templates for *Brick* and *Clock Face*
- Links to video resources for additional lettering styles
- Full color versions of the images showcased in each chapter
- And much more!

**Did you know...**
Neuland offers four lettering style exemplars you can download for free at www.neuland.com/handlettering

How-to videos for these styles are available through the *Unlock Your Neuland Markers* free video series available at www.LetsLetterTogether.com

**Other resources available:**
At the time of the printing of this book, there are several other online and virtual lettering courses available at www.LetsLetterTogether.com, including
- *Write Like an Architect*, self-paced, online
- *Letter Like a Sign Painter*, self-paced, online course, zine
- *Lettering with the Masters*, self-paced, online
- *Level Up Your Lettering*, virtual cohort, in-person workshop
- *1:1 Virtual Sessions* - customized for your lettering needs

**And coming up:**
- *Bold and at the Top of the Page* - titles
- *When Composition Matters* - composition and color
- *Listen, Letter, Draw Together* - virtual workshop and integration course
- *Lettering Journey EXPRESS* - in-depth videos to accompany this book

**More online learning resources:**
Let's connect on social media! You can find me here:
- www.facebook.com/CorporateGraffitiArtist
- www.youtube.com/user/GraphicFacilitation
- www.gumroad.com/corpgraffitiart

**Collaborating with others**
I love lettering together! If you are a student of Christina Merkley's, she offers a variety of my materials to her students in the SHIFT-IT® School. Check out her online resources for links, downloads, videos and discount codes here: bit.ly/shiftitresources.

Sandra Dirks has invited me to be part of her *Advents Special* and *Winter Session.* Search for these titles:

- *Twinkle* - a fast and fun serif style using any marker nib, designed with the FineOne Art in mind
- *Thick/Thin Script* - using the No.One marker

Watch more of her videos here: bit.ly/sandradirkslettering

# ANATOMY OF A LETTER

Here is a quick overview of just a few anatomical terms defining the different parts of a letter.

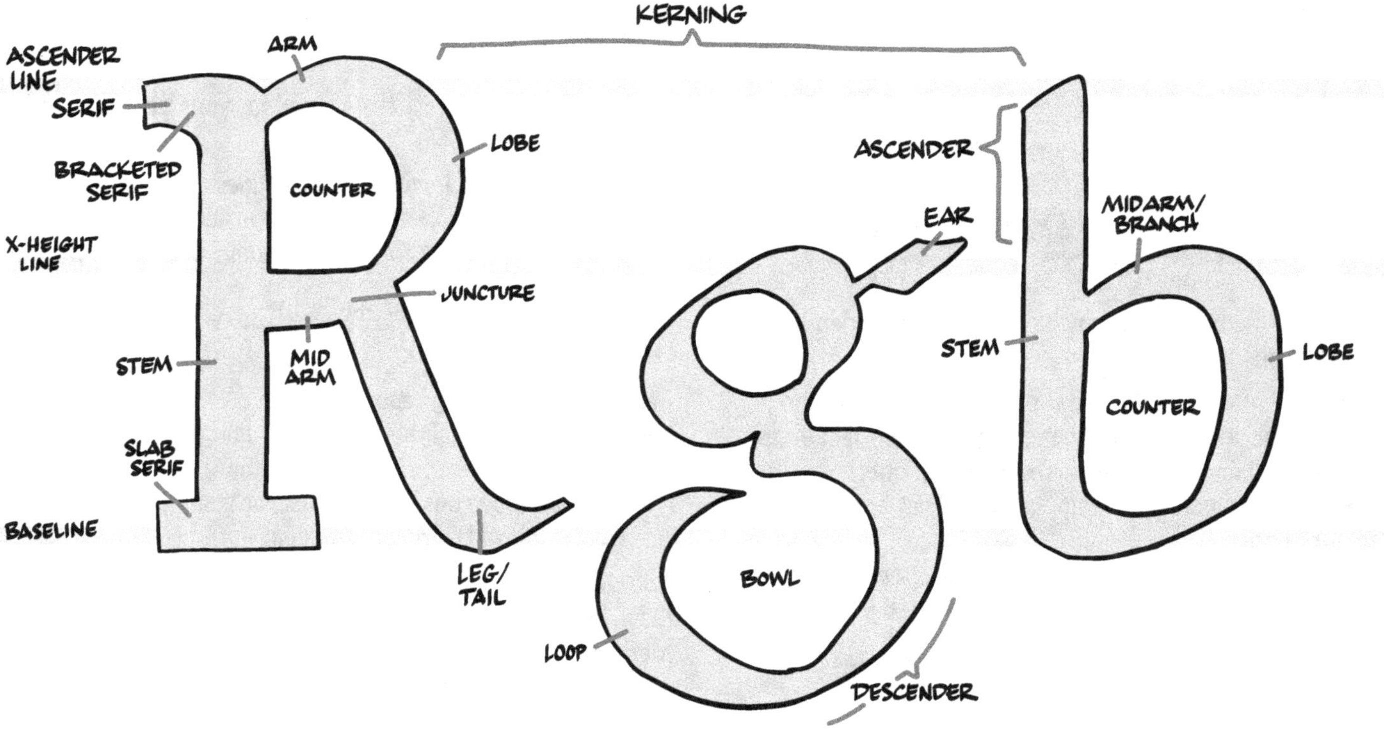

Video available about the anatomy of a letter—important terms to know when watching demo videos on lettering.

# GLOSSARY OF TERMS

Many of the terms found in this book are frequently used by calligraphers, sign painters, type designers and graphic designers. I am defining them here based on the original definitions and how they are applied in our field of work. This is by no means an exhaustive list of terms.

**baseline**    The line that letters "sit" on. See Anatomy of a Letter on the opposite page.

**ductus**    Lines and oftentimes numbers that denote the direction and order of strokes when writing a letter.

**exemplar**    Example or model of letterforms in a particular lettering style.

**font**    The combination of typeface and other qualities, such as size and spacing, that is delivered by mechanical means. Not to be confused with lettering style, script or hand, which is created by hand.

**juncture**    The point at which two or more lines come together in a letter.

**majuscules**    Capital, uppercase or large letters of an alphabet.

**minuscules**    Non-capital, lowercase or small letters of an alphabet.

**pangram**    A sentence containing every letter of an alphabet.

**nib width scale**    Several marks made to show how tall (or less commonly wide) a letter should be, determined by the nib's width. Also known as a pen scale to calligraphers who use pens in their work.

**perpendicular**    At an angle of 90° to a given line, plane or surface.

**terminal**    The start or end point of a stroke in a letter.

# CONCLUSION

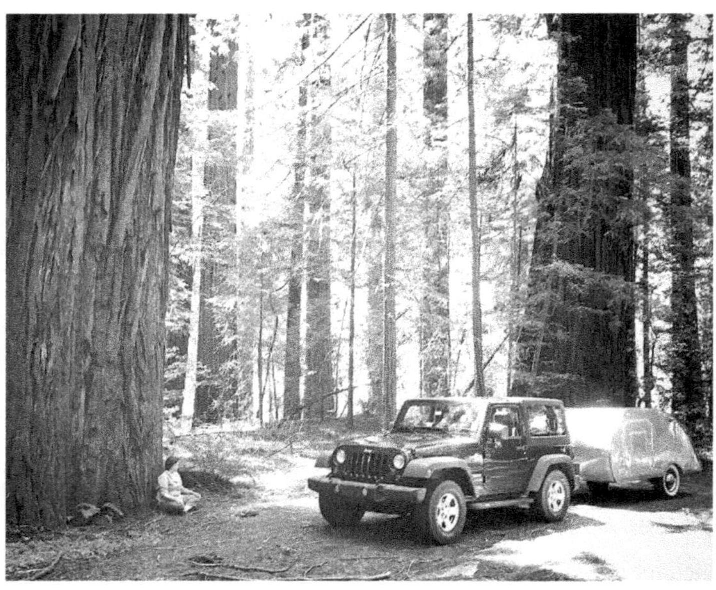

Meditating under a redwood tree in northern California, with Flo nearby, before heading back on the road and to the next lettering workshop in the Bay Area.

Yes, I'm a bonafide tree hugger. To see more photos and read about our adventure, visit www.OnTheRoadWithFlo.com.

## Phew! We did it!
## That was a lot of letters!

Thank you for joining me on this crazy lettering adventure.

My favorite part was being inspired throughout our trip across the country and translating what I found into lettering styles just for you. With over 13,000 miles on the odometer in just six months, I'm ready to hit the road again. Who's with me?

With Neuland® markers in my bag and a sketchbook full of dreams, this is just the beginning of what is to come. I'm already thinking about the next few projects inspired by the lettering tours I offer in conjunction with my in-person workshops around the world.

I hope our journeys cross paths so we can letter together—again and again.


Your Friend in Lettering,

Heather

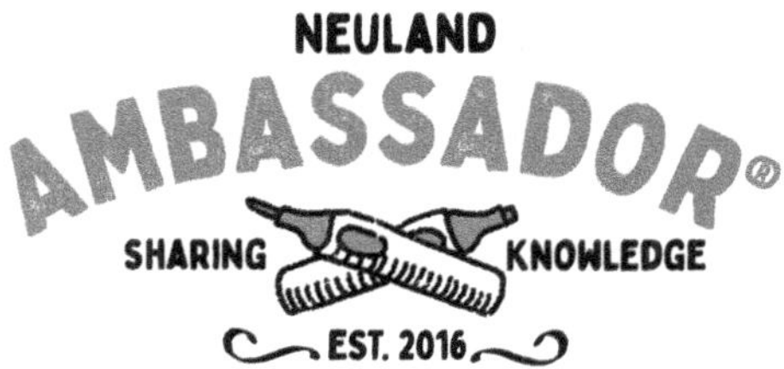

*denotes Neuland Ambassador

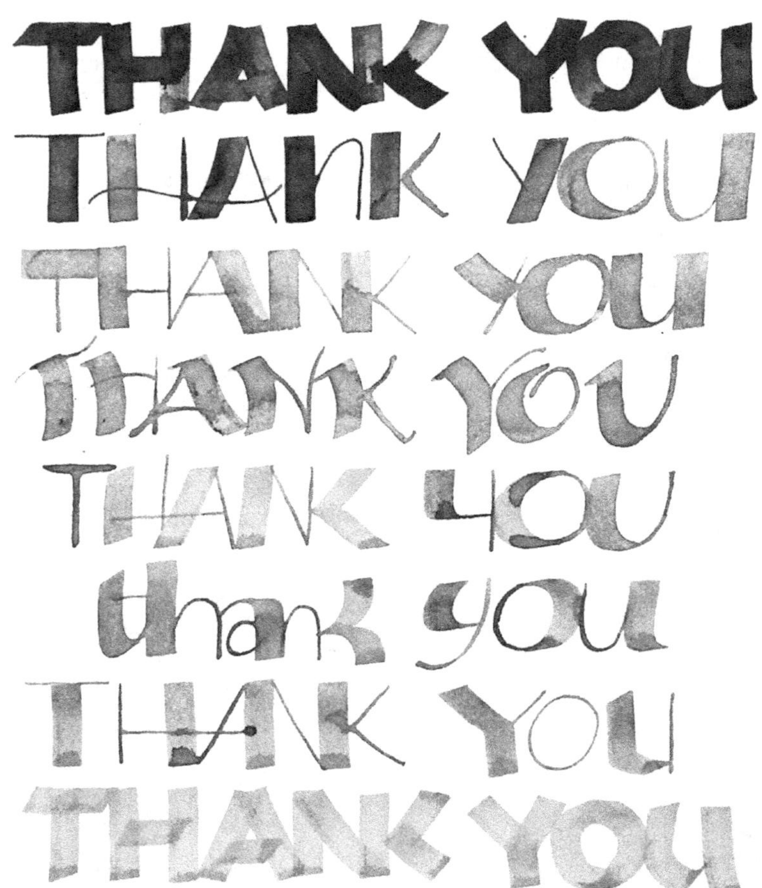
THANK YOU
THANK YOU
THANK YOU
THANK YOU
THANK YOU
thank you
THANK YOU
THANK YOU

# ACKNOWLEDGEMENTS

To my mom, who first taught me how to hold a pencil correctly and whose handwriting I've always admired.

And to my dad, whose first brick-and-mortar business included a lot of hand-painted signs. I used to watch that sign painter for hours. Thank you for investing in him and in me.

To Hermineh Miller, my first calligraphy teacher, who had the patience to work with me when I had no clue what I was doing—but thought that I did.

To Carol DuBosch, master calligrapher/role model/ friend, who put a pen in my hand and encouraged me to see and make letters in ways I never expected. Her encouragement changed my career path, and her generosity has afforded me opportunities that I could never have imagined.

To Mike Meyer, master sign painter, whose kind and encouraging ways will always make me want to pick up a brush. I'll be back!

To Kelvy Bird, Mike Rohde and Brandy Agerbeck for sharing wisdom from your book-writing experiences.

To Kyla Jenkinson, my studio mate and creative partner of all dreams possible, thank you for being witness to most all of my creative endeavors.

To Guido Neuland and Verena Hanke-Neuland, of Neuland, for believing in the power of the handwritten word and for making such wonderfully engineered tools to help us do our jobs well. Thank you also for asking me to become an ambassador. It has been a dream opportunity. I love collaborating with you and your team.

To Amy Sparks, Tina Abert, Dana Wright-Wasson, Carlos Valdes-Dapena, Christina Merkley, Elizabeth Kinahan, and Antonio Iturra, who have tolerated me through the production of this book and who have given me encouraging and critical feedback.

To my friends and family, who continue to support me though they may not understand what I do for a living.

To Patricia Burk who has helped me write the next chapter of my life everytime we get together.

To Gawkie, who always had breakfast waiting even though I missed many of them to work on the book. I look forward to next Sunday's homemade green chili and tortilla.

To my students, who invest in us lettering together.

And to my husband Ray for going on adventures with me. We always find ourselves in the most peculiar places. You are my favorite person to write love letters to.

*pictured opposite*
"Thank You" written with a Pilot Parallel pen and alternating Winsor & Newton dark blue and ochre inks. It was after learning Jubilee from Carol DuBosch that I had the confidence to really play with the different edges of the broad edge/wedge nib.

# Thank you for taking a Lettering Journey with Neuland products!

**Save 10% off your next Neuland order!**

Use coupon code:
**MyLetteringJourney**

* This voucher is only redeemable once and not combinable with literature items and other vouchers.

**Want to share the *Lettering Journey* with others?**

*Lettering Journey,* the book, is available in two versions. Get yours **in color** directly from Neuland at www.neuland.com or in black and white at www.LetsLetterTogether.com.

**Visit Neuland**
www.neuland.com
www.facebook.com/neuland
www.instagram.com/neulandcom

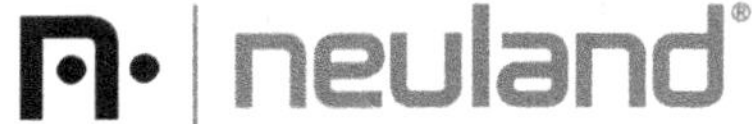

**These are a few of my favorite Neuland products:**

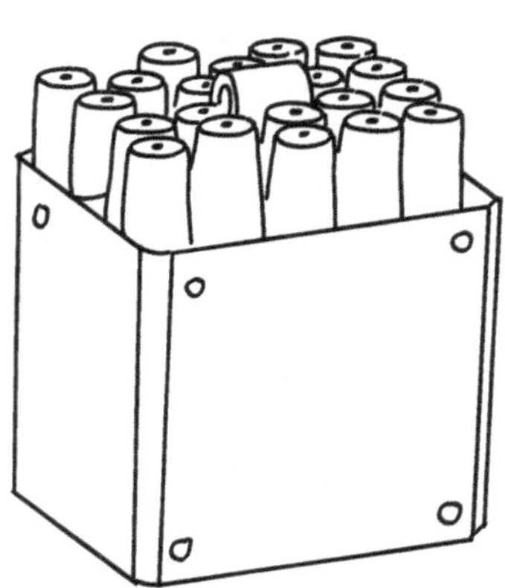

Novario® No.One-Box
Item no: 8030.0001

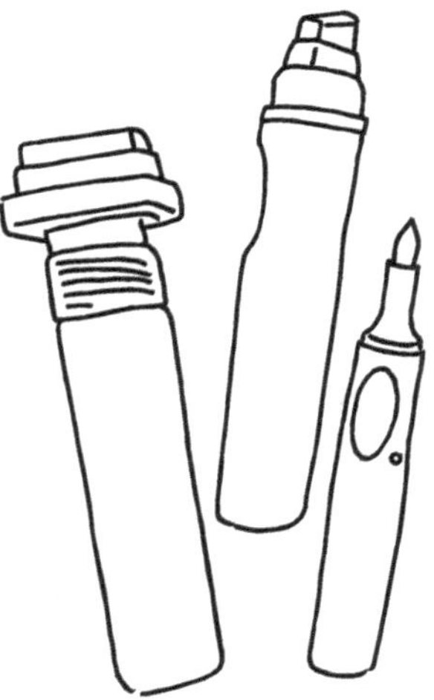

FatOne 30mm, Item no: 8061.3000
*with* Neuland Ink RefillOne, Item no: 8044.0500
Neuland BigOne®, Item no: 8042.0010
Neuland No.One® Art, Item no: 8059.0305

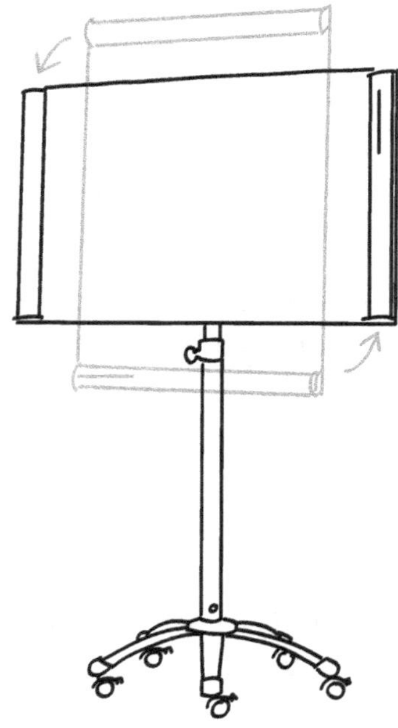

sketch@work FlipChart
Item no: 8309.0230

# COLOPHON

This book was typeset in Formata, Bernd Möllenstädt's first type design, released in 1984. The font was chosen for its extensive weight range, which includes normal and condensed versions. Like the tools we use as visual practitioners to show hierarchy in lettering, the breadth of this font family makes it an excellent choice for a wide range of applications, from bodies of text to attention-grabbing headlines.

Formata is trademarked by Berthold Types Limited.

The section titles throughout the book were handwritten in the lettering style of that chapter.

The cover and headings in the book were handwritten using a Neuland No.One® Outliner with a brush nib for a dry brush effect. The lettering style is my own handwriting inspired by *Architect* and *Roman Hand*.

Illustrations were drawn with Neuland FineOne® Outliners and digitally.

Letters were drawn with the markers outlined at the beginning of each chapter.

The ductus for most exemplars was superimposed digitally using an Apple pencil and Adobe Draw.

Layout and design of the pages were created in Adobe InDesign on a Mac. Photographs were prepared using Adobe Photoshop. Graphics were prepared using Adobe Illustrator. In all cases, the 2018 versions of Adobe products were used.

Ideas for the book were sketched out using a Palomino Blackwing pencil.